Play Till You Hear the
WHISTLE

My Face-Off Against Cancer

To Melissa & James,
Nice meeting you both.
Hope you enjoy!

[signature]

Marc G. Mitchell, DVM

drmarc@comcast.net

ISBN: 1500307947
ISBN 13: 9781500307943
Library of Congress Control Number: 2014918901
CreateSpace Independent Publishing Platform
North Charleston, South Carolina

For Harryman

Table of Contents

Prologue

I wasn't sure this book would ever come to fruition. There were several reasons that I actually got enough gumption to sit down and finally get it done. The first one was the real driving force. Just before my dad passed away, I promised him that I would write another book. I didn't know what it was going to be about but I made him a promise.

Since my first book was about the farm, and racing horses during my late teens and early twenties, I thought it would be kind of neat to go backwards chronologically for the second book and talk about my childhood development during our time on the farm; kind of a retrospective to *Hoofprints in the Sand.* It would try to convey that life on the farm was different than most of the kids I went to school with, who would go to parties and afterschool events, while I went home and worked the chores. I would tell anecdotal stories about how it spawned my idea to become a veterinarian and what events truly led me to my decision.

I wrote a fair amount, but felt it was boring and a bit redundant. Sure, there were a lot of good stories still left untold and perhaps one day I will get around to finishing what I started, but in the meantime, I wanted to tell my story about me and my dad's struggle with cancer together. Not knowing how much time I really have left had something to do with it, but not entirely. Maybe the real reason was that I didn't want my second book to be an unneeded prequel to my first one.

The second reason I felt I needed to write it was for catharsis. I needed to get out all the thoughts and ideas that ran through my head during those most difficult times. I felt that if I could convey them on paper, it could help me both deal with hard times should they arrive in the future, and give me an appreciation of what I went through. Writing it and rereading it certainly has given me the strength to carry on and not want to go through it again, so healthy living and abiding by the rules seems paramount.

Thirdly, and perhaps most importantly, I thought that if I told my journey through my battle with cancer, alongside my father who struggled with his, it could be somewhat of an inspirational piece to help others who have been diagnosed with terminal cancer. It's hard to go through this type of thing alone, even if you're surrounded by people you love. In essence, the battle is done from within. Hearing what someone else went through before you go through it yourself could be just what you need to get by. Knowing that there are others that have done it and pushed through the darkness can only help.

Having people tell you that you're going to be just fine isn't very comforting when you're lying in a hospital bed wanting to opt out. You need to know there can be some light at the end of the tunnel from someone who has been out the other side. Someone who understands the pain, the fear, the angst, and the knowledge that their life will likely be cut short. I'm not saying it isn't incredibly heartwarming to feel the love and strength given to you from family and friends, but the perspective is different. They aren't "in it."

The hardest part about writing this book wasn't reliving those awful days of treatments and hospital visits. It was not having my dad (I will often refer to him as Harryman; it's what we all called him) to help me create it. He was nothing short of my biggest fan. While writing my first book, each night I would e-mail him whatever I had written that evening, usually sometime after midnight. It could have been a few pages, or if my mind wasn't sharp, it was just a few paragraphs. He would be up waiting for the next installment, and in a few minutes, I would get an e-mail critiquing what I had sent him.

Sometimes he would say something like, "I like it Cope," (using my nickname). Or he would say, "Not bad, but could use some work in that middle part. Keep it up. Good stuff." He was always there. A constant muse. Once he was gone, my sounding board was gone. It was just me and a blank computer screen. No one to send it to. Certainly my wife, Jen, my brother, Doug, and my mom were all more than willing to have a look whenever I felt like giving them what I had, but no offense to them, they weren't Harryman. He taught me how to write. He was with me through every term paper, every speech and every short story I had ever written. I leaned on him every time. His style oozes out of my prose, minus the sarcasm. That's all me.

I found it depressing to finish writing a segment and not having him on the other end of the computer to read it. But I had made a promise, and he would have been pissed if I didn't do it because of self-pity. So I pressed on.

His work ethic was second to none, and I felt I owed him at least the effort. If I found myself getting down, I would picture him in his tractor, pushing manure around for hours and that would put a smile on my face. Harryman and his tractor. Sitting in that seat may have been his favorite spot in the world. He logged over 9000 hours in that beast of a machine. That's over a year of his life.

He baled thousands of bales of hay, dragged miles of track smooth of bumpy hoofprints, dug trenches for drainage, pulled trees out of the woods, loaded manure for ten bucks a load to locals for fertilizer, buried horses (dead ones of course), bush hogged the back 40, filled thousands of wheel barrows full of sawdust for the stalls, plowed snow in the winter, and countless other chores that only he could find useful for the tractor, even if it wasn't necessary or very safe. Often times I just sat back and watched Doug and him and just shook my head, but somehow they always got it done.

HARRYMAN AND HIS TRACTOR

One day, my brother and I wanted to carry a picnic table down to the pond and were just about to do so when he boomed out, "Hang on, I'll get the tractor and we'll chain it on!" Both Doug and I just rolled our eyes, knowing we couldn't stop him. We easily could have had it done by the time he started the thing and made it over to us with the chains, but we let him do it anyway. When we were done, he said, "See, wasn't that easier?" Honestly, not really, but we just nodded. He so loved using that machine. So, when I was writing, I pictured him in his tractor, where he was at his happiest, and that brought me comfort. I would talk to him while I was writing, as if he were there, listening. Sometimes I could hear him talk back. It was as if he was with me throughout the entire book.

One of the things that I wanted to mention in this section was what my illness did to me psychologically. It made me more cynical and intolerant to the little things. It made me someone different. My thought process was morphed. Although I am cynical by nature, it was amplified when I was in the hospital. Little things bothered me more. I had a terrible case of hyperacusis (intolerance to noises). I was more easily annoyed by just about anything. That behavior is quite obvious throughout the book and I wanted to be as honest as possible when I wrote it, not leaving out my shortcomings during that time.

When I wasn't sick, I wouldn't say I was the life of the party, but I feel like I brought life to the party. During my bone marrow transplant, that spark inside of me was gone. I couldn't find it. I tried to stay positive, and for the most part I did, but I was a mere shadow of what I normally was. My point is that the disease made me someone else. It took away some of my humanity, my humor. But it didn't take it all. I found ways to stay focused and upbeat.

Hopefully, this book will convey the essence of what it is to go through a rigorous chemotherapy protocol along with a bone marrow transplant and still stay away from the darkness. The alternative is to give up. Don't give up. Don't ever give up.

CHAPTER 1 – DREAMS SHATTERED

I was having one of those dreams. It's one where I'm in a car, or worse, a van. I find myself in the backseat and can't imagine why I'm there because I'm supposed to be driving. Somehow the vehicle is staying on the road for the moment. No matter what I do, I can't seem to get myself back to the driver's seat. Inevitably, my car crashes, and I finally wake up realizing that it was only a dream. To become aware that it wasn't real is an overwhelming relief.

In this particular dream, I can't see where I'm going, but I feel my car jump into the air as I crash into something. The noises are surreal and horrifying. Because I can't see the road, I know I'm dreaming and that at least I'm going to wake up. I hear glass shattering and the unnerving sound of metal crunching. From outside my dream, my conscious mind wants to wake up and is urging my slumbering unconscious to enter reality. It feels so real; so much so that I'm anxious to get back to the tangible world. I need to wake up to prove to myself that I'm dreaming.

Finally I feel myself breaking away from the nightmare. My eyes feel heavy, and it's a struggle to open them. As my vision clears, I see that I'm not lying in bed but actually sitting in a chair. Seconds later, I realize that the chair is the driver's seat of my car. I can smell acrid smoke, and an airbag has deployed in my face. The car is still rolling slowly to a stop, but my foot is not on the brake. My worst fear has come true. The dream is in fact reality. My mind won't believe it. I think quickly, *Maybe it's a dream within a dream.*

As I become more aware of my surroundings, that possibility slips away as an understanding of what's real begins to set in. In a fully conscious state, you are certain of reality. It's only within a dream that you really ever question whether or not you're dreaming.

My brain was trying to piece together a picture it didn't want to see. It was becoming clearer to me that I'd been in an accident. I had no idea what had happened. I didn't know if there were other cars involved or even if I had hit a pedestrian. Something was burning inside the vehicle, and it was filling up with smoke. The car had come to rest on the right side of the road along the soft shoulder. I tried to open my door, but it had been badly damaged in the crash. There was glass in my lap and the airbag was in my way. I needed to get out of the car.

Unbuckling my seat belt, I managed to get the door open a crack and pivoted my body so I could kick out the driver's door enough to squeeze onto the side of the road. I was still trying to wrap my head around what went down. I looked back up the street, my vision somewhat impaired, perhaps from the dust from the airbag, or just from trying to regain consciousness. I could see something lying in the road. It was about five feet long and lying motionless about a hundred yards back. It looked like a body.

My immediate thought was that I had hit someone. It had to be what I ran over that caused the car to jump into the air in my dreamlike state. I tried to focus on it, forcing myself to see it for what it really was rather than tricking myself into believing it was a person.

I staggered toward the mystery object, and it began to take shape. It was the front bumper of my car. I exhaled in relief. I must have been holding my breath. When I blacked out, I had crossed the road through oncoming traffic and into a stone wall. The momentum carried the car into a tree and then ricocheted back across both lanes of the road before finally coming to a rest on the right side. The bumper must have been torn away when it glanced off a giant oak. Somehow I wasn't T-boned by oncoming traffic, nor had I hit any pedestrians.

As my mind cleared, I replayed the events leading up to the accident. Three days previously, I'd undergone a biopsy on a swollen lymph node. I'd been avoiding having it checked for several months. It was just above my right shoulder. The surgery had gone terribly awry, causing my neck to swell up grotesquely. Jen and I were planning on traveling to Oregon to visit her parents, but the swelling in my neck was so bad that it wasn't going to happen.

The morning of the accident, I remembered waking up completely soaked from a horrible night sweat that was somehow related to the lymph node issue. I was wallowing in my worries, looking like half a linebacker from the unilateral swelling in my neck. We had made the right choice. I was in no condition to fly. The pain from the biopsy was making it even harder for me to sleep, and I felt as if I was getting weaker by the day. I couldn't tell if it was because of the post surgical trauma, or if whatever was causing the lymph node to pop up was creating other problems.

THIS PICTURE WAS TWO DAYS AFTER THE BIOPSY WHEN
THE SWELLING HAD COME DOWN SOME.

A few days following the surgery, when I was feeling just a little bit better and the swelling had come down by applying a ridiculous amount of ice, I decided to get out of the house. It was Columbus Day, and our animal hospital was closed for the holiday. It was simply gorgeous out. Temps were in the eighties, and there was just a hint of a breeze in the air. I thought it might be a nice idea to go to the driving range and hit a few golf balls one last time before the weather turned. Maybe swinging the clubs would loosen up the knots of muscles torturing my neck and also make the swelling come down.

We New Englanders who play golf never want to call an end to our season, even though we know it's pretty much over once October hits. Sure, there are a few days scattered here and there, but the sun only hangs around for a cup of coffee, and for the most part, it's too cold. Mind you, some of us morons still play into November, but it's more to spite Mother Nature than anything else. There are so many reasons *not* to play golf in the late fall. It's usually freezing out, the ground is hard, the putting surfaces are usually aerated and bumpy, and all kinds of debris has blown onto the greens. And you can forget about finding a ball in the leaves. Yet we play. I told you, we're chowder heads.

I'd had enough sense not to play a round that day, although it had crossed my mind. Imagining the worst from my biopsy, I thought it might be my last chance to play golf. So instead I drove to the driving range in the nearby town of Newfields. It was one of my usual haunts for practicing. After a few swings, my neck hurt like hell. After about eight hits, I got a little lightheaded and decided I better stop. I could feel the pulse pounding in my head, and it worried me. I left a perfectly good bucket on its side with a bunch of balls strewn about. What a waste. I didn't really care about the five bucks; I was just upset I couldn't hit them. It was official, my season was over.

I sat in the car for about ten minutes gathering myself. I couldn't believe how rapid my heart rate was after hitting a handful of golf balls. That was way out of form for me. I normally could hit a hundred and not break a sweat. Something was seriously wrong. I just needed to go home. Once my breathing returned to normal and I couldn't hear the swooshing of blood in my skull, I started back for the house.

Route 85 is a small country road that passes through the center of Newfields, New Hampshire. It's your quintessential New England town. I passed the country store on the right that sells fresh sandwiches, homemade fudge, and whoopee pies. It's an old colonial house with hardwood floors converted into a store. It has two bay windows trimmed with white panes on either side of a glass-paneled front door, a door with an old-style brass handle and thumb latch. A real quaint little place.

I always watched my speed through Newfields because there's a lot of foot traffic. It's a fairly busy place for a small town, with bicyclists, dog walkers, shoppers, and joggers. I cruised past the police station on my left, and that's when I started to feel a bit funny. Not funny ha-ha. Funny in a bad way. The world was quickly getting brighter. It was as if the sun had broken free of the clouds, except there weren't any in the sky.

I immediately thought that I needed to pull over. That's when everything went black. The next thing I knew, I was on the side of the road, trying to figure out what had happened.

People told me later that someone must have been watching over me. Some say I must have had an angel riding shotgun. Perhaps, but I sure wish she were watching over me before I blacked out. It would've been infinitely more convenient to avoid the accident altogether rather than miraculously not hit anybody, or get hit by another car while unconscious behind the wheel.

Slowly it all started to come together. I remembered feeling odd, then hearing the sickening sound of crunching metal and my body being tossed about. I was trying to come to grips with the fact that it really happened. I did a quick body check for broken bones and lacerations. Fortunately I was for the most part unscathed, but I was very weak and shaken. I stepped clear of the car and the possibility of an explosion, because we all know from watching TV that every car that crashes explodes. I slumped down a safe distance away on the side of the road and waited for help. From the sound of the sirens, they were close.

I may have been unconscious for a longer period than I thought, because in no time at all, a young gentleman in a uniform was standing over me. He had a fair complexion, medium build, dark hair, and good looks, and he seemed oddly familiar. I was still shaking out the cobwebs, trying to gather my thoughts when he spoke.

"Marc, are you okay?"

"I think so. Yeah, I'm all right. What happened?"

How did this guy know who I was? My mind drifted off, confused as to how he knew me. *Did I tell him who I was a few minutes ago and not realize it?* I didn't remember blacking out a second time, but it was entirely possible that I had. He was talking again, but I wasn't really paying attention, still trying to make sense of it all.

"…and relax. Just lay back and let the paramedics take care of you," he said as I refocused on what he was saying.

The EMTs were all business, treating me as if I'd been hit head-on by an eighteen-wheeler. They were taking no chances. They had me lie down on the side of the road and started with the neck brace. Then they placed my hands on my chest and slowly rolled me onto my side and slid a backboard underneath me. I was trying to tell them that I was fine and didn't need the spinal injury treatment. I had taken bigger hits in hockey.

But it was as if I wasn't speaking. As they were doing their thing, the officer kept asking me questions.

When my head cleared, I realized that he was indeed someone I knew. His name was Jim Fletcher, and he had worked for me a few years back as a technician in our animal hospital. He was a good kid. When he left us, he intended to pursue a career in law enforcement. Apparently he had succeeded.

"Hi, Jim. Man, you got here fast," I said.

"I was right around the corner." He smiled and pointed over his left shoulder. "Do you remember anything about the accident?"

As I became more lucid, I described all the events in detail. I explained how I had gone for a biopsy on my neck three days prior, and that perhaps the outrageous swelling may have pinched my carotid artery, causing me to black out. It happened so fast that I didn't have time to pull over, even after I realized it was probably a good idea to do so. The thought of stopping had been so fleeting that it was the last thing I remembered thinking. After that, I remembered waking up while slowing down on the side of the road.

"Have you had anything to drink?" Jim asked.

"No, nothing. I took something for the pain like eight hours ago, but no, nothing," I responded, not liking where his line of questioning was going. I tried to explain to him again why I thought I might have passed out. I told him that they had found a tumor in my chest. I'd had x-rays done just a day before the surgery that confirmed some sort of growth.

He commented on my neck, and I repeated my story about the biopsy. He wrote a few things down in a little notebook and told me everything should be fine and he'd take care of it. He implied that I wouldn't be charged or issued any kind of a citation as this was an accident in the truest sense of the word.

It was comforting to have an ally at the scene like that. But as he assured me everything would be okay, I couldn't help feeling uneasy. The last time someone said something like that to us, my father ended up with a year's suspension from harness racing.

Back in the early nineties, our family raced standardbreds. My father, my mother, my older brother Doug, and I would make trips four or five nights a week to Maine or Massachusetts to race. My father was listed as the trainer, Doug was our driver, and I was the groom responsible for all the tack and preparation. Later on, when I became a veterinarian, I was still the groom; a groom who injected joints to promote healing, gave medications, and treated all the other issues that came along with owning fifteen head of horses.

I'm pretty sure I was the only veterinarian who still held the role of groom. I didn't mind a bit. Besides, I couldn't drive a horse the way Doug could. Our mom (who we call by the nickname Mama Pajama), in the early days, when Doug and I were too young to help, did an incredible amount of barn work. Later on, when the two of us became useful workers, she came along mostly as a cheerleader, but helped out whenever necessary. We had quite a team. We almost never went to a track without the four of us.

MAMA WORKING THE HORSES IN THE EARLY SEVENTIES WITH DOUG BY HER SIDE.

Back then most tracks were, and still are, testing horses for bicarbonates, or baking soda. Crazy as it sounds, using a few pounds on a horse before a race can have a profound performance-enhancing effect on them. But not all horses responded in a positive way. In fact, some suffered the opposite effect by colicking after receiving such a large amount of the stuff.

They call it "milk-shaking" because when you mix it with water and sugar…you guessed it, it looks like a milkshake. The real problem was the fact that some trainers took it upon themselves to use a nasogastric tube (passed through the nose and into the stomach) to get it into the horse instead of hiring a vet; or, more simply, just giving it to them orally in a paste. If the tube were to go into the lungs instead of the stomach, then you had a dead horse. Sad, I know. That was probably one of the leading reasons the practice was banned, but not the only one. Another was because it was considered a performance-enhancing drug, or PED, so most tracks made it illegal and began handing out fines and suspensions if anyone got caught.

In its infancy stages, the testing was sketchy at best, and the allowable levels were set too low. Our stable was one of the first in the state of Maine to be "caught" allegedly using the stuff. We had been using baking soda as a supplement in small quantities for our horses for years, but we never "milk-shaked" our horses. Once they started testing, we even stopped using the tiny amount in their feed for fear any substance being in their system. Nevertheless, one of our horses came back with a high level. We still don't know why his levels were over the limit that day, but even though this was our first offense, my father was banned from racing for a year.

I remember Mike Lynch, one of the test officials we knew very well, talking to my dad during the whole incident. It was a beautiful summer day at Scarborough Downs, and we had two or three horses in to go. To Bad Honey was the name of the horse that had the positive. He came back high not once but twice on the machine. He was scratched immediately and banned from racing for thirty days. The other horses that were racing that day also got scratched, even though they were never tested. It was madness.

We were all pretty distraught. Mike was seemingly very sympathetic to us and tried to placate my father.

"Don't worry about it, Harry. We'll take care of it."

His words are still clear in my head. He took care of nothing. He joined in the witch hunt to prosecute anyone who even had baking soda in their freezer.

As ludicrous as the whole thing was, and the fact that we never used the stuff, didn't matter. We were out of racing. It was devastating.

On the side of the road, as Jim was writing down all the details, his tone was eerily familiar.

"It'll be fine, Marc, I'll take care of it," he said.

His voice was so compassionate, so caring, yet I had heard that tone before only to have the gavel come down. Take care of it? Take care of what? I didn't do anything wrong. What was he saying? Could I be in trouble for having cancer and a swollen neck? At that moment, I could feel myself standing in the sun at Scarborough Downs outside the little test trailer with my heart pounding out of my chest with anger.

I had to try to forget that. There was nothing I could do about that now. That was in the past. It was so long ago, yet I was feeling the same emotions, and it was affecting me physically. My heart was racing and I was agitated. It wasn't helping my head. It was throbbing along with my pulse. As I calmed myself down, the hammering in my ears subsided.

The EMTs were holding a pen light to my eyes, making me follow it back and forth. It was more of a nuisance than anything. I could see at *that* point. It was when I was unconscious that I had vision problems.

No one asked me about the crazy swelling of my neck that made me look like a freak. Maybe they thought it had happened in the crash and that's why they were so attentive to my spine.

They strapped my neck down good and tight, but when they did, a buckle from the headgear got stuck at the base of my head. When they cinched me up, that thing stuck into my skull like a dagger. Over the past few days, I'd been taking such careful steps to not touch my neck for fear of pain. When they tightened me down, the neck brace drove deep into the site of my biopsy. Just moments after the accident, I'd been fine. There was no pain at all. Once I was on that stretcher, everything changed. There I was with a buckle from a neck brace buried into my skull *and* a major soft tissue injury clamped down on for good measure. I was waiting for a wet towel to get thrown over my face and have them start water-boarding me. I was not happy.

Just before they put me, mummified, on the gurney, I was able to Houdini my cell phone out of my back pocket. I needed to call my wife, Jen. With my arms crossed I managed to hold the phone near my face and call to tell her that I was okay but had been in an accident. I tried my best to sound chipper and unhurt so that she wouldn't worry en route to the hospital. I don't think I was very successful. We had met in vet school and been together for over twenty years. She knew me too well to be fooled by my charade.

She in turn called my parents and brother, who probably assumed I was dead, and raced to the hospital before they could slap on a toe tag and zip me up. As I lay on my back in the ambulance, I gazed at the ceiling thinking about all of the events that had transpired over the past week. A botched biopsy, a tumor lurking in my chest, my car totaled, and I'd nearly been killed. If he existed, I knew the Almighty could hear me, even though I whispered it.

"Is that all you got?" I asked, not really wanting an answer.

In my head I heard his response. "Pal, you're still alive. Don't push your luck."

"Maybe I'm just tougher than you thought," I snarked back.

I decided that was enough conversation for the time being. It was probably not a good idea to get into a pissing contest with the "Big Man."

The ride to the hospital was anticlimactic. No high speeds, no screeching tires, no sirens. Not so much as a *boop-boop* going through an intersection. Come to think of it, we may have even stopped at a red light. It was my first ambulance ride, and quite frankly, it was unimpressive.

The doctor who saw me was fantastic. First off, she got that buckle out of my head and released the pressure on my surgery site. She was quite thorough and even ordered an ultrasound of my neck to see if there were any obstructions of blood flow secondary to the inflammation. I would describe her to you, but I can't remember anything significant other than that she was a woman. I guess I was still a little woozy. They checked my blood pressure, took some blood, and did some cognitive tests by asking me questions.

Come to find out, the bloodwork showed that I was severely anemic and moderately dehydrated. The ultrasound indicated that there was a mild narrowing of my carotid artery and jugular vein, but not a complete occlusion. It was a perfect storm. The anemia meant less red blood cells and therefore less oxygen to the brain. The dehydration and constricted carotid meant less blood as well. Good thing it wasn't summertime. I was a couple mosquito bites away from flat-lining.

They kept me for a few hours for observation and then let me go home. The Lincoln LS that I had been driving for the past eight years was no more. I really liked that car, although when we had snow it was nearly useless. It had rear-wheel drive and almost no weight in the back, making winter driving a real challenge. But in the summer, it was a pretty sweet ride. It was a 2001 model, but didn't look a day over three. In the end, she took a bullet for me. What more could I ask for?

THE LINCOLN LS IS DEAD.

Lying there in the hospital, staring at the lights, I couldn't help but wonder how I got to this moment. Only a week before, I was playing floor hockey and looking to win another championship. That was all gone now. So far away. My mind drifted back, and I found myself on the court, standing on the right wing, desperately trying to catch my breath. I knew something was wrong. Something was horribly wrong. I retraced the events leading up to the accident.

CHAPTER 2 – LOSING THE GAME

"Are you going to take the skirt off and play or what?"

My friend, Paul, stared at me incredulously from the center dot of the street hockey rink with a grimace and a hint of a smile. My brother, Doug, was on the left wing wondering the same thing, but let Paul say it. They had every right. I was way off my game. I was playing a step behind everyone. I was losing every battle in the corner, every race to the ball.

Now I'm no Usain Bolt, but I'm not the slowest guy on the floor. What I lacked in speed, I made up in tenacity. That wasn't there either.

The week before, during the quarterfinals, the owner of the rink thought it would be a good idea to do some renovating using a couple of tractors inside. They were in the process of ripping up some old flooring and trying to lay down a new indoor soccer field. He was lamenting that the crew was already a week behind, and he couldn't afford to shut them down since he was losing money each day his new floor wasn't done.

A blue haze hovered inside the arena, and the smell of diesel punched me in the face when we walked in. My eyes started burning in just a few minutes. The heavy air hit my lungs, and I could taste the exhaust. All the players and refs who'd been there before us seemed to have gotten used to it. I was surprised no one had already succumbed to the fumes.

It was something you might hear about in a third world country with people getting carbon monoxide poisoning. This type of thing shouldn't occur in the United States. We have regulations; OSHA and all that crap. This guy didn't seem to care if people died, as long as the job got done. Not only was it unsafe, the sound of the tractor engines were distracting to the game. It made it hard to communicate on the court, and hearing the whistle was a strain. Someone had to say something. That someone was me, of course.

Even after my two- or three-minute diatribe on how wrong the situation was, he would not concede. The engines stayed on. And the haze got worse. There were two giant exhaust fans high on either end of the building that sat motionless. I inquired if they could be turned on, but the reply was that no one had wired them in yet. Brilliant. The place had been operational for ten years, but no one had hooked them up.

I found a fairly large floor fan in a closet nearby and ran an extension cord to the bench area, so that at least we could draw some air across the players to get some oxygen stirred up. It was more of an effort to appease my common sense than anything worthwhile. It was simply awful. It was one of the worst playing conditions I have ever been a part of.

Years ago, we played in an arena that had to be over a hundred degrees inside. One of the goalies almost passed out from heat prostration and was carried off the floor. It didn't stop us. We found another net-minder and kept playing. That was when we were in our early twenties. Now we were in our midforties. At least this time I *knew* we were insane. Back then, I never gave it a second thought. I would have been pissed if someone even suggested not playing because of the heat. Ah, youth; if it didn't kill you, it probably should have.

So in a smoke-filled, carbon monoxide pit of death, we played street hockey. We lost the game 3–2, and it had a huge impact on me physically. My head was pounding, my legs felt like anvils, and I couldn't lift my arms over my head. The effects of the toxic air weighed heavily on me. I asked Doug and Paul on the way home if they felt the same. Neither complained of any similar aftereffects. They admitted that it had been hard to breathe during the game, but they couldn't honestly say they were feeling what I was.

I chalked it up to getting old and being out of shape. We wouldn't have to play in those conditions again. The next week, they would surely be done with the renovations, and we could get back to competing in a normal atmosphere and not the equivalent of playing on the red planet. But just in case, the three of us decided that we wouldn't play if the same scenario unfolded.

When I say the three of us, I'm referring to myself, my brother Doug, and our friend Paul Lesiczka. We'd been playing street hockey together since sometime in the late eighties. We met Paul playing against him back when we played pick-up games at the Newton middle school nearby. That was when I thought I was Gretzky on parquet. This guy, "Paully," as they called him, was killing us. He was scoring these circus goals and had ridiculous speed and stamina.

At first I thought he was just lucky. Of course I would. No one was better than me. Let me tell you something I learned that summer. One, it wasn't luck. He was a freak on the street hockey court. Two, I wasn't as good as I thought I was.

Mind you, I'm not that bad. I'm just no superstar. I have a knack for play-making, can play hard against anybody, and have fairly soft hands around the net. But this guy was sick. At first I fought it. I didn't want to believe that someone could be that much better than me. Then I came to accept it. When he finally agreed to play for us, I embraced it. My brother has a similar skill set as me, but has sneaky speed for a six-footer and a wicked one-timer from his left wing position.

We became known as the Kingston Rats and went on to win championships in many a venue in the Northeast. And we also lost. But we had more fun than was probably legal. The rides home in the car with my dad tagging along are some of the fondest memories outside of racing horses I have. During the pinnacle of our career as a line, we were almost unstoppable. At times the chemistry was magical.

We had some amazing wins, including a championship series that had us down one game to none in a best of three. Facing elimination with a minute and nine seconds left on the clock in the third period, we were down 6–3. During the face-off, Paul glanced to his left at Doug, then over at me on his right. His left sleeve was torn off at the shoulder from a bench-clearing brawl ten years before. He probably hadn't washed that thing twice since he'd been issued it some fifteen years earlier. The dark emblem of a vicious black rat holding a stick with drool coming out of his fanged mouth was faded and dirty. The right shoulder of his jersey was blackened from countless dives on the floor sacrificing his body for the game as a human Zamboni. Sweat glistened on his face, and in a matter-of-fact tone, he said through a clenched jaw, "This ain't over. There's a minute left. We gotta bring it to another level."

Doug and I just stared ahead and said nothing. He said it all. *"Play till you hear the whistle."*

In fifteen seconds, Paul scored to make it 6–4. Twenty seconds later, I got us within a goal. With less than a second remaining on the clock, our big defenseman, Chris, scored with a vicious slap shot from the point, to tie it 6–6. We went on to win in overtime as Doug buried a quick one-timer from the high slot three minutes into the extra frame.

A week later, we trailed again in game three and tied it up once more with only three seconds left on the clock. We finished them off in overtime again with Doug sneaking one five hole. It was something that could have been written for a movie. I'm not sure anyone would go to see it, but nonetheless, it seemed scripted. Except no one would believe it was possible. Not only was it possible, but it happened, and we have it on tape to prove it. It was the best of times.

Rats 2009 Champioship:
Back row left to right: Chris Janozs, Paul
Chauvin, Doug Mitchell, Jay Emerson
Front row left to right: Jeb Sayer, Ron DesRosiers,
Marc Mitchell, Paul Lesiczka

But we were much older now. The game had slowed down for us, but we still loved to play. The teams that were gunning for us were comprised of twentysomethings and late-model teenagers. They were all trying to dethrone the old regime. The three of us (plus Harryman) made the trip back down for game two of the semifinals, assuming that the construction was done and we wouldn't have any confrontations with the rink owner about noxious gases. We had been calling my father Harryman for many years, as somehow he had gained the title when he was Doug's music agent and went by the pseudonym Harry Mann. The name stuck. Besides, he was "the man."

When we arrived, the sound of diesel engines drifted out into the parking lot, as did the blue smoke through the doorway as we entered. Seriously? After all of our discussions the week before about how unsafe and unhealthy it was for people to play in there, they were back at it. Not to mention the fact that it was illegal and that we threatened to pull our team from the playoffs if the rink owner didn't stop the construction during games.

This guy was either one stubborn son of a bitch or just plain stupid. One of our players left. He was one of the smarter ones. The rest of us started in on the owner, telling him that we couldn't play under those conditions. He had to shut off the machines. After a few minutes of heated debate, he finally conceded to have them take a forty-five-minute break for our game. You would have thought we were asking him for a kidney.

The air was still toxic. There were dangerous levels of carbon monoxide in there, and to be honest, we should have walked out. But even in our forties, with all that we know about the hazards of those situations, we still wanted to play the game. We loved it that much. So we played.

After the first period, we trailed 3–1.

"Are you going to take the skirt off and play or what?" Paul asked now.

I was bent over with both hands on my stick, resting it on my knees, just trying to catch my breath before they dropped the puck again. For hockey's sake, I call it a puck, but we played with an orange street hockey ball.

"I'm trying, Paully. I'm just getting warmed up. Something's not right, man. Never mind, I'll be all right. Just get ready," I replied, breathing heavily.

"Another level," he chirped back.

In agreement I answered, "Another level. Gooch, you ready over there?" calling my brother by his nickname.

He nodded once with a dark glare back through the smoky-yellow visor of his helmet from his spot on the left wing. In all my years playing, he was the only one I'd seen wearing a visor that wasn't clear. He said it was because it didn't fog up as much. It certainly gave him a menacing look.

For the next shift, I gave it everything I had. My legs were betraying me. But I pressed. Gooch did a hesitation move at the blue line, freezing the defensemen, and then dished over to Paul, letting me get ahead of the play. Paully then slipped me a sweet pass that gave me an easy snap shot for the score. The push paid off. We were back in the game. But in those two minutes, I was done.

"That's more like it." Paul slapped me on the helmet. "I thought I was going to have to pull that extension cord over there," he said, pointing to the fan that was blowing the blue smoke around, "and shove it up your ass to get you charged up."

I smiled, recognizing his joke, but inside I was collapsing.

"Yup, I'm back," I said quietly, worried that I had nothing left.

It *had* to be the carbon monoxide. Once again, it was taking its toll on me. Between periods, I ran outside and drank in as much oxygen as I could in the two-minute break. It wasn't enough. My muscles ached, and I couldn't catch my breath. But I had to get back in there. Retirement from this young man's game was becoming depressingly imminent. I thought, *This could be the last time I'm here, on the court, playing for a title.*

I made my way back in and sat on the bench, letting the other line get out there, hoping they could hold their own until our scoring unit got back on the floor. Doug and Paul played as hard as they could with me lagging behind, unable to make the plays to set them up as I normally would. It wasn't there. My mind was writing checks my body couldn't cash.

Despite my poor performance, the team rallied and won 5–4. One more win and we were in the finals.

Soon after the game, I realized that it didn't really matter. Paul had already told us months ago that he would be away the following week. It just so happened that his trip landed on game three of this best-of-three series. Had we taken care of business as we should have and won the first two, we would have made it to the finals with a bye week coming up. We couldn't win without him. That wasn't being pessimistic; it was just reality. To tell the truth, removing any one of us from our line would have been devastating, let alone our best player. We were doomed.

On the way home, I was exhausted and lay down in the "way back" seat of the van as the other guys sat up front. My arms felt like they were tied down. I elevated my feet on the side glass and rested my heels on the bottom of the window. My fingers found my neck and started feeling around the swollen lymph node on the right side of my throat. I took a few worried swirls around it with my thumb and middle finger. It wasn't going away. Fortunately it wasn't getting any bigger, as I had been keeping a close watch on its size. About two centimeters.

I had been taught to use my fingers this way during school while I was training to be an equine vet as it was a prerequisite for palpating mares that were going to be bred by feel. The clinicians had taught me how wide my fingers were and how to measure small objects by feeling them. It was imperative to be able to measure things like that when sizing ovaries in mares.

Oddly, as a right-handed person, I always used my left arm when rectally palpating them. Yes, I said rectally. The idea of sticking nearly your whole arm into the back end of such a large beast at first blush seems not only counterintuitive but downright suicidal. It takes a gentle, slow touch to get in there without getting your head kicked off. Believe it or not, most mares will stand for the procedure without too much protest if you are a gentleman.

A nicely lubed, coned hand is ideal. Gloved, of course. They call it a palpation sleeve. It's just a sliver of plastic between your flesh and the end product of equine digestion. Inevitably your arm smells like manure for the rest of the day despite the protection.

You start your approach with just your two center fingers, and with your hand shaped like Kermit the Frog's mouth, you ever so slowly make your way in. Once inside, we were taught to contort our bodies and reach around and find the right and left ovary from within the rectal walls. Sounds impossible, right? It felt like it too…for about twenty or so tries, until one day…I felt it. I was actually holding an ovary in my hand through the intestinal wall. It was quite a triumph. And then you start feeling for follicles and hope you find something bigger than two centimeters or so. Follicles that big meant the mare was ready for the stallion.

My lymph node was almost ready to be bred. Ignoring it wasn't making it go away. The antibiotics I'd tried nearly three months previously had had no effect on it whatsoever. As a vet, I'd felt dozens of these types of lymph nodes. It couldn't be good. But I was only forty-five, too young to get…cancer. I said it out loud in my head. *I probably have cancer.* I stared at the van's headliner thinking about how awful I felt at that moment.

"Great game, guys," I croaked from the back. "Either of you two feel like shit like I do from the fumes?"

My brother started, "I feel it a little, but not bad. Why, what's up?"

"I feel great. I could play another game," Paul quipped.

I could feel him smiling even though I was still staring at the unlit dome light.

"You'd play another game if you were dead," I replied. "I felt like I was running in quicksand. Something isn't right. I have to make an appointment to have this swollen lymph node checked."

"You still have that?" my father chimed in from his usual position in the driver's seat. "I thought you said it was getting smaller."

To save everyone from unnecessary worry, I had kind of downplayed the whole thing. No sense getting all worked up over something we knew nothing about. I would get it checked in due course. I think I was just worried about what I might find out and, quite frankly, didn't want to know. Ignorance is bliss. Unless you're dead. Then you're just ignorant. Even worse, you're just dead.

"Yeah, I still have it."

"Jesus, I can't believe you're that dumb," my father said. "Get that thing checked."

"Yeah, I will."

"Tomorrow. Do it." Harryman finished his sentence abruptly.

"I know, I'll call my doctor and set it up. First thing."

"You're a dink. Don't just say it, do it!" my father responded emphatically, implying that I might not follow through.

Harryman knew me better than anybody. He had seen me procrastinate with the best of them. He was my mentor, teaching me how to write, even in the very beginning. Many a time he saw me wait until the last possible moment to finish a writing project, but willingly helped me get it done, no matter how late it was. He wasn't wrong in thinking I would once again put something off without his urging.

I was quiet for the rest of the trip home, only occasionally jumping in when Doug and Paul verbally recreated the goals we scored, reliving each pass, each shot, as if it were the Stanley Cup we were playing for. We would have played for a Dixie cup. It didn't matter. We absolutely loved the game. I was thinking the worst about my situation and became saddened that perhaps I had just played my last one. Self-pity enveloped me.

CHAPTER 3 – SEARCHING FOR ANSWERS

The diagnostician in me took over. I started laying down all of my symptoms, starting with the first: the lymphadenopathy. One swollen lymph node. Okay, what does that mean? Well, just one. That's good. If it's cancer, it's likely contained. Let's see. It could be an infection.

But I had already tried a broad-spectrum antibiotic, and it did nothing. No, I didn't see a doctor. I self prescribed one from my pharmacy shelf hoping it would just go away. It was not only illegal, but by not getting it checked early when I should have, could have cost me my life. Not smart. Maybe a resistant bacteria? But there was no fever. I was grasping for an easy out.

It's probably cancer.

More self-pity.

Back to diagnosing. What other symptoms? We have to find a disease that fits that isn't malignant. I used the term "we" in my thought process as if I were in rounds at school addressing students. "We have the lymph node. What else, anyone? Anyone?" (I don't have to write it…you said it in your head already. Just admit it, you said Bueller.)

Fatigue. I could barely keep up during the game. I was winded after one shift, and my muscles were quivering on the way home. It was probably the carbon monoxide. I was trying to explain it extrinsically. I was just fooling myself. No one else in the arena had complained about it; just me. It didn't make sense.

Good, fatigue, what else? Let's put the fatigue on the table. That might be explained by the fumes, but it's also a symptom. The night sweats. Oh man, I completely forgot about those. They were horrible. For the past month or more, I'd been experiencing nearly sleepless nights that had me changing my bed three and four times a night, throwing the wet linens in the wash at three in the morning and having another set ready for the next episode just two hours later. I was completely soaking my sheets and pillow. Repeatedly. It was so bad that Jen had bought a special fan that attached to the foot of the bed (just under the covers), which tried to cool me off and prevent sweating. It was a sweet thought. It failed miserably.

Okay, that's definitely a symptom.

Jen couldn't take my restlessness, as with all the flipping and flopping I did, she was getting just as little sleep as I was. She started sleeping in the extra bedroom at the other end of the house. Well, it is actually a double-wide trailer that looks like a real house, so it is fairly long.

One night, during the first episode of my true night sweats, I panicked a bit. There I was, exhausted, lying in a puddle of perspiration, with no idea what was going on. Even my pillow was soaked. I was shivering uncontrollably from the heat loss. I thought I was in big trouble. I started calling for her to come help me. I was too cold to get up.

"Hey!" I softly yelled out, hoping Jen would hear me.

The first time I called her, it wasn't that loud. I didn't want to freak her out; I just wanted to get her attention. Then I did it again, this time with more volume. Three times. Still no response from the other end of the house. She had to be hearing me; my voice was booming. Finally I really yelled out in desperation.

"HEY!!!!"

And I mean it was loud. I was freaking out. The thing is she had heard me the first couple times and had been slowly making her way toward my room. On the last yell, she was standing right next to me in the dark.

"WHAT!" she screamed back (quite angrily, I might add).

Well, I just about jumped out of my skin and let out an "AHHH!" Then she jumped back and yelled the same thing. We had scared each other half out of our wits. I almost had to change the sheets for a different reason. Looking back, it was quite comical, but at the time, neither of us was laughing. She graciously helped me change my sheets after understanding why I was screaming for her, but she still wasn't very happy about being roused out of bed at three in the morning by a madman yelling "hey" repetitively in the dead of night.

Two hours later, my sheets were soaked again. I changed them myself.

I wanted to stop searching for problems. It wasn't painting a pretty picture. The more I thought about it, the worse I felt. If I had a dog with these symptoms, I would be trying to pacify the owners, getting them ready for the bombshell that was about to be dropped when we finally got around to the answer we didn't want. Cancer.

My muscles didn't ache just that night. They ached every single day. It was a chore just to get out of bed in the morning. My ribs hurt, my back hurt. Hell, everything hurt.

"Paul, you really not playing next week?" I snapped out of my little bubble of worry in the back of the van to get out of my own head.

"Yup, got a parts show in Pennsylvania," he replied. "You guys will be fine."

Paul was into old muscle cars, more specifically Pontiacs circa 1970. He was probably looking for some NOS parts for some rare GTO or Judge that he was working on.

"We're screwed. It was a good run. What the hell is a parts show? You know what, never mind. It doesn't matter."

Doug chirped in. "That's just great. A friggin' parts show," he said in a sarcastic tone that both busted his chops and implied an understanding of previous plans.

Secretly I was relieved. I couldn't play three more games after the next week, even if we won. I was completely gone. The way I felt, I would be lucky to make it up the stairs of my house.

The next morning, hearing my father's words in my head telling me I was stupid, I reluctantly made the call to my doctor. He couldn't see me for a week. Had I been persistent, he probably would have seen me sooner, but I was still fighting it, not really wanting to know that there was a major problem.

A week came and went. Doug, my father, and I made the trip back down to the hockey rink without our star center. In over twenty years, Paul had never missed a playoff game. Everything felt off. I was physically and mentally beaten. Without Paul, and with me functioning at 50 percent or less, it would be nearly impossible to pull off a win. The only positive about the whole situation was that there was no construction going on.

I was right, but the game was closer than expected. We lost 3–1. Ironically, I scored the only goal for us, but it was in the first two minutes of the game when I had just enough energy to compete. After that, I was useless, taking one-minute shifts and coming off the court desperate for air. My brother gave everything he had, but I gave him no help. It was depressing to watch, and I was helpless to affect the outcome. It was a shame. Our last realistic chance to win a championship ended like that.

Jen covered for me in the animal hospital that we had opened together in 1997. I drove myself to Manchester, New Hampshire, to my doctor's office at the Queen City Hospital.

Nothing good could come from this, I thought. I had already convinced myself that I had some sort of malignant condition, but I was hoping they'd find something that would be fairly easy to treat. Based on the rudimentary differential diagnosis list I'd made using veterinary medicine as a baseline, I hadn't come up with anything I liked.

The top two on my list were both forms of lymphoma: Hodgkin's and non-Hodgkin's. I had done a fair amount of research on these diseases and decided that Hodgkin's was my best choice. It's the first string of cancers as far as name recognition. It's the one that

Mario Lemieux had. I figured if he was still alive, it was a fair assumption that it was treatable in some instances.

Non-Hodgkin's disease is a catchall term used for all the lymphomas that aren't specifically the Hodgkin's variety. If you start trying to figure out which cancer you might have, and you're not an oncologist, you will most likely be wrong.

In the non-Hodgkin's category, they break it down into two groups. One is called T-cell lymphoma, and the other is B-cell lymphoma. Under those categories are numerous different variations of horrible things that can go wrong when cells mutate, and they have names for every single one. Just trying to remember the names alone can be a difficult task. Now try to study each disease and learn all the mechanisms of action, possible causes, symptoms, and the best ways to treat it. I give those doctors a tip of the cap when it comes to their grasp on these illnesses and the ability to keep up in an ever-changing world of neoplasia.

As I read some of the prognoses for the dozens of cancers that were listed, I started getting more and more concerned. If I had to choose, I guess Hodgkin's was as good a choice as any. They had named it all by itself, so they had to know quite a bit about it. When you start reading about second- and third-string cancers like the little-known nodal marginal zone B-cell lymphoma, it makes you wonder how much is really understood about it. Just the name alone is confusing. It doesn't have a catchy moniker, at least not one that anyone could ever say in passing conversation. And let's face it, it doesn't sound very hip. Perhaps if they made an acronym for it, it would have more cachet, like NoZoLympho. Nah, that still sucks. The more obscure the condition, the less money goes into research. Less money, less survival.

But you have to be careful what you wish for, even if you're trying to pick the lesser of a hundred evils. Plenty of people have died from Hodgkin's disease who were told they had a reasonable chance of survival. That's why they give percentages. Some poor bastard always falls into the category of mortality. It's just the way it goes.

It was making me nervous to be almost requesting a certain disease. I needed to pump the brakes in my head and just let fate deal me whatever cards she had. There was no sense to it anyway. It wasn't going to change the inevitable. I cleared my mind and decided to let it all unfold without my prejudice.

Dr. Milakis had been my primary care physician for many years. We shared a Greek heritage, but neither of us spoke the language. Both of my parents spoke Greek all the time in our house growing up. They used it as a secret language to be able to talk behind our backs, right in front of us, rather than try to teach us. If we were smart enough, we would have picked it up. Neither Doug nor I was able to decode and learn. His brain is musical, and mine is mathematical. When it comes to languages other than our own, let's just say they were foreign to us.

Dr. Milakis doesn't look "greeky-greek," and you might confuse him for any one of the other Mediterranean breeds out there. He does have the smaller stature and dark features of our group, but his nose is not nearly as big as most of us Cretans. He had a salt-and-pepper professional haircut that featured a bit more salt than spice. His right hand had a large patch of vitiligo that was blanched and devoid of any pigment. I'm guessing he had other blotches elsewhere, but I never saw the man naked. The one I could see looked like some Eastern European country, but I couldn't tell you its name. I told you, math is my forte, not geography. His slightly overweight body was well hidden under a classic white doctor's lab coat.

There was a stretch of ten years where I didn't see him at all. I'm not stating this because I'm proud of myself for not getting checked. It's both a reflection of my male stubbornness to get a physical and my general state of wellness during that time. I was young, healthy, and indestructible. At least I thought so.

He started in with the typical history taking, with nods and uh-huhs, as I told him what I was experiencing. His somber demeanor made me even more nervous when he started feeling my lymph node on the side of my neck. His seriousness was only confirming my own worries. He wasn't giving me the, "Oh this little thing? Don't sweat it, Marc, it's probably nothing." Oh no, he never said anything like that. It was more like, "I don't like the looks of this; we need to set you up for a biopsy…as soon as possible."

Beautiful, a biopsy. Yup, I knew it. It's cancer. But he wasn't saying anything I didn't already know. He was merely endorsing my theory by saying it out loud. In the meantime, they took about ten vials of blood and shipped it off down the hall to the lab. After telling me how concerned he was, the doctor accompanied me down to the reception area and made sure the nurse made my appointment with Dr. Shultz for the very next day. He was one of the best. Aren't they all? They never say, "We're going to set you up with a surgeon; he's just mediocre."

"Tell Dr. Shultz that I want it done tomorrow," Dr. Milakis told his nurse sternly.

"He's very busy, Doctor," the nurse replied. "If I can't make it for tomorrow, is next week all right?"

I thought to myself, *yeah, next week is fine. I've had this thing for, like, four months, so two or three days are no big deal.*

"No, tell him I want it done tomorrow. He'll work him in," he snapped back.

Lovely, it was worse than I thought. If he had his way, I'd be getting laid open on the table as we speak. I was screwed. Next, he sent me down to radiology for x-rays. You know, just some routine chest films to be sure everything was clear in there. Just a precaution.

Ten minutes later, I was sitting in his office waiting to go over the films. His office had recently gone digital, so the results were almost instantaneous. Well, the images are done right away, but sometimes it takes a few days for a radiologist to read them. As I sat there, I took a peek at the last patient's films that were still up on the screen because I was nosy, and we vets think we can read any x-ray you put in front of us. At least some of us do. Truth is, we can't, but that's how we egotists think.

As I looked at the view of this guy's chest, a rush of fear flooded me. *Please don't let that film be mine. It can't be mine,* I pleaded to myself. There was a relatively big white mass in the center of the film just above the heart that couldn't be anything but a large tumor. Even a veterinarian who had never looked at a human x-ray could see that it was not supposed to be there. A feeling of doom crashed over me. I began to assume that it was me up there on the screen. I felt my chest, then the lymph node. Nothing was wrong with my chest on the outside, but it didn't matter. The x-ray told a very different story.

Please don't let that be me. Please don't let that be me. I kept saying it my head. I was staring at it from my seat from about eight feet away, too scared to get up and check the patient's name in the upper left corner of the screen. It was too far away to read from my chair.

Then the doctor came in the room. He had a look that told me the answer. It *was* me up on the screen.

"Are those my x-rays?" I asked before he could even close the door behind him.

"I'm afraid so. It's not good. We'll know more once the blood-work is done and the biopsy is taken tomorrow."

The tumor was clearly obvious. It was perched just over my heart. I approximated it to be about eight centimeters in diameter, and it had fairly indistinct margins. For those of you unfamiliar with the metric system, that's about the size of a tennis ball. And it was fuzzy like one. That fuzziness, in my professional estimation, meant it was probably fairly aggressive, because it was spreading out unevenly instead of growing in a nice regular fashion. That, of course, is open to interpretation with any given type of tumor, but in general, the fuzzier it is, the worse it is.

"Do you think it's lymphoma?"

"Most likely, at your age, something like that. It's not good to make any diagnoses without confirming it with other things like bloodwork and a biopsy. Hopefully we'll find out soon, and we can get started with some sort of treatment plan." His tone was apologetic and sincere.

"Yeah, I know. I knew it was something bad. It sucks being right all the time," I said in a somewhat sarcastic tone.

He shook my hand and told me to try to think positively as he saw me out. What more could he do? It wasn't his fault. Don't beat the crap out of the messenger, right? I know, I know, don't shoot the messenger. I didn't have a gun.

On the way home, I called Jen and explained the findings to her. The gravity of the situation was finally beginning to sink in. Our worst fears were being realized. I had cancer. Now they had to figure out what kind. My doctor was fairly certain it was lymphoma.

Then I did probably the worst thing that any patient can do. I googled it. The Internet is a wonderfully horrible thing. It can be so helpful if you want to find out how to get to a destination, get reviews of certain restaurants, or just troll around Facebook to see what your neighbors and cyberfriends are up to. But when it comes to playing doctor, it's best to leave that to the doctors.

If you want to scare yourself to death and misinterpret information, it isn't very hard. I started looking up morbidity and mortality tables for all the different kinds of lymphomas and tried to figure out what my odds were for survival based on my age and the size of the tumor in my chest, along with other factors. The problem is, I'm not a doctor. Sure, I'm a veterinarian, but last I checked, I wasn't a dog.

After about an hour of self-torture, I solemnly shut down my browser and tried to fall asleep. That's when I started to think I could feel that thing growing inside me. A little alien trying to make its way out of my body, slowly taking over in an effort to destroy me. I just wanted to reach inside myself and yank it out. I felt so helpless. I was almost certain I could feel it getting bigger.

After a night of impossible sleep, I stirred to the reality of going for the biopsy of the little friend on my neck. I made the trip back to the Queen City Hospital by myself early in the afternoon while Jen worked the clinic. Should have been easy. A quick biopsy, a butterfly bandage, and I'd be heading right back home. It was October 7. There was nothing fun or good about the trip. I was extremely anxious, not so much because of the procedure, but for the potential outcome. The results couldn't come back quickly enough.

Dr. Shultz had the personality of a feral cat that had gone to boarding school—just refined enough to get by, but his true character seeped out of him. He was aloof and abrupt. Everything he did seemed mechanical and sterile. I guess sterile is good for a surgeon, but it's better suited for instruments and not your persona. He had pale skin, blue eyes, and thinning white hair. He was probably younger than he looked, but the stresses of being a surgeon had likely aged him prematurely. I assumed he was of German decent from his name and looks. Nothing about his speech suggested that lineage. I was just making an educated guess.

This was to be an outpatient procedure. No sedation, no big deal. They escorted me into the surgery room that was easily thirty feet by thirty feet and had a huge bank of surgery lights in the center of the ceiling about fifteen feet up. They were the new LED style that are blindingly bright. There was a surgery table in the middle of the room and an instrument tray next to it. That's it. The open space was odd. It felt big enough to be one of the surgery rooms we had in the equine ward at vet school, except there weren't padded walls and the table was five times smaller.

For the procedure I was about to undergo, it seemed like overkill. It was me, the doctor, and a nurse in this monstrous surgical suite. It was a room where they might perform a heart transplant with a team of twenty. Our voices echoed in the absence of people. A single machine was hooked up to my right index finger, and the beep, beep, beep of my heartbeat filled the empty space.

Most of the surgeries I did during my large animal days were done on conscious horses. As a surgeon, it is important to possess a certain feel or finesse, especially if the patient is awake. With the horse, a gentle technique may be more for self-preservation than anything else. This guy had no touch whatsoever. I knew from the first stab with his needle carrying the local anesthetic that he was heavy. Now I'm not saying he was a butcher, but there are some surgeons who have a soft feel and some who are as subtle as a hammer. He was the latter.

As he opened up his incision, I felt the warm blood run down my neck under the drape. I wasn't giving him an A for smoothness, and now his grade for hemostasis was seriously in jeopardy. He spent a few moments tying off the bleeders he had encountered and moved on. He then went in for the lymph node. He was pulling and twisting and jerking at it quite vigorously.

My neck was being yanked around, and I could feel him tugging at the tissue attached to my throat even though it was numb from the meds. I then realized why I was not anesthetized for the procedure. I found myself trying to anchor myself down with my hands to keep from physically moving. Had I been asleep, he would have hauled me right off the table. You would have thought he was extracting an impacted wisdom tooth. I was waiting for him to throw his left leg up onto my shoulder to get better traction. Definitely German, I thought, and a direct descendent of Dr. Mengele.

I could tell it was giving him more trouble than normal with all his grumblings and how often he was asking his nurse for gauze to dab away the oozing blood. After about a half hour, he was mercifully finished and closed the wound. I give him credit for that; the finished product looked great. But then the swelling started.

If you punch someone in the face repeatedly, chances are you will get some edema. The less-than-gentle technique that he employed on my tissue was about to fight back. In three minutes, I could feel the tightness forming around my neck. In four minutes, my head was pounding and I could feel the swelling with my hand. At five minutes, I was frantically calling the nurse for ice as I could tell it was going to get worse. A minute later, she came back in with one of those "crack and go" ice packs that get about as cold as a stick of butter in the fridge. It was about the size of a saltine. Then she proceeded to wrap it in a terry cloth towel that couldn't possibly let the cold through it. Basically, she wrapped it in an oven mitt.

I just stared at her in disbelief. This is the ice she gets? Clearly a joke. I promptly removed the insulating pad she had it encased in and placed it on my quickly enlarging neck. She immediately scolded me, saying that I couldn't take the cover off the "ice." It was hospital policy to not let patients put that directly on their skin for fear of causing some sort of frostbite effect. Frostbite? This stuff wouldn't even nibble me. I told her that I would abide by the rules if she got me some real ice and called the doctor.

Meanwhile I was swelling by the second. It was scary how fast it happened and how large my neck was growing. By the time the doctor came back in to check on me, it was far too late. The damage had been done. Eight minutes had transpired. He told me that this never happens and all that happy horseshit. Blah, blah, blah. That's something I have heard all my life in so many instances. "You're the first person this has happened to." Right. Typical.

If something can go wrong, or anything goofy can happen, look no further than yours truly. For me, it's been a way of life. This was just another gem in the jewels of ridiculousness I have been graciously adorned with along the way. I don't let it get me down, I just keep plodding along. I know there are people out there that understand this. Maybe a lot of people feel this way, like stuff just happens to them.

They never did bring me any real ice. I just sat there with a luke-cold cracker pressed onto a swelling that was four times its size. Funny, in a morbid, sad kind of way. Quite pathetic actually. Most people in the medical field know that ice is your best friend when it comes to soft tissue injury and swelling. It seemed that the Queen City Hospital didn't buy into that whole theory. But I'm not angry. Not bitter at all. No, not me. It might not have been so bad but for the events that unfolded as a result of this debacle.

I really should have had someone escort me there, because it was nearly impossible to drive myself home. I was unable to move my head to either side from both the pain and the constriction due to the swelling. They probably should have admitted me for observation, not knowing how bad it could potentially get. The doctor was quite flippant about the whole thing and told me to go home and get some rest. I wish I could have channeled the pain into his body that night. Get some rest. Not likely. He was officially off the Christmas card list, since he was partially responsible for the car wreck that nearly killed me.

Over the next day, the inflammation got worse and the pain increased. The night sweats continued, and my head pounded constantly. As I lay awake in bed at 3:30 a.m., fleeting thoughts of overdosing on anything crossed my mind. By 3:35 a.m., I had come to my senses and decided to tough it out. Moments later, my frustration was pointed at my surgeon, and thoughts of hitting him over the head with a baseball bat crept in. By 3:41 a.m., I was picturing myself in a jail cell with night sweats and a swollen neck. Perhaps I didn't think that through well enough. The seconds ticked away agonizingly. Pain, boredom, fear. They were all my friends that night.

As Friday rolled along, Jen and I started to discuss the trip we were supposed to be taking on Sunday to visit her parents in

Portland, Oregon. They had retired out there after spending quite a few years in Cleveland where Jen's dad was a prominent surgeon at the Cleveland Clinic. As I felt the thumping in my head and the tightness of the skin stretching down to my shoulder, I thought how nice it would have been if he had done my biopsy instead of the guy I drew here at home.

John H. Raaf, MD, was an oncology surgeon who specialized in pancreatic tumors. Talk about needing a soft touch. The pancreas is probably the most cranky and cantankerous of all the organs. It is pale yellow, soft, and doesn't really have a distinct shape, although I'm sure Jen's dad would quickly dispute that. He would assure me that it most definitely has an identifiable shape and also has lobes and nooks that have names and all that. Sure, to an expert. For someone like me, who just glances at the pancreas while removing a spleen or biopsying a liver in a dog, it's just a creamy, scalloped blob that hides out near the stomach.

If you don't handle the pancreas with absolute respect, it will get very angry. You can't even give it so much as a disparaging look without the thing getting upset. When I'm doing abdominal surgery in a dog, I take notice and give the little guy a wide berth. No telling how long he'll stay pissed after you aggravate him. He can hold a grudge for weeks.

Ah yes, it would have been nice to have her dad on my neck that day. Instead, we were now faced with the real prospect of canceling our trip because of post-surgical complications. Jen's mom, Heather, is also a doctor. She went back to med school and was in her residency while we were both in vet school. Quite impressive. However, she would be the absolute last person I would want working on me. Before they moved to Portland, she was a forensic pathologist for the city of Cleveland. If you saw her, you were cold, dead, and belly up on a slab of stainless steel. No, she was not the person I wanted working on me. Not yet anyway.

JEN'S PARENTS: JOHN H. RAAF, M.D. AND HEATHER RAAF, M.D.

We were supposed to fly out on Sunday. When Saturday morning came, my neck wasn't much better. There was minimal improvement, the pain was still fairly significant, and my range of motion was nearly nonexistent. It was becoming clear that we wouldn't be able to go. We had told Dr. Shultz about our plans to travel before I was discharged that day, and he was quite certain I would have no problem flying in a few days. So now we had a heavy-handed *and* a delusional surgeon.

Jen and I started going through the logistics of travel and weighing out our reasonable options. We had been planning this trip for a year. The two of us rarely got to go away for an extended period of time together because of the constraints of owning a single-doctor veterinary practice. One of us usually tended the store while the other did his or her thing. Sure, we got away for long weekends, but for both of us to take a full week off was not an easy task. We were finally getting that chance.

On top of having a home in Portland, Jen's parents also owned a cabin on the Rogue River in Agness, Oregon, that had been passed down from Jen's grandfather. Andaddy, as they called him, was a prominent neurosurgeon; a real pioneer in his field. I imagine he was one pretty smart dude. I mean really, there's even a saying about it. He and his cronies had purchased some land in the remote recesses of the Rogue River where road access wasn't yet available. They got there by boat and had to trek up a steep one-hundred-foot embankment to get to the lot where they cleared some trees and built a log cabin using the native lumber. It was quite a site in its day.

There was just one big drawback to its remoteness. If you ever broke a leg or had a heart attack, or, say, got pancreatitis, there was no way in hell you were getting out of there in a hurry. You didn't have to be...well, Jen's grandfather, to figure out you could be in trouble out there with such limited access to medical attention. Fortunately for the group, none of them ever required such help.

A VIEW FROM THE BOTTOM OF THE ROGUE RIVER. HARD TO
IMAGINE THIS RIVER ROSE OVER 100 FEET IN 1969.

As the weekend rolled on, it was becoming increasingly obvious that we weren't going to make the trip. Not only was my neck still puffed out, but there were all the other issues I was experiencing as a result of whatever it was that I had. I was still soaking my sheets at night, my body ached all over, and I was exhausted every waking moment. And although I was tired all the time, it was nearly impossible to get a good night's sleep because of the pain and the sweats. I was beginning to realize that even if the whole biopsy catastrophe hadn't happened, we wouldn't be making a trip across the country.

To be completely honest about all this, I must admit that what happened to my neck very well could have happened under anyone's surgical blade. It's just so much easier to point the finger at someone rather than to think it was just bad luck. I guess you'd call it human nature.

I once did a simple cyst removal on a dog's hock (back ankle) that should have gone routinely. After surgery, even though the animal was wearing one of those silly cones on his head, and the surgery site was bandaged, he was able to almost chew his leg off. What ensued was a disaster. With no cost to the client, I ended up keeping the dog in my hospital for almost four months, doing daily bandage changes and a skin graft to ultimately fix the damage that was done. We ended up saving the limb and healing the wound, but lost the client as soon as the dog left the hospital. He apparently blamed me for what went wrong, no differently than what I had done with my surgeon. Maybe I should have packed the dog's leg in ice.

I think my ire toward the whole lymph node fiasco was based on the lack of ice offered in my scenario. The truth is that surgical catastrophes are part of the landscape. Sometimes things just go sour. The fact that they didn't give me an adequate supply of ice certainly didn't help my situation but it wasn't the only reason it transpired. Like I said, sometimes things just go bad, but I threw the surgeon under the bus for good measure. What can I say? I'm human.

After much consideration, we cancelled our vacation. Let's be clear, I still blamed the doctor for not going. Off the record, there is a high likelihood I would have been miserable had we gone, but that biopsy blunder never gave me the chance to find out. Okay, maybe I am a little bitter.

Don't get me wrong, I was miserable at home and I don't really think it would have been worth going given my situation. Besides, I'm sure Jen's parents didn't have enough sheets in their extra bedroom to accommodate me. I would say I was sweating like a pig, but it's not only cliché, it's incorrect.

Pigs don't really sweat. That's why they wallow in mud—to cool off. So, in fact, the old adage is completely erroneous. If you wanted to say you sweat like an animal, any animal at all, the pig is quite possibly the worst choice to use. Who knew? Apparently the expression has something to do with the smelting of pig iron. But alas, the poor swine pays the price. You can't always trust those old sayings. Sort of like, "I wouldn't wish that on my worst enemy." Of course I would. It's my worst enemy.

Now I know what you're saying: Marc, it's an expression. It's so bad you wouldn't want any human to endure it. I say nonsense. Whatever you're referring to—let's say being slowly cooked to death on a spit by cannibals, having your eyes plucked out with sewing needles, or being forced to watch anything with the Kardashians in it—that's exactly what I would want for my worst enemy. He's my worst enemy. I want him to suffer. Maybe the expression should be "I would only wish it on my worst enemy." Now that makes more sense. As far as the perspiring thing and the pig; just leave the pig out of it. It doesn't work.

Chapter 4 – Diagnostics

The days that followed were agonizing. My neck was killing me, the night sweats continued, we missed our vacation, my car was junk, I was achy all over, and I was getting frailer by the day. The final straw was that I had the absolute realization that I had cancer. Through it all, like the stubborn Greek that I am, I continued to work in our veterinary hospital. When I was too tired, Jen would fill in and take the reins.

I had to stay busy, at least mentally, if not physically. Practicing veterinary medicine allowed me to do both. Waiting for the results of the lymph node biopsy was excruciating. Knowing that I had a tumor the size of an orange in my chest that was most likely the root cause of all the symptoms made me very uneasy. Okay, maybe it was more like a nectarine, but it was pretty big. Every day I waited, the malicious disease inside me was digging in deeper. Every hour that went by brought me closer to death. I just wanted an answer, good or bad.

The not knowing was difficult. I was desperate for a diagnosis, a name. The worst part of all, however, was that a treatment plan hadn't been implemented yet. Whatever that thing was, it was surely getting bigger and stronger as I got weaker. When I swallowed, I started to hear saliva gurgle in my throat as my esophagus was getting bullied by the growing tumor.

Most of my clients who have their animals' tumors biopsied have the results in two or three days. We were at day ten with still no word. It was extremely frustrating. I wondered if I had been the son of the surgeon, how long would that biopsy take to get back? I'm guessing not even remotely close to a week and a half.

The ironic thing about my impatience was that I had no problem waiting like four months to get my lymph node checked, but I was out of my mind with anxiety that they were taking more than a week. Perhaps if I just looked in the mirror, I could have found the right person to blame for my worry. Even when I thought about it, I was still blaming them for taking too long. Funny how the mind works to deflect anger.

This thing in my chest, this malignant evil, was slowly spreading, and there was nothing I could do about it. They say early detection is paramount in combatting cancer. I had already waited too long to have it checked out. Now that it had been detected, we were letting it grow. Every night I lay awake in my bed wondering how much it would grow overnight. In a week, how big would it be? At what point did it get so big they couldn't get rid of it? Were we at that point now?

Ten days. Nothing.

Finally, at day twelve, the hospital called. They still didn't know what I had. They said there were a lot of plasma cells and odd-looking lymphocytes. It might be lymphoma, it might be a plasmacytoma, and they couldn't rule out multiple myeloma. So after nearly two weeks, we still didn't have a treatment plan. They scheduled me the next day for a bone marrow biopsy.

I don't know if you've ever had one, but one thing is certain: don't put it on your bucket list. It's not a barrel of laughs. In the right hands, the procedure is almost tolerable. Fortunately, for the four or five I've had, I've been more than impressed. All of them so far have been delicate and efficient. No matter how gentle they are, though, they can't blunt the sensation caused when they extract the marrow from the bone.

Bones have two basic structures, the cortex, or hard outer part, and the medullary cavity, which is the marrow and is mushy. The thought of my father sucking the marrow out of a chicken bone in the old farmhouse still creeps me out. Mmmm, have a nice helping of reds and whites. That's okay when you're talking about wine, but when it's a heaping serving of lymphocytes and red blood cells... holy crap, that's just disgusting.

When doing a biopsy of the marrow, the hard bone has to be driven through first. This takes a fair amount of force. The operator of the sharp metal bit has to twist back and forth in a clockwise–counterclockwise fashion to bore through. Sometimes you have to lean into it pretty good to do the job.

I'm not sure which scenario makes it worse, having a background in medicine and knowing exactly what they're doing, or being completely in the dark about it. The unknown certainly has the fear factor, but the knowing has the heebie-jeebie element. As they passed a harpoon-sized trocar through my hip, I was worried that the doctor might slip and drive that thing clear through to my bladder.

So there I was, lying facedown on a bed with my butt exposed to the world. A nice young nurse, I assume in her thirties, came around to the front and held my hand for support. Mind you, I didn't ask her to do this; I just assumed that it was protocol to have someone there to literally hold your hand through the procedure. I really didn't care one way or the other, but I certainly wasn't going to offend her. It seemed to be her job to stand there, so I went along with it.

The doctor blocked the skin with some Carbocaine or Mepivacaine, which most people still think of as Novocain. They don't use Novocain much anymore because it contains epinephrine and isn't as effective as the newer generation of drugs. Although epinephrine helps to constrict blood vessels and control bleeding at the injection site, which was very useful for dental procedures, it made some people a little jittery, since it is very similar to adrenaline. Most people can't detect the small amount in the solution, but some patients who were very sensitive to even a minute dose responded with a rapid heart rate and nervousness. That's not exactly what you're looking for when you're trying to relax during a stressful procedure. So, years ago, they switched to a more potent drug without epinephrine in it, but many lay people today still call it Novocain. That brand name has become almost synonymous with any drug used as a pain-killing injection. Sort of like Kleenex is used for any facial tissues, or the term Band-Aid is applied for any of the bandages used for small cuts.

After the doctor numbed up the skin, she started torqueing the trocar back and forth into my hip bone. The bone isn't completely blocked from pain but doesn't hurt as much as you'd think when they burrow into it. Sure, it isn't pleasant, but it's not awful. I could feel her going through the hard cortex. The sensation was changing, and somehow I could feel the point of the bit engaging into the softer, meatier medullary bone. I quickly told her she was close, as I imagined her breaking through and driving that sucker clear to the other side. I wanted her to be sure she started backing off the pressure when she was about to reach the core.

She had probably done hundreds of these procedures before, and she almost certainly rolled her eyes to the other people in the room as if saying "like I really need his help." Listen, all I know is that when I'm drilling through a piece of oak and leaning on the drill, there are times I've buried the hosel of the chuck into the wood when the bit breaks through. I realize I'm no piece of wood, but the mechanics are the same. I didn't need any blunders as she penetrated through the outer bone.

She didn't need my help. She backed off perfectly and slipped in with precision. It was quite a relief. That was the easy part. It's the harvesting of the marrow that really isn't very nice at all. I couldn't see what the instrument was, but it was some sort of metal loop, like a miniature bubble blower. She slipped that into the bone marrow and starting sweeping it back and forth to collect some nice fresh cells. Not fun.

Since it was my first time, I had no idea what kind of sensation to expect. Usually when a doctor is about to perform a procedure on a patient, he or she says something like, "this won't hurt that much," or "it will be over before you know it." Nope. Not for this one. She actually said that it would hurt. I've had plenty of experiences when the doctor says it won't hurt, and it hurt like hell. Now she was telling me that in fact it would. That made me nervous.

And it still didn't prepare me for how it felt. It was like a deep, painful, hot electric shock inside my hip. It isn't very often you can feel pain within your bone. It is a strange feeling indeed. I made some sort of snide remark and grimaced at the first pass with her devil hook.

The skin of the nurse who was holding my hand started to feel a bit clammy. Her grip on my fingers loosened as the doctor went in for sweep number two. When I looked up at her, her eyes were distant, and her face was bloodless. She was dropping like a sack of flour. As she passed out, I was left trying to keep her from smacking her head on the floor, so I did my best to hold on as tight as I could. There I was, with a metal probe in my hip, trying to keep this lady from cracking her skull open. As I braced myself, my body shifted, and the doctor reprimanded me for moving. Well, geez, what the hell?

"A little help here," I said, imploring someone to help this poor woman.

One of the assistants came over and settled her down on the floor. The doctor apologized for what she had said and for the unconscious nurse. I didn't mind. These things happen to me. Par for the course. The very person that was supposed to be keeping me composed and calm passes out. Good stuff. Perhaps she should have been cleaning the instruments or something.

In an ironic kind of way, she did her job. With all the hoopla surrounding my limp supporter, my focus was averted from the procedure. After the doctor finished waving her little metal wand about ten or fifteen times back and forth in my marrow, she put a butterfly bandage on the hole the drill created. Done.

Jen drove me home, and the waiting game began again. They said it could take up to a week to get the results back. I wasn't going to hold my breath. I went back to work the next day and tried to immerse myself in everyday life. But that was virtually impossible. The fatigue was brutal. My muscles were betraying me as I withered with each passing day.

My neck was still swollen on the outside, and the tumor continued to grow from the inside. I could tell it was getting worse, because the noises that were made when I swallowed were getting louder. As saliva tried to pass through my throat, it found a constriction and gurgled there for a while. I would open my mouth and make the letter O, trying to amplify the sound the liquid was making, just for kicks. The soft glug, glug, glug the spit made sounded like a tiny little man was pouring wine into a glass in my throat. If I didn't know why it was happening it would've been kind of cool.

I really should have gotten some sort of award for working. It was a struggle. No, that's not the right sentiment. It was fucking horrible. At the end of the day it felt as if someone had thrown potatoes at me for eight hours. Everything ached.

On Wednesday that week I was visited by my friend Jim, the police officer who had been at the scene of my accident. I thought he was there to ask how I was doing. He knew that I'd been diagnosed with some form of cancer from our discussion that day. But alas, that was not his reason for coming in. He was there to serve me a summons.

Wait, what? I distinctly remembered hearing him say that he was going to take care of whatever he felt he needed to take care of. I was certain he was just busting my chops and that he would soon drop the ruse and indeed ask me how my health was and give me a smile and a firm handshake. Instead, my mind drifted back to Scarborough Downs and milkshakes. I was being deceived all over again.

"The chief says I have to charge you with something. If it were up to me, I wouldn't be doing this," he said, not looking me in the eye.

"What am I being charged with?" I asked, not believing what I was hearing.

"Reckless driving."

"Seriously? I was unconscious! Technically I wasn't driving at all. My bumper was in the middle of the road. Is he charging me with littering too?" My tone was angry and sarcastic.

"No, just the reckless driving," he replied, perhaps not understanding my cynical retort and clearly not seeing how absurd this all was.

"Thanks for stopping by and checking in on me. I have cancer, by the way. This really should help in my healing process, you know, positive energy and all that." I was trying to make him feel as bad as he should have.

"Sorry, Marc, I wish I could help."

And with that, he left. I wish I could help. *You could start by growing a set of balls and telling your chief that this is bullshit.* Reckless driving. Any citation at all was ludicrous. I would have been okay with crossing the yellow line or something trivial like that. The reckless driving charge was preposterous. It carried a $500 fine and a loss of license for six months. All because I was lucky enough to develop cancer. I told you before—this is the kind of stuff that happens to me.

Do you think the guy who has a heart attack and crashes into a store gets cited with reckless driving? Or how about the woman who goes into a diabetic coma and slams into oncoming traffic? It's an *accident*. That's why they're called accidents. These are unfortunate events that happen beyond our control. Reckless driving implies a lack of concern for the well-being of yourself or others around you. Did they think I wanted to pass out and almost get killed? It was insane. Yet it was happening nonetheless.

After another week of waiting, I finally got a phone call from the hospital. They needed to send my sample to Boston for special staining. Special staining? Oh boy. That probably meant I had stumped some oncology pathologist, and we were dealing with some red herring. Suddenly my friend the nodal marginal zone B-cell lymphoma was a distinct possibility. Whenever they have to do something special to diagnose a disease, it's never a good thing.

The days passed. The gurgling sounds of the miniature waiter doling out drinks in my throat were getting louder. I swear I could feel that thing inside me. At least I couldn't play with my friend the lymph node that used to be on my neck, since they'd ripped it out of me. I wanted so badly to take another x-ray of my chest to see where I stood. Was it growing? I needed to know. I had to know.

Our animal hospital is a modern facility. Although small, we have a lot of bells and whistles. One of them is a digital x-ray machine. Instead of waiting several minutes for an automatic processor to send film through a machine, we now can produce an image almost in real time. Years ago, we had to dip them in the developer and fixer by hand. Just dreadful. In fact, I now have a suspicion that the cancer I have may be related to inhaling the fumes from those processing fluids for many years. But that's just conspiracy thinking. I have no real basis for that, just something my gut tells me.

This new digital technology is quite remarkable and fun to use. Images can be magnified, rotated, written on, lightened, and darkened…hell, I can even delete them as if they were never taken at all. That got me thinking. I could take a picture of myself, look at it, and then delete it as if it had never existed. Hmmm. If it never existed, then maybe I was never exposed to those harmful gamma rays. I had it all figured out and had rationalized my way into convincing myself it wasn't ethically or morally wrong, let alone detrimental to my health. I wasn't going to let a $100,000 piece of machinery just sit there staring me in the face. Or, in this case, my chest.

Conveniently, or inconveniently, depending on the day, our clinic is located right next to our house. My commute consists of walking eighteen paces from the back door of my house to the back door of the clinic. I say inconveniently because there have been times that clients have knocked at my front door with an animal emergency. Not convenient at all. They must think I'm a nephew of James Herriot or something. I did read his books, but that's where our connection ends.

Late that night, after they sent my tissue down to Boston for further testing, I made my way to the animal hospital. I had to go out there anyway to walk Cody and Jazzy, my two hospital dogs that live out there. We call them the goons. Cody is a collie that was surrendered to us because he was unruly as a puppy. No kidding, an unruly puppy. Who knew? Then there's Jazzy, a Maltipoo, given to us for similar reasons. Both turned out to be very nice dogs and prefer to live at the hospital rather than in our house. We tried a few times with the collie, and he ended up peeing on our rug and puking on the couch. Contrary to the old Lassie shows that depict the breed as some superintelligent canine mastermind, the collie can be quite dumb. Affectionate and sweet, yes. Smart, no. My apologies to all the collie owners who have brilliant dogs. Seriously, to both of you, I am sorry.

"The Goons": Jazzy and Cody.

Because I knew what my intentions were, I felt as if I was breaking in. As I crept across the threshold, I found myself looking over my shoulder to see if anyone was watching. The dogs greeted me in their typical fashion, circling around my legs like sharks around chum. Then the little one started jumping up and scratching my calves while "long nose" jammed his beak into my crotch. Same routine, different night. Much different.

It's peaceful in the hospital late at night. The animals are quiet, the blood machines aren't whirring incessantly, there are no clients at the front desk, the washer and dryer are asleep, and I can hear the clock ticking on the wall in surgery. Occasionally the phone rings and breaks the silence. Probably a call from a frantic client whose dog has been vomiting for five days and needs to be seen immediately at one in the morning. I am compassionate and want to help, but I told you, I'm no James Herriot. That's what we have emergency clinics for. Besides, for ten years as an equine vet, I did that whole emergency thing and had earned my stripes. Those days were over.

Looking over my shoulder one more time out of some sort of subconscious guilt, I found the switch for the x-ray machine and turned it on. In the quiet dead of night, the hum of the 220 power surge softly filled the room. I calculated that I was somewhere between a Labrador and a Mastiff. I set the KVP at 72 and the MAS at 10. After doing this for almost twenty years, I had a pretty good idea what the settings should be.

Pushing the red button to light up the collimator, I lay down on my back and tried to line myself up as best I could. I draped a lead-lined thyroid collar over my neck and covered my nether region with a lead apron. I was being illicit and perhaps a bit unethical, but not reckless. Holding the foot pedal that triggers each picture in my hand, I took a deep breath and squeezed. The rotor in the machine fired up and got ready to shoot gamma rays into my body.

When it finally built up enough power, the machine beeped and sent the radiation through me.

In less than five seconds, the demon inside me was revealed. The good news was that it hadn't grown that much. The bad news was that it was still there, and I still wasn't being treated. It was a surreal moment. Just me, the dogs, and an image of myself I never imagined possible. I had taken the radiograph with perfect technique. I looked over at Cody.

"I nailed those settings on the first try, huh, boy?" I said proudly.

He just looked at me and cocked his head inquisitively.

"Just looking for something positive, pal. That's all I got right now."

After measuring the tumor's size, I shut the machine off and deleted the image. It never happened. I fed the dogs, told them to be good, and switched off the lights. I paused at the back door in the darkness wondering if this was all real. A feeling of dread and loneliness overcame me. The end could very well be near. I set the alarm and locked the door behind me.

At that moment, I knew that my life would never be the same. I was depressed, physically exhausted, and mentally drained. The last thing I wanted to think about was a fight against whatever this was, but that's what I had to do. I wasn't angry. I never asked why. I thought back to when our prize filly, Honey's Best, lost in the Maine Stakes final over twenty years ago when she was sick. It would have capped off an undefeated season and her twentieth win in a row. It was a loss that still hurts to this day but inspired me to write my first book. I remembered how hard she fought even though she was struggling to breathe from an upper respiratory infection. Don't give up, don't ever give up. Even if you lose, you go down swinging. Bring it on.

Chapter 5 – The Diagnosis

The very next day, I received a call from the hospital once again. It seemed they finally had a diagnosis. They told me that I had multiple myeloma. Although I had heard of the disease before, I had no idea what it meant for my future. Was it treatable? Was it terminal? And the most pressing question of all, how long did I have?

This is the question asked by just about everyone stricken with a terminal disease. It's probably the hardest one to answer. Most doctors today try to avoid giving any hard numbers unless the answer is obvious. If a doctor tells a patient he has between six months and two years to live, the patient will assume that he has at least two years. On the flip side, if that same patient lives a full two years, he will proudly tell everyone that the doctors only gave him six months. Because of this, it's difficult to get them to tell you just how long you might have left. So before meeting with my oncologist, I once again did something foolish. I looked it up on the Internet.

What a horrible idea. Based on what I found, I questioned whether they had made the right diagnosis. First of all, according to my source, the average age for a patient with multiple myeloma was seventy years old. I was forty-five. Secondly, one of its hallmarks is an elevated calcium level. Mine was normal. Thirdly, most patients with my advanced form of the disease were in kidney failure. Thankfully, I was not.

There was no way they were right. How was it possible? I didn't fit the top three criteria to make the diagnosis. I continued reading. I had only one question on my mind. How long did I have? From my discussion with the doctor who called me, if they were indeed right, I was in stage III. That was of course the worst possible scenario. There is no stage IV. On second thought, I suppose there is. It's called death.

How long did I have? I was frantically looking for the answer. Finally, at the very end of the article, I found it. Twelve to eighteen months. Once I read that depressing tidbit, I was certain they had made the wrong diagnosis. I quickly scrolled back up to the top. I reread the bullet points. Average age is seventy. High calcium. Kidney failure. What the hell?

There was no friggin' way I had multiple myeloma. Average age was seventy. Seventy! High calcium! These guys were crazy. My heart pounded in my chest.

My appointment with the cancer specialist wasn't until the next day. As it was, the night sweats already prevented me from getting much sleep. This news ensured that I would get none at all. I couldn't read about it anymore. I tried to convince myself that they were wrong and in the morning would tell me that I had something else. Anything else. I closed my laptop and stared at the ceiling. It was a long night.

They set me up with a doctor at Exeter Hospital. His name was Donny Hobbs, MD. He was an oncology specialist with a fair amount of knowledge regarding multiple myeloma. He just so happened to be only ten minutes away. I thought to myself, *How about that? I have a specialist just down the road. I really am one lucky bastard.*

When I walked into his office, I felt as if I was walking into a sentence hearing. He got up from his desk and extended his hand.

"Donny Hobbs, nice to meet you, Marc," he said with a smile.

When he stood, he towered over me. He had to be at least six feet five inches. He was as thin as he was tall, easily weighing less than me. Everything about him was skinny, and it seemed improbable that he could even walk on two legs. He looked as if he should've been a foot shorter but somehow got stretched out, as if you were seeing the reflection of the man standing in a circus mirror. His fingers were long and thin; an awkward fit for my fat, meaty hand that I put forward.

His straight brownish-gray hair swooped to the side. I imagined that he never used a comb but just brushed it over his forehead with his hand. His face matched his body—frail and long. His smile was warm and inviting. It was a smile I imagined he used to comfort many terminal patients.

He started rambling about a four-month chemotherapy protocol followed by a bone marrow transplant. He gave me details about how the disease was in many cases treatable and that some patients had a good response. I desperately listened for him to say the word "cure." He talked about sending me to Dana Farber for a stem cell transplant if I responded to the initial phase of therapy. I was getting impatient. Sure, I was anxious to get started on some sort of treatment program, but it seemed as if he was stalling. As if he didn't want to tell me what I really wanted to know. How long did I have?

"Okay, Doc. Tell me this. Should I sell my practice?" I asked coyly.

He knew what I was driving at. Let's face it, it wasn't that veiled a question. Besides, he knew I would come at him for some answers. If he told me that selling was a good option, then I was in trouble. His response was almost exactly what I expected.

"Well, I'm not sure I'd do that just yet." He smiled hesitantly.

Perfect. I had tried the front door, and that was locked. That could mean just about anything...except that it wasn't looking good for the long haul. If the big picture looked good, he would have unequivocally told me not to even think that way. So I did get something out of him. It was as ambiguous as it was unnerving. Clearly I was going to get nowhere with this line of questioning. I went in for the kill shot.

"Do I need to make out a will within the next six months?" I asked directly.

I figured if the answer was yes, I probably had less than a year to live. On the other hand, if he answered, "oh, that's just crazy talk," then I probably had some time before I checked out. His response was somewhere in between.

"Well, let's not get ahead of ourselves," he said, dodging the question.

I pressed, trying to crowbar through the closed door that would reveal my life expectancy. "I read online that my form of this disease has a mean survival rate of about fourteen months."

"Oh yes, those were statistics gathered from 2001. Since then, they have developed several medications that have extended survival times by a fair amount."

A fair amount, I thought. This guy should be a politician. What the hell did that mean? Two months? Six years? It was becoming very clear that I wasn't going to get a solid answer. In his defense, he probably had no idea. Every patient is different. Some respond very well to therapy and others crash and burn.

I didn't say much as he explained about the treatment plan. He never got into the disease itself, as to what might cause it, or what happened when the treatments ran out or failed. He used terms like "response to treatment" and "your case is considered high risk." I assumed that high risk probably meant high risk of dying. What other risk was there? We weren't playing the stock market here. He didn't use the term "remission," and not once in our conversation did he mention the word "cure." Because there isn't one; at least not now.

It didn't sound very optimistic, but at least there was a plan. After hearing him speak for about fifteen minutes about my plight, I still had that burning question on my mind. How long did I have? It's clearly what everyone wants to know. How about a ballpark figure? Anything would be better than these sidesteps he was taking. I knew there was no way in hell he would give me a number. Maybe I could get in through the back door. I decided that I might pick the lock of prognostication by asking a question that could give me a hint as to where I stood.

"Other patients like me that you diagnosed, say, five years ago, are they still alive, or have most of them died?"

"It depends. Some are still doing well, whereas others didn't have a good response to treatment."

There it was again, that response to treatment thing. But I did get some good intel with my hard-nosed line of interrogation. I deduced that I had somewhere between two and ten years. Since the new treatments started in 2005 or 2006, there were still a few people kicking around who hadn't died yet, so we didn't really know how long they could make it. I supposed that was comforting. The two-year possibility was a cold water blast to the face. I guess it was better than what I had initially read, but it was still sobering.

CHAPTER 6 – STARTING TREATMENT

He laid it all out for me, the grand plan for the next six months. When he started in, all I could hear was the line from the movie *The Terminator*. The line goes, "Dyson listened while the Terminator laid it all down." I laughed to myself. That was me, Dyson, and he was Schwarzenegger. Then I thought, wait a second, Dyson dies at the end when he can't keep his hand from triggering the explosive. Well, that mental analogy sucked. I should have come up with something more positive, but it was the first thing that popped into my head. I couldn't help myself. That instantly switched my mind over to another movie, this one with Dan Aykroyd, when he unwittingly thinks of the Stay Puft Marshmallow Man. His famous line goes, "I couldn't help myself. It just popped in there." I laughed again inside. *Ghostbusters*, that was more like it. I then mentally recited one of the final quotes at the end: "We came, we saw, we kicked its ass!" There, much better. Okay, Dr. Hobbs, you were saying?

They would implement what they called the RVD protocol. It consists of R (Revlimid), V (Velcade), and D (Decadron). The first is an oral nightmare of a drug that I affectionately refer to as Devilmed instead of Revlimid. Don't ask how it works. Frankly, I don't care. Even as a doctor, I don't care. They tell me to take it because it will help me to live longer. Good enough for me.

At the twenty-five-milligram-per-day dose they started me up with, the drug is just plain evil. It is taken orally in three-week cycles. It's a daily capsule taken once a day, every day, for twenty-one days. Then they give you a break for a week. They do that because your body would likely implode if they kept you on it full time. It has a whole host of side effects; literally too many to mention here, but I'll list a few. I easily had a dozen of them in the first week, and they continued for the entire four-month initial phase of treatment. Constipation, nausea, rash, muscle pain, muscle weakness, low white cell counts, low red cell counts, fatigue, and oh yeah, diarrhea when the constipation breaks. Those are just a few of the lovely things it causes. Weight loss was also on the list. Of course my body shrugged that one off. I gained weight like Elvis in the seventies. The steroids (the D of the RVD protocol) had a lot to do with that.

Then there's the Velcade, the breakthrough drug that will hopefully keep me from being a statistic from the 2001 article I read prior to my visit with Dr. Hobbs. You know, when I was all smart and looked it up online. Velcade is an injectable poison that is given twice a week for three weeks, and again they show mercy and give you a week off. Then they start you back up again for four or five cycles, depending on your "response to treatment."

What does it do? I have no idea, other than hopefully shrink the tumor in my chest and keep me from dying young. It is evil in its own right, but quite different in its attack. Its list of fun side effects is even longer than my first friend. Some of them include back pain, blurry vision, difficulty thinking (nice), hives, nausea, diarrhea, and many, many more. The worst one, in my opinion, is called neuropathy. This is defined as pain, burning, numbness, and tingling of the hands and feet. All of which I encountered.

On October 10, I smashed my car and, seemingly along with it, my dreams of growing old with my wife. For better or worse, till death do us part. Those words seemed so rhetorical during our ceremony, so distant. Yet now, it was hauntingly apparent that those ceremonial words which were no more than idealistic oration to a young man, were now becoming a reality. It was a devastating thought.

It took nearly six weeks after my diagnosis for them to start my treatment plan. It was late November when the first catheter was tunneled into my arm, and the fight was on in earnest. Twice a week, someone would drive me to the Exeter hospital for my chemotherapy. It was usually my brother. I think he wanted to spend as much time with me as possible. He probably thought I was going to die and figured this might be precious time that we could have together. He could have been right if things went poorly. The thing is, we're all going to die. It's just a matter of when.

Oddly enough, even before all this, I never thought I was going to live a long life. Even though three of my four grandparents lived to nearly a hundred and both of my parents were cruising along in their late seventies, deep down, I felt that I would die fairly young. I know it sounds strange and morbid to think that, and in no way was I pessimistic about living a shortened life; I just had this weird feeling. Maybe a lot of people feel that way. And now it was becoming quite possible that my self-fulfilling prophesy could come to fruition.

It was a very dark time for us as a family. The four horsemen. We were as tight as any family could be. The thought of losing any of us was disheartening to say the least. We all know that the circle of life is a constant. We live, we die. No one gets out alive. But there is supposed to be a balance in life. Parents shouldn't ever see their children die. It's just not the way it should be. In the natural order of things, the parents go first.

In late November, when I was in my third week of chemotherapy, my father was given the news that he had lung cancer. It started with some indigestion and what they thought was gastric reflux. After two months of treatment with no improvement, he developed a bit of a cough. For some reason, the doctors were reluctant to take a chest x-ray, since they thought it was a digestive issue. After I insisted that one be taken, they found a large irregular mass in his lungs. The natural order of things. Perhaps it would work out that way after all.

It was hard to fathom. I told him that he really had some nerve getting cancer and not letting me be the martyr. He laughed his typical Harryman laugh, full of sincere appreciation of the irony.

But somewhere in that laugh was a look of worry. He knew we were both in trouble. We were now in the fight of our lives together.

He didn't need this. We didn't need this. Through the years, we had been through so many trying times. We had been screwed over by many injustices during our lives. The number of episodes that left us wondering how it was that we could be so unlucky was astounding. We had our huge moment in the sun with Honey's Best, a mare we foaled ourselves at the farm. She went on to win nineteen straight races (fifty-five lifetime), and a fair amount of money that allowed me to go to vet school. She alone could have been enough to offset all of the bad that ever happened. But we suffered some painful heartaches during her career, heartaches that could have been avoided had it not been for bad luck.

We also lost several court cases throughout the years, most of them brought on because of something egregious somebody had done to us. There was the time our neighbors cut down a few hundred trees on out property so they could get a better view of the farm (and they took the wood!). We had distant cousins steal land in Greece by forging documents. And of course there was the baking soda tragedy, which we brought to court, but the long arm of the law brought down the hammer on us.

Ugh. Bad pun, I know. But bad puns have been spewing from my mouth since I was about thirteen. I think *Mad Magazine* was the culprit. Ever since then, my mind just churns them out by the dozens and I have to decide whether they're worthy enough to become a verbal reality. Hundreds a day pop in there. I might throw out eight or nine on any given day. I might get *one* laugh. And even though I do screen them for humor, most of them are just terrible. Even the ones I think are funny and come out of my mouth, usually end up getting me a stare from Jen that tells me how bad it really was. I can't help myself. If she only knew of the ones that I suppressed, she might divorce me. Well, you know what they say, the pun is mightier than the sword. See what I mean? Awful. That one should have stayed locked up.

There were other litigations as well. Not once did we win any of those cases where we were clearly in the right. More often than not, if there was a very good chance that things would work out well, they would go the other way. It was discouraging for sure, but we plodded along.

We never let it get us down. Every once in a while, something good would happen in our favor, and we would all be stunned. We would laugh at our good fortune because it hadn't turned out the way it usually did. But through all of our trying times, we always had each other, and more importantly, we had our health. During many dinners together, with just the four of us, Harryman would make a grand proclamation and raise his glass and say, "We may not be lucky in money, but we are the luckiest people around." True enough. Until now.

HARRYMAN

That all changed in a matter of two months. We were both diagnosed with terminal diseases. My brother and mother were in the worst possible spot. I think it's harder for the people who aren't sick. It's such a helpless feeling. I couldn't appreciate it until Harryman was diagnosed. I found myself worried about my own fate, my dad's fate, and, worst of all, the fate of Jen, Doug, and my mom. What would happen to them after we were both gone? It was a disturbing thought.

With each successive dose, the neuropathy got worse. I was set up for twelve weeks of treatment. That consisted of two injections per week for two weeks, followed by a week off. All said, it was twenty-four injections over the course of four months. During that time, the neuropathy intensified. It started with just some numbness, but then progressed to constant pain and burning. During my down week, the symptoms abated some, but when they started me back on the treatment, they were worse than the previous session. Dr. Hobbs kept a close tab on me and asked me every time if things were tolerable. He explained that we should decrease the Velcade dose if it was getting really bad, because the neuropathy could, and likely would, be permanent if we didn't back it down at some point.

It was quite a dilemma. Risk permanent neuropathy that would be a bitch to live with, or reduce the dose of a drug that could potentially allow me to live to complain about it. I decided I would suck it up and keep my mouth shut. I would keep telling him that everything was fine to ensure the maximum dosage to fight this thing off.

At some point, he caught me waddling down the hall like a penguin, shifting my weight back and forth to relieve myself from the pain. It was somewhere around week ten or so, and he called me out. In so many words, he told me I was an imbecile for not coming clean. When I explained that the pain was fairly unbearable, he rolled his eyes as he ordered the nurse to administer a lower dose.

"I told you not to man it out," he said in a condescending voice.

I'm pretty sure he meant "man up," or maybe "gut it out," but he was so exasperated that it came out wrong.

"Yeah, I know," I replied sheepishly.

I told him that my brother and I had a saying when we were racing horses. I explained to him that there were times when you had to pull your horse and go, no matter if it seemed like the wrong time to do it. At some point, it would be too late and you'd be trapped in traffic and the race would be lost. You might not win because of your decision, but the lack of a decision would result in a certain loss. We would say, "This is the race." It wasn't tomorrow. It wasn't ten seconds from now. This was the race, right now. Pull and go. Otherwise victory was unattainable.

This was the race. I figured I had one shot at beating this thing and this was it. Right now. "If I told you to back the dose down, I may not get another chance to win," I said.

"Yeah, well, this isn't a horse race. It's bigger than that."

"Uh-huh." I felt like a child being scolded by his father. "Do what you have to do," I said quietly.

Although his harsh words resulted in a somewhat lower dosage, I still was hard set on going to every single one of my sessions. Somewhere during the third month of my dosing scheme, when I had only two more treatments left, I developed food poisoning from who knows what kind of bacteria. I think it was from some cream sauce at a local restaurant. The day after the ingestion of the Salmonella- or Staph-laced slop, I felt pretty good during the morning. I was due for a dose of intravenous Velcade the next day, and I was going about preparing one of those premade fish and chips dinners that are so healthy for you.

Listen, when you're going through chemo and you feel like absolute dog shit, the last thing you want to hear is that you have to eat right and get three square meals. I was just trying to survive.

The idea of preparing healthy foods was not on the radar screen. Not even close.

I had struggled through a morning of work in the clinic, each day now becoming worthy of a Congressional Medal of Honor for just showing up. Maybe that's a bit lofty since I wasn't in any war. I would have accepted the Presidential Citizen's Medal though. Still too much? How about an Eagle Scout pin?

I popped my frozen fish and chips dinner into the microwave for exactly three minutes and thirty-three seconds. It's not just because tapping 333 is pretty easy, it's actually the perfect time to heat the thing up. Go figure.

Anyway, I can't look a french fry in the eye without a pound of ketchup to keep it company, so I slopped it on my plastic dish right alongside the little pieces of fish. Ketchup goes with just about anything fried, so I dipped the fish in it too. Those little dinners aren't much, maybe 250 calories, and they're more a snack than a meal, but the steroids I was on was making me put on pounds like a Russian weightlifter. I figured a light lunch would do me well.

I scarfed it down in less time than it took to heat it up. Even with the ketchup, it was what you would expect from a microwave fish and chips meal. Crap.

In less than an hour, I knew I was in trouble. The bacteria from the night before were finally gaining in numbers in my small intestine and winning the battle of the bulge. Beads of sweat started to form on my cool forehead, and the queasiness in my gut was ramping up. It couldn't have been the fish and chips. No bacteria works that fast. Well, they do in some science fiction movies, but not in real life. It had to be from the something I ate the night before. The churning. The gurgling. I knew it was coming.

Before the puking started, I thought how ironic it was that after twenty-odd doses of chemo, I had cruised through without so much as an acid reflux burp from the drugs. Other patients were wrenching their guts out. Not me. I was eating like a champ and packing on the pounds. In my defense on the weight gain thing, they told me to eat when I could, because once I got into the stem cell transplant, I would need the extra heft since eating would be difficult due to the inappetence caused by the drugs. Lies. I gained even more during that time. Once again, while everyone else around me was bowing to the porcelain god, I was ordering cheese pizzas and eating Oreos by the dozens.

I could feel the fish, more so than the chips, swirling in my stomach. And why did I have to use so much damn ketchup? Otherwise I might have had a fighting chance.

Out it came, and with a vengeance. And with the smell of each heave, it just made it easier to heave some more. If you tried to create a smell that would induce vomiting, I found it: rotting fish and ketchup. Yup, that's your winner. And finally, when I thought the devil of self-exorcism had left my body, the deep bumping and grindings from the bacterial party lower down the tract were getting ready to leave the dance floor and head for the exits.

I think you know what happened next. It was quite a show, man. During a brief respite from either venue erupting, I was able to track down an orange Home Depot bucket for my front end while I stayed seated on the toilet. I sat there for at least an hour. Time lost all meaning. I was in survival mode. The smell of the fish. My God, the smell of the fish. Each time I puked, that stench was probably the worst part. I couldn't tell if my stomach was bleeding or it was just the absolutely ridiculous amount of ketchup that I had put on that awful frozen dinner still finding its way out. Who uses that much ketchup? Jesus. Well, probably not Him, I was just cursing.

As I sat on my throne of death, I could see myself in the mirror. Mouth agape, drool hanging from my lip, pale, face puffed out like the doughboy from the weight gain, and for a moment I thought...this is how I'm going to die. Not from the cancer but from food poisoning. Kill me now. Just do it. What are you waiting for, man?

It was not the longest night of my life—that was still to come—but it was a doozy.

At one o'clock the next day, I was due for my next Velcade injection. In the morning, I started drinking Gatorade to begin the rehydration process. I was in rough shape. Since the nausea was gone, I was able to really start putting down the fluids, but I was physically weakened, and my hands were shaking from the electrolyte imbalance that was clearly a result of nearly being turned inside out the night before. But I wasn't going to miss that treatment. I thought, *This is the race, goddamn it. This is the race.*

I walked into the clinic at 12:45 p.m. and said hello in as cheerful a voice as I could muster through the dryness of my mouth to Kelly, the front desk lady who nearly always greeted me. She asked how I was feeling with genuine concern rather than how most people greet each other with idle banter. She really meant it. "How are you doing today, Marc?"

I sensed that she could tell I was clinging to life from my hell night and that I was trying to keep it together so they wouldn't send me home without my treatment. I'm not sure what gave it away, but it may have been because my olive Greek skin was in fact a shade of green. My eyes were slightly sunken in and I must have had a vacant stare.

"Oh, I'm okay, just had a little food poisoning last night, but it shouldn't keep me from getting my chemo today." I really tried to ham it up that I was feeling fine, but I feared my face was telling the story of my near death experience the night before. *Just act natural,* I said to myself. I felt as if I was shoplifting or something. I signed in, took a seat, picked up a random magazine called *Coping,* and acted as if I was reading it. Maybe I should have actually read it.

The nurse called me into the back lab area and drew my blood to check my kidneys and red and white cell counts. They also took my temp and blood pressure. Same old shtick. Take my vital signs, ask me how I'm feeling. Almost every time the nurse would say, "Just a little prick." I kid you not. That's what she'd say.

On that particular morning when she said it, I quipped back, "What did you just call me?" I'm sure she'd heard it a hundred times before, but I couldn't help myself. Too easy. I'm sorry, but if you throw a softball like that, I'm going to take a swing at it. She gave me a hint of a smile to acknowledge the overused joke. Probably heard it a thousand times. Maybe it just wasn't funny. It's funny, right? Well, I thought it was.

She commented that I must be in good shape because my pressure was 110 over 65. I told her I used to work out a lot. Amazing how that dehydration thing can lower blood pressure. The bloodwork came back unremarkable, but they seemed happy with my slightly higher red cell counts this week. Huh, imagine that. Take away a few gallons of water, and voila, my red cells went up. I probably should have said something, but I didn't. Two more treatments. Just two more.

They took me back to the treatment area and stuck my arm again with the catheter. The slow drip of Velcade started. The venom once again entered my vein. A wave of warmth washed over me as it made its way into my bloodstream. It was a sensation that was disturbing yet powerfully enlightening. As it hit my brain, a fuzziness and an odd ringing filled my head. It almost sounded like someone turning the volume up on an amp as it hums white noise. Then it got turned back down again; over and over with each heartbeat. I could feel it working its way through my body and attacking the tumor inside. The downside is that it also attacks the good guys. In the army, they call it collateral damage. The doctors call them side effects. I had other names for it. None of which I care to express here.

I couldn't turn back now. If I wanted to win, this was my chance. This is the race, I thought. This is the race.

During all this time, Doug usually drove me to my appointments. Sometimes Harryman took me in. It's not that I *needed* anyone to drive me, but it was a hard time, and as I said, I think they just wanted to spend some time with me, not really knowing how much time we had left. There were plenty of times that I wish I could've just driven myself. When I went in alone, it seemed less dramatic. I drove in, got my medication, and went home. No big deal. When I had a chauffeur, it was a constant reminder of how brutally real my situation was.

During my third month of treatment was when things got a whole lot worse. That's when Harryman also got diagnosed with cancer. In a matter of two months, a family that had been blessed with almost no illness to speak of suddenly found half its members stricken by a terminal disease. My father and I joked about who would go first. We kidded with each other that the over-under was about six years. If only that was even close.

We both had our initial chemotherapy at Exeter Hospital. They had a decent oncology department, and when we needed more expertise or more invasive treatments, we went to Dana Farber in Boston.

One day while sitting in my chair getting my poison (I had driven myself in this time), three chairs down sat my dad. He and my mom were together as he too was getting infused. It was a surreal moment. He didn't look good. He had lost about fifty pounds and was pale from anemia and bald from the chemo. It was the first time I had ever seen him without a mustache. In a way, it defined him. It draped around the corners of his mouth and was fairly full. I had seen it go from a dark black when I was a child, to completely white as an older man. Without it, he no longer looked like the Harryman I knew. The cancer had stolen part of his identity.

He caught my gaze and gave me an uneasy, closed-mouth grin and a single wave of his left hand that had the catheter in it. I smiled back and shrugged my shoulders. I said to him fairly loudly since he was a fair distance away and was a bit hard of hearing, "Are we having fun yet?" This time he answered with a wide, exaggerated smile, showing his missing teeth, and gave me a thumbs up. Always positive. Always hopeful.

He was an amazing man. Never complained. Never moody. Never once did he want to stop fighting. I asked the nurses if they ever had a father and son team together in the facility. None of them could remember a situation where two family members were ever being treated at the same time. Lucky us. Can't win the lottery, but we sure as hell can both get cancer and get stuck being treated in the same room at the same time.

HARRYMAN AND JEN JUST A WEEK BEFORE HE DIED. JUST AFTER THIS
PICTURE WAS TAKEN, HE LAUGHED FOR THE LAST TIME.

CHAPTER 7 – NOT KNOWING

Sometime in late December and January, during my twelve-week chemo regimen, from time to time I would secretly take radiographs of myself late at night. Just me and the dogs. I needed to know if this thing inside me was going away. I needed some positive reinforcement. They told me that they would reevaluate me before my stem cell transplant that was slated for March, but that was too far off in the distant future for my liking. I just *had* to know. If it was getting smaller, I felt that the positive energy would help in my recovery. Not knowing would only cause me anxiety and give me negative chi in my head.

Two weeks into my session, around midnight, I slipped into the clinic with my cloak and dagger. I lay back on the x-ray table once again. Same settings as before, 72 KVP, 10 MAS. I hadn't written it down or anything; I just have a thing for remembering numbers. Names, not so much, but give me a number, and it's locked in my head. Just one of those idiot savant things.

If people had numbers instead of names, I'd never forget anyone. Ah, but they don't, which often leaves me in some very awkward scenarios, where I have no clue what a person's name is when I clearly should know that person quite well. There I am trying to introduce my wife to this…this…this, whatever the hell his name is. In a pinch, I'll try to be sneaky and use the third-person intro technique. "Hi, this is my wife, Jen!" and hope the person then introduces himself as my wife holds out her hand to greet him. By golly, sometimes it works. "Hi, Jen, I'm Jim, nice to meet you!" Yes! It worked, weaseled my way out of that one. Jim. Jim. Jim. How could I forget that? It can be quite humiliating when they sit there and wait for *me* to introduce them by name while I am drawing a blank.

These can be people I see once a week, not just people I haven't seen in two years or something. It even happens with my employees.

I just blank out. It's astonishing. I could tell you their phone numbers, but their names...sometimes there's nothing there. Like I said, idiot savant. I really can be an idiot. Have to work on the savant more.

Lying on the table with the foot pedal in my hand, I hesitated. What if it hadn't changed? Then what? Was that it? I had read on the Internet (yeah, I did it again) that patients with my high-risk stage of the disease responded favorably about 30 percent of the time. I didn't like those odds. For you math-deficient people in the crowd, that's less than a one in three chance of working. And what exactly was a good response? Was it a complete reversal of the disease? And those other 70 percent, were they helped at all, or did the drug just do nothing? I had no answers. Just thousands of questions as I lay there holding the pedal, not sure if I wanted to see what was going to glow on the digital screen above my head in a matter of seconds.

My hand squeezed the trigger, and the rotors started up. A long beep followed, and the picture was taken. I stayed there for a moment, knowing the image was there. "How's it look, Cody?" I asked the dim-witted collie that poked his nose into my ribs, wagging his tail. No response. Stupid dog. Can't even read a simple x-ray. But he gave me comfort nonetheless. He stood by me, waiting for me to get up and pet him.

When I'm working, he is always next to me in the clinic. Never leaves my side. I think it really pains him when I go into appointments with my patients because he can't be with me. If I don't completely latch the door behind me when I go into an exam room, he uses that snout of his to push his way inside to be close to me. Cats don't take too kindly to his interruptions. And the dog-aggressive dogs don't particularly care for his antics either, although it is remarkable how many of them don't go after him. He just waltzes in and is, like, "What's up, guys?" The owners are amazed that their dogs don't attack him the way they do others.

Perhaps they can sense that he is just a bit slow and leave him be. He is a kind soul, and maybe those bully canines can somehow recognize that.

There's a saying in Greek called *colo ke vraki*. Simply translated, it means "your ass to your underwear." It describes how perhaps two lovers are together all the time; like hand in glove. That's me and Cody: *colo ke vraki*. He's always there. He really is a good dog.

I finally gathered the courage to get up, and Cody stood right next to me, grumbling a bit as collies do when they talk. He probably wanted to play and didn't like the fact that I was just lying there on the table. I clicked the button to digitally enhance the picture and waited for it to do its thing. Then I finally took a look. It was smaller. Not by much, but damn it, it was smaller. I had measured it before, and it was 8.1 centimeters across (I told you, I remember numbers). I measured it again this time…7.4.

I petted Cody's head. I wasn't ecstatic or anything, but I was encouraged. It was a step in the right direction. I knew it couldn't have been a monumental change, because the gurgling in my throat was still there when I swallowed, but this affirmation that the drug was working made me feel that at least there was something good going on. The next eight weeks weren't necessarily going to be in vain. If this change could happen in two weeks, then who knew what would happen after twelve.

Two weeks later, I did the same routine. I know what you're probably thinking. Isn't that illegal? Uh, hell yeah. Of course it is. Just writing this could potentially lead the government to have me cease and desist all radiographic capabilities. But if you had access and know-how to use such equipment, wouldn't you be tempted to do the same? And of course there are those people who would tell me that the extra radiation could be harmful and an unnecessary stress to my body. Listen, when they did their whole work-up on me, they took seventeen x-rays and two CAT scans, including injecting me with a radioactive dye. So tell me, what's two x-rays more going to do? Kill me? Okay, maybe it was four additional x-rays. All right, five. Whatever. I'm already dying, give me a break.

The fact that it was shrinking gave me hope. Driving in for my chemo twice a week seemed less daunting. It was helping. If after twelve weeks the size of the tumor was unchanged, the whole ordeal would have been useless. Not only useless, but a strain on my body that it didn't need to endure. At least now I felt there was a purpose to my visits. My thoughts were positive, my attitude brighter toward going in. I've always felt that positive energy goes a long way in healing. This could only do me good.

I waited four weeks before taking the next one. At that point, I was just curious rather than anxious. How much smaller was it going to get? Could it go away completely? At least visibly. I knew the disease wasn't ever really going to leave my body, but maybe it could be shut down for a while. The CAT scans had already shown that it had infiltrated my ribs, spine, skull, shoulder blades...well, it was just about everywhere. It's just that the biggest one was in the center of my chest. They called it a plasmacytoma. I jokingly referred to it as a plasma-screen-cytoma, due to its enormity. It's funnier than the little prick thing, so give me a break. Laughter is the best medicine, after Velcade, that is.

My next x-ray "that never really happened" showed the tumor to be almost half the size it had originally been. That Velcade stuff was really working. But it was taking its toll on me. The neuropathy in my feet was almost unbearable and the fatigue was overwhelming. It made working each day a monumental act of strength. Although Jen had unofficially retired from practicing medicine (she took on the administrative part of the business), she started working some morning appointments so I could sleep in a bit. She had slugged it out for thirteen years up in Rochester, New Hampshire, at her own clinic working six days a week nonstop and another two and a half years at a nearby clinic to help an injured veterinarian. The burnout factor for veterinarians is extremely high. She was cooked. Our profession is ranked number four in the country for suicide rate, that's how stressful it can be.

Filling in those early hours was a great help, but at some point we would have to hire some relief vets to come in, since my stem cell transplant was looming on the horizon, which would essentially take me out of the game for almost four months. Until then, I kept getting my treatments and worked as much as my body would let me. They started me on Gabapentin for the neuropathy, which took some of the pain away. Without that drug, I'm not sure it would have been tolerable. At times I almost couldn't walk, the pain was so intense. That's about when Dr. Hobbs scolded me for not telling him how bad I was getting.

On February 1, 2012, I received my last dose of Velcade. That's when they finally decided to x-ray me again for real. The tumor in my chest wasn't there anymore. At least not grossly (to the naked eye). I'm sure a few cells were still kicking around in there, but for the most part it was gone. It was incredible news, but I knew my journey was really just beginning. Another bone marrow biopsy needed to be done, and then they would need to set me up for the bone marrow transplant.

Now the name "bone marrow transplant" can be confusing. I often will refer to it as a stem cell transplant because in my head it makes more sense. They are one and the same. When I consider a transplant, my mind thinks of a heart transplant, a corneal transplant, or a kidney transplant. This is obviously when they take a specific organ from someone and surgically put it into someone else to replace a failing one. When they say bone marrow transplant, it isn't quite the same deal. They don't take a scoop and gather marrow out of someone's bone and then stick it in your bones, but that's what it sounds like.

What they do is collect blood (more specifically stem cells produced in the bone marrow) and then transfuse you with them. In essence, they take the cells that are in the bone marrow and give them to you via the bloodstream. They destroy your marrow by chemical warfare first, and then they put the new stuff in. Hopefully that takes away some of the confusion of what they mean when they say bone marrow transplant.

I was going to get an autologous transplant. What that means is that they would harvest my own stem cells instead of getting them from a donor. I can't tell you why some people need to get other people's bone marrow for some diseases and some can use their own, but in my case, they were going to use mine (well, I might be able to explain why, but it would be way too technical and I'd have to go on Wikipedia or something and do some research. Not going to happen). For autologous transplants, the recovery time is about a hundred days before you can go back out into the world and be with other humans again. The risk of infection is too great to be introduced to an environment full of germs and viruses, where someone with almost no immune system would quickly get sick and likely die.

The other type is called an allogeneic transplants (popular with leukemia patients), which requires a donor. The recovery time for that is about a year out of the general population.

For a few weeks I was off the Velcade, off the steroids, and finally feeling a bit stronger. The thought of the stem cell transplant was all consuming. I just wanted to get it done. And then there was the biopsy again. The waiting was just brutal.

Even though I was off the steroids, they had done a real job on me. With the weight gain also came fluid retention and a generalized body weakness. Another fabulous side effect was that my throat got fatter along with the rest of my body. It created some of the worst sleep apnea I have ever encountered. I was snoring while awake, just breathing. I swear the diameter of my airway had been cut in half. My tonsils were swollen like a couple of plums, and my uvula (that little thing that hangs down in the back of your throat) took a beating when I snored. In the mornings it hung down like a punching bag in a gym. Same color too.

There were some nights that I had so much trouble sleeping, that the thought of a self-tracheotomy crossed my mind. I had even decided what size endotracheal tube to use. These were of course just fleeting thoughts from a delusional mind that was desperate to get some sleep, and it worried me that I could even think of doing something like that. I envisioned Jen finding me dead in a pool of blood in the clinic bathroom holding a number eight trach-tube in my hand and a scalpel in the other. Yeah, that was a bad idea. Thankfully, it was nothing short of a fantasy. It was more like a wind-pipe dream.

Not helping my weight gain was my worried brother, who insisted on dropping off care packages at my back door at random times. I would get a text that there was something for me at the bottom of the steps nearly every day. He'd bring blueberry muffins, cookies, bananas, grapes, apple pies, and all sorts of other tasty treats to keep me going. Who was I to refuse that? I scarfed them down. The double fudge ice cream certainly wasn't helpful, but I ate it anyway. Listen, they said I was going to lose weight, remember? I threw caution to the wind. I felt like an actor getting ready to play the role of Jackie Gleason. It was working. I just kept getting fatter.

I would get about ten minutes of sleep and then wake up gasping for air. I tried lying on my side, on my stomach, propped up in a chair; it didn't matter. I would wake myself up because I snored so loudly. Jen slept in the extra bedroom. No human could sleep through the noises I was making. My brother ordered me one of those mouth guards that makes your bottom jaw stick out to help open the airway, but it was cumbersome and made my mouth hurt. I would have been better served if he stopped bringing me those damn snacks. Besides, the mouthpiece only helped by letting me sleep for maybe twenty minutes at a time instead of ten. I would look at the clock and see every hour of the night: 1:30, 2:22, 2:57, 3:41, 4:17, 4:43, 5:15, and so on. Some nights a whole hour would go by, and I would be excited to have slept for so long.

It was crazy. This went on for weeks. The night sweats had stopped, but the apnea took over, and often I wouldn't get to sleep until about 7:00 a.m. from overwhelming exhaustion, only to have to get up in just a couple hours. During work, I was the walking dead.

I can remember sulking toward the exam room door, barely alive and wondering how I could gather the strength to put on a game face. I would laugh to myself thinking back to my dad when I was maybe four or five years old. He would put a long frown on his face and hold his hand horizontally just below his chin. With a slow sweeping motion upward he would contort his face into a huge smile as his hand reached the top of his head. He would then sweep his hand back down, and the frown would reappear from beneath his hand. He would repeat this five or six times to get me giggling.

That's how I felt walking into appointments, except the door was his hand. The clients would have no idea how bad I was feeling, and I would put on the top hat and cane and dance for them. When I opened the door, I smiled and greeted them as if nothing was wrong. My performances left me exhausted, and as the door closed behind me, the frown quickly flushed down my whole body. I couldn't keep it up much longer. I was becoming weaker from all the chemo, and my mind was getting foggy from them as well. On the bright side, my act would end soon since my stem cell transplant was just a month away.

CHAPTER 8 – COFFEE WITH HARRYMAN

Some days Jen would have to work the whole day, while other days I had enough strength to do it myself. One thing was steady through all this, though; Harryman would always bring me a morning coffee. For the past sixteen years, there weren't many working days that he didn't come over around nine o'clock and bring me a Green Mountain coffee in a plain white cup from the little convenience store just up the street. There was a Dunkin Donuts right next door to it, but Harryman liked to give the little guys his business. He was old school that way.

He disliked the big chain stores. He thought of them as the demise of the American dream. In a way, I think he was right. So he would stop in at the little store owned by a Pakistani family, and he got to be quite friendly with them. I affectionately called the place "The Cell," joking that it was probably a front for Al Qaeda. Yeah, I know, it sounds racist, but I really was just kidding with him. Who knows, maybe it was. No, really, I'm joking. But, you never know, right?

Anyway, every morning, no matter what the weather, or if he was feeling crappy from his treatments, he would bring me my coffee. Another one would be in the car that he would bring to Doug back at the farm, and they too would have a similar "sit-down" session in the barn. I had a little chair in my office that faced my desk, and he would plunk himself down with his own cup of joe, and we would chat for a while. Sometimes he would stay for just a few minutes, and other times he would stay for an hour. We would discuss all kinds of topics. I cherished those moments. He was so insightful, so informative, and so well read.

We would discuss politics and religion and anything else that was currently relevant. We both stood slightly to the left side of the middle politically, so the discussions were never heated, just thought provoking. Neither of us liked the two parties that represented the country. We agreed that both sides were fundamentally flawed in their thinking. He read the paper every morning from cover to cover. He was my own little newscaster. He would tell me about stuff going on in Syria and about a gas line leak in Boston. As we both knew we were terminal, we often discussed the concept of God and whether one existed or not.

We both grew up believing in a God, because that's what we were taught. As we aged and processed information scientifically and philosophically, our beliefs became radically different. We both felt there probably was some sort of entity or force that created everything that existed, because our minds couldn't fathom that it could happen out of nothingness. But what that power or source is was certainly up for debate. Since there are hundreds of different religions that all have completely different ideas of who God is and what the rules are, we both determined that most likely none of them had all the answers. That didn't mean a God didn't exist, he just didn't exist the way man had created him on paper.

Evolution is real. I have no doubt in my mind about that. The fact that some religions rebuff this idea makes me question everything and anything they say to be a truism. If they think that man was created in a single "day" by a single being, then I have to just flat-out laugh. After studying the physiology of animals for as many years as I have, I have come to the conclusion that there is no way something so complex could have come into being all at once. No way. Now, could God have had his hand in evolution? Sure, that's a possibility. Feel free to disagree. I didn't say I was right. I'm just telling you my beliefs. And Harryman echoed my thoughts. Or maybe it was me who echoed his. The fact remains that he did have an enormous impact on my way of thinking. It was refreshing to be able to talk to someone with similar sentiments and political views rather than butt heads with some right- or left-wing radical.

We talked about climate change and how people were turning a blind eye to it. Facts are facts. Our climate is changing. You can argue that it isn't, but that would be like saying gravity doesn't exist because you can't see it. You can argue whether *we* are causing it or whether it's just happening as a natural course of things, but it is changing. We talked about overpopulation and how no one wants to even bring up the topic. We talked about growth hormones in our food and how boys today are taller than we've ever seen and how twelve-year-old girls look like Dolly Parton. There was nothing we left off the table, including our own mortality and what might happen to us when we were gone.

We all hope there is something after this life. Many insist that there is. They are *sure* of it. I guess they call that blind faith. Just because someone wrote it in a book a couple thousand years ago wasn't quite enough for me and Harryman (or my brother and mother, for that matter; they just weren't at this coffee table). I really don't know if the Bible is fact or fiction. I can take it on the word of the church that it's all true, but let's be honest, none of us were around to see it written. If someone in the year 500 AD read *War of the Worlds,* they would likely have assumed it was real. In fact, many people who heard the story on the radio in 1938 believed it was happening. My point is if they want me to be certain of something that no one has physically proven, I have a hard time just believing it on faith alone.

The church tells me that when I die, if I've followed the rules, I get to go to heaven. I sure hope that they're right, but believing it just because they say so is hard to swallow. On the other hand, I don't dismiss something after this life either. To say that nothing exists would be both hypocritical and ignorant on my part. I can't prove that either, so I want to believe that there is. Such is how my mind works.

Coffee with Harryman. These were how our mornings went. Sometimes we talked about lighter things like the farm and work, but we could go pretty deep. They were fascinating discussions. Too bad we didn't get them on tape. They would have made a great memoir. We never judged other people's beliefs because we didn't know any more than the next guy. We could only assess what we believed. For all we knew, *we* were wrong, and any one of the hundreds of factions of religions is right. Maybe on some level we are all right. It's just a matter of interpretation. If there is a God, and he in fact did create the brain that's in my head, then he certainly understands why there is doubt. He's God, he would realize this. I'm banking on it, come the day I ever have to face him and he says, "So now you want in, huh?"

CHAPTER 9 – MAKING STEM CELLS

On March 2, they started me on a drug called Neupogen. Its purpose is to stimulate the bone marrow to produce stem cells. Now stem cells are really cool. They are the primal cell of each and every one of us. Any stem cell made in the bone marrow has the potential to become anything. And I mean anything (well, not an elephant or a tree), anything encoded in its DNA that is. It could be a white blood cell, like a lymphocyte to ward off infection. It can become a red blood cell to deliver oxygen. That's what happens in all of us. All mammals really. Probably birds too, but I skipped most of my avian classes. But the really cool thing is that they have the potential to become an arm, or an ear, or a tongue— even another you. They have all of the DNA to do it; they just need the right signal to be told what they're supposed to become.

How the body does this is really the miracle of life. Which cells become what, and how many, and when? That is the question geneticists have been asking themselves for years. Sure, they think they have an understanding, but the intricacy of how it works is mind boggling. How do you tell a cell to become skin for grafting? Well, you throw it in a petri dish with some actual skin cells, and it figures out where it is and becomes skin. Does that mean we know how it does it? I don't think so. Maybe *they* do, but I sure don't.

Anyway, this drug, Neupogen, tells the bone marrow to make stem cells and at a rapid rate. They grow so fast, in fact, that they don't have a chance to become anything else yet. They're just stem cells. Sure, a few of them convert over to some white cells or red cells, but for the most part the bone marrow just keeps churning out stem cells like crazy. Ah, the advancements of medicine. Playing God. But I'm not going to complain, because it's supposed to lengthen my life. But get this, they're not even sure it will. This stem cell transplant is just the standard protocol they're using now for my type of cancer (and many others). It's still in the trial phase, and they aren't certain if it helps.

There was some discussion with my doctors as to whether it needed to be done at all. Studies are inconclusive so far, since we don't have data on the people that have tried it yet. Some have died anyway, but some have lived longer. Again, the jury is still out. The whole idea behind the transplant is to harvest a bunch of cells, and put them in storage to be later transfused back into you. Then, once they have them safely bagged away, they completely wipe out all of your white cell line, leaving you without any immune system whatsoever. Nothing. The common cold would kill you.

In some cases, this type of procedure can cure cancer (like certain forms of leukemia and lymphomas). For mine, it can't wipe out what's still hiding in the bone, tucked deeply away. The hope is to quiet it down for as long as possible by killing the bad guys lurking in the bloodstream. For multiple myeloma patients, one day those bad cells that are bunkered down in the skeletal bone will mount a coup and return. The question is just a matter of when, not if it will happen. In the meantime, the idea is to take chemotherapy for the rest of my life until that day comes. It's so heartwarming.

After they have your cells neatly packed away, they give you this stuff called Melphalan, which is like napalm to the bone marrow. You are rebooted from all your immunity, including any vaccinations you ever received. You are as immunely naïve as the day you were born.

So why don't infants get sick as soon as they enter into existence? They are born with no immunity at all. Because of good old mama, that's why. Her first milk is so rich in immunoglobulins that a baby's first drink gives him or her all the immunity that Mom has. It's really an ingenious design. As those antibodies slowly die off over the weeks and months ahead, the infant's own immune system starts making its own antibodies to fight off the world.

Unfortunately for stem cell patients, we don't get to drink that magical colostrum that would instantly allow us back into civilization. Even if they gave it to us, it wouldn't work. Only a newborn's intestines are capable of processing the stuff. I told you, it's ingenious. We have to wait for our own bone marrow to make new cells from scratch (if it turns itself on...they tell me there is a 2 percent chance it never will, and I think you know what that would result in), and then slowly start to make antibodies against everything again. That's why patients stay away from the public for at least a hundred days for autologous transplants and a year for the allogeneic ones.

Being somewhat altruistic, I opted for a clinical trial. There were three forms (or arms as they call them) of the trial I could potentially be placed into. The first was to get just a stem cell transplant, then take no drugs at all afterward and take my chances. The second was to have the transplant and then be placed on an indefinite regimen of my friend Revlimid, which would hopefully continue to slow down any regrowth of cancer cells. The third was to have another transplant six months later. That last one was called a tandem trial, which sounded just ridiculous to me. They had very few patients who had gone through it, but it seemed to be me that they wanted more. They insisted that all the trials were random.

Which one do you think I got chosen for? One guess. Right, the tandem trial. Of course I did. Random my ass (I told you I was cynical). I figured they just wanted to funnel more people into that study since so few had gone through it, and so they "randomly" put me in it. Maybe it *was* done by chance, but my sardonic mind has a hard time believing that. The good news was that I could voluntarily bow out of the trial at any time if I felt it was in my best interest. Well, there was no way in hell I was going through two of those back to back. I hadn't been subjected to the first one yet, but I knew I wasn't doing it twice in six months, which would essentially put me out of circulation for over a year. I thought that if I were unlucky and only got to live two more years, I didn't want to spend half of that time down and out. I didn't tell them this at the time, but it would come to pass that I'd respectfully decline.

As part of the trial, they would also be able to take bone marrow biopsies now and then to check on my condition. Sure. Check on my condition. No, they just wanted my cells so they could play around with them in the lab and try different drugs against the defective cells to see which ones might work against the malignancy. You know, throw some mud on the wall and see what sticks. This, however begrudgingly, I did agree to. I figured some poor bastards must have done the same thing before me so that Velcade could become a reality. And for those who did, I am forever grateful. I didn't like the idea of multiple "unnecessary" trocars being buried into my hip, but for the good of science and to maybe help someone ten years down the road be cured, I signed on. It certainly couldn't hurt my resume for some sort of afterlife inquisition either, if you know what I mean. Seriously, that had to outweigh some of the sinister stuff I'd done right? Ah, probably not. Hard to fool the big guy.

After enduring the first transplant, I was certain my decision was the right one. It was sheer hell. But we'll get to that part in a little bit. In the meantime, they started me on the injectable Neupogen. Because I'd put on so much flab, instead of one injection every day, they decided that my new weight class required two injections each day. Lovely. Had I stayed at 180 pounds where I started, I would have been all set for just one a day. But I had ballooned up to 205 and now needed the extra dose. Lucky me.

The injections had a cool space age design with needles that retracted back into the syringe so you could just throw them into the trash. They looked like something out of a Bond film that would knock out a bad guy if you stuck it in his neck. Spring-loaded, shiny glass, and a nice thick shaft. Real cutting-edge technology. They failed to make it not hurt like hell when they gave it, though. It stung like a bitch. I *so* looked forward to giving them to myself— something I had lobbied for instead of driving to their office twice a day, since I was pretty familiar with giving injections. Besides, it seemed to hurt less when I did it to myself. Although most of them were gentle, one of those nurses really jabbed it in there quite cavalierly. We weren't trying to land Moby Dick, for God's sake, it was a simple injection. If I did that harpoon routine on a Rottweiler, I'd probably get my arm bitten off.

And so began my ten-day stint of injecting myself twice a day. I would stab myself in the belly fat and give it subcutaneously. I had developed a fairly big target. The goal was to produce 6×10^6 stem cells. So that's like six million. Well, it's exactly six million. And they counted every single one in a fancy machine. If I failed to make that many, I would have to start over again, which would push my transplant forward who knows how many weeks. The thought of another round of twice-a-day Neupogen was far from appealing. It had better work the first time.

They warned me that when the cells started to build up in my bone, things would begin to get rough. Eventually, because so many were being produced so quickly, the bone marrow couldn't put them into the bloodstream that fast, so they would start stacking up in the bones. When the numbers escalated and it got too crowded for them all, they would bubble over into the bloodstream all at once. Kind of a jailbreak of stem cells. That, they told me, was when it would become painful.

How painful? Well, they said it could be anywhere from a two or three, all the way up to ten. I wondered if it could even hit eleven. I would be remiss if I didn't quote the line from the movie *Spinal Tap*: "That's one more than ten." I was really looking forward to that moment. But it wouldn't be just a moment. The process of the bubbling over takes about twenty-four to thirty-six hours.

I've never been afraid of pain. As a matter of opinion, I'm pretty sure I have a higher pain tolerance than most. But since most guys would probably say that, maybe I don't. Even knowing I could handle pain fairly well, I was worried. I had "heard" dreadful stories from other people. One woman said it was ten times worse than child-birth. I had to hope that she'd given birth to a three-pound preemie, or perhaps a chipmunk. How did I hear about these testimonials? You guessed it. I googled it. Still hadn't learned my lesson about the Internet. There was story after story about how bad it was. Guys like me saying how they could handle pain, but this was the worst they ever had. I just had to do it, didn't I? Couldn't leave well enough alone. Had to go look on the Internet, the information stupid-highway.

On day six, I started to feel the pressure. It was building slowly. Day seven, two more injections. With this much Neupogen, my bone marrow was filling like the testicles of a celibate monk. Something had to give. Day nine. I was walking up the stairs from the basement and felt a twinge in my back. I've had these twinges before, since I'm a man, and seemingly all men my age have bad backs. It's that twinge you get right before your back considers going into a full spasm that lays you out. You hope it just stops there, but sometimes it goes into a complete lockdown, and you know you'll be out for at least a couple days, lying in bed, living off Ibuprofen, and packed with ice. Real ice.

But it stopped. Then tweaked again. This was different. It was deeper than muscle. That's when I started thinking the boiling pot was getting ready to blow. A few hours later, I felt it in my right hip. It was happening.

During this time, I was writing in a journal, a diary of sorts, and I will now transcribe the exact prose that I wrote that fateful night.

March 9th
8:01am
The bone pain associated with the stem cells has arrived. Not good. The concern is not the pain I'm in, but how bad will it get? Tough saying, not knowing. It started in my lower back, much like when I get a spasm. And at first that's what I thought it was since I had an episode of that about a month ago after bringing in eight 40-pound bags of water softener salt. But now,

I can feel it in my hips and my legs. My legs feel hot, and the pain is making me sweat a little bit. Not good. And I thought I was useless before. At least I was on the bench before, now I'm in the press box. Not in the game at all. This blows.

March 10th

1:20am

The bone pain is excruciating. 8 out of 10. At times 9. Most of the pain is in my lower back, very similar location to where I get back pain from time to time. But this is way worse because there is no position that relieves it. There is no possible way I sleep tonight. Zero chance. I can olny (pain is so bad, I misspelled 'only') hope the stem cells break through and there is relief at some point. I've already taken too many pain meds and have to wait before I take more. Not sure they're even doing anything. Not good. Nope. Not good at all. You would kill yourself if life was like this without a doubt.

11:55pm

Last night was probably the hardest night I have ever physically had to endure. Harder than the time I had pericardial effusion from a hit in floor hockey when each beat of my heart sent searing pain shooting through my chest. Mind you, it could have been worse. Like I said, the pain held at an 8, and it was sustained for at least twelve hours. I think it actually could have been more painful. Thankfully, the pain has eased. Now, I'm at a 4-5 out of 10. Wouldn't want to go through that again. Got no sleep. None. Just like I predicted. Went to bed at 8pm tonight and woke up twenty minutes ago. Three hours! Already got more sleep tonight than I did in the last day and a half. Tandem transplant my ass. No way I go through that again. No way.

The pain really was exquisite. If I could just lie as still as possible, it was almost bearable. If I moved at all, any joint that had motion caused me to recoil and want to let out some expletives. It's funny how swearing can somehow make it more tolerable. But at four in the morning, I didn't want another repeat performance of Jen appearing next to me yelling "WHAT!!!" so I clenched my jaw and mentally f-bombed like a madman.

I will now return to my journal to give you an idea of where my head was at. I haven't edited anything I wrote at the time; I thought it would be more authentic that way. It gives you more of an idea of how disjointed I was mentally.

March 11th
12:01am
Should be a better day tomorrow although my hips still ache. Damn stem cells. I'll tell you what, they better not kill me with this procedure 'cause I'll be pissed if I went through this in vain.

11:30pm
Turned the clocks ahead today. Can't we just leave it like this? Seriously, who benefits from turning them back in the fall? Money *has* to be at the root of it. It ain't for the school kids to not go to school in the dark. Please. The government couldn't give two shits about them. It's the money. Darker early, more lights, so more electricity, more money. Those big companies have some pretty strong lobbyists. There's no way we do it for the 'good' of the people. It has to be money. Man am I cynical.

Anyway, crappy day. Again. Nothing new. Going in tomorrow to get a Hickman line put in my neck. Yay. Have to fast for six hours because they're going to somewhat sedate me to do it. They have to perform a "cut down" on my subclavian artery/vein to make sure it's right. Should be fun. Then they can start vampiring my blood out and harvest the stem cells.

It just keeps getting better. Pain is still present but not like the other night. No sir. That was bad. Real bad. The kind of stuff you actually wish on your worst enemy. But I've been over this before.

Fortunately the pain has abated some. Going to bed. Really looking forward to this line placement thing.

March 12th
11:00pm
Had the Hickman like put in my chest today. Supposed to be sedated but I've been on so many narcotics, the amount of Fentanyl they used barely even touched me. I was partially awake for the whole thing. It went well, but took all afternoon. Had a 1pm appointment; they didn't roll me into the surgery suite until 3pm. Some lady (it could have been a dude) was having a meltdown next to me about pain. She sounded like a complete wuss. So they tended to her and put me on hold. I wanted to smack her (or him) a good one and show her real pain. Faking self-centered piece of shit. What? Too harsh? Whatever. If you had to listen to her, you'd feel the same way. She went on and on and on and on.

"Owwwwww, owww, owwwww, ohhhhh, owwwwww, ohhhhh." Please. Shut your pie hole. We all have pain. And none of the doctors gave her anything for it, so you know they knew she was faking. Probably drug seeking. All I know is that she cost me a couple hours.

So now I'm home. Gotta go back in tomorrow at 7am to harvest my blood for ten hours. That means we leave here at 5:30am. Yee haw. Doesn't get any better than this.

During the procedure of putting the line in my neck, I could tell they were having issues. They were pulling my arm straight out and torqueing it here and there trying to get the catheter in. At one point I heard one of them say that "this jugular is blocked." Well, what do you know, that quack Dr. Shultz had come back to haunt me again. It seemed that when my lymph node biopsy went sideways, my right jugular vein got occluded or at least narrowed.

I knew something was up with it because I could feel an awkward pulsing in my neck when I was in certain positions, and I often have to unblock my right ear canal every two or three hours from pressure build up. Man, that guy really did a number on me. And here we were again, facing the consequences of his masterful work. But I'm not bitter. They had to use a different vein than they normally would, but they assured me later that it was something they encountered now and then. Not often, of course. I'm sure the percentage is extremely low; I'm just a lucky kind of guy.

The Hickman line is pretty cool. It has to be a foot long inside your body, although I didn't see them put it in. It has an inflow line and an outflow line all in one, with two ports that split from it as it exits your body. This way, they can either take blood out or put stuff in like meds or fluids or a transfusion. In the case of the stem cell harvest, they pull blood out and put it back in at the same time in a closed circuit.

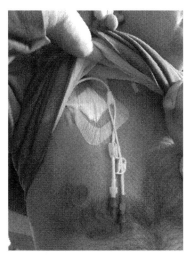

THE HICKMAN LINE INSERTED IN THE RIGHT SIDE OF MY CHEST.

Crazy as it may sound, Jen's dad, John H. Raaf, MD, who was a pretty bigwig director of surgery at the Cleveland Clinic at one time, almost got the patent for a similar catheter. But this guy, Hickman, beat him to it. Otherwise, they would have been putting in a Raaf-Cath instead. And Jen's father would be a very rich man today.

I am not a morning person. Never have been, never will be. Even when we worked the farm, I never got up before 8:00 a.m. unless there was some kind of an emergency. I know that certainly sounds contradictory to what most people think about farmers, but we weren't just farmers. We were farmers who also raced horses. This required us to drive an hour and a half or more to tracks in Maine and Massachusetts and race until as late as midnight. We often got home at one or two in the morning. This type of behavior does not jive with getting up at the crack of dawn.

We had our schedule. It worked for us. Harryman would always get up early anyway, even though he was up late the night before, and feed the horses around six in the morning. I don't know how he did it. I guess afternoon naps were his answer. Doug and I would roll out of bed around nine or ten and go straight through the whole day and night after that. Back then, I never napped. Not the case anymore. I almost *have* to nap nowadays. Probably because I don't get to sleep until at least two in the morning most nights. The drugs have really screwed me up.

The night before my harvesting was no different. I didn't get much rest. Maybe two hours at the most, and then there we were, off to Boston at 5:30 a.m. I couldn't believe how many people were on the road at that hour. What a crazy world we live in. Humans are not supposed to be up and about that early. It's sheer madness.

Jen drove while I head-bobbed my way in and out of what I guess you could call sleep. Every minute not awake was welcomed. She dropped me off for the day and would pick me up at the end of the procedure. It was going to be a ten-hour ordeal.

Chapter 10 – Stem Cell Harvest

As I figured, they really didn't need me there that early. They made me wait about two hours before they hooked me up to the machine that would syphon gallon after gallon of my blood, plucking out every painful stem cell that burst out of my bone marrow, and then give back my precious blood in a giant cycle. If all went as planned, I would be back in four days to get blasted with the chemo that would reboot my system.

Knowing that in just ninety-six hours I would essentially have no immune system left, I decided to wear a mask so that if anyone had a cold or flu, I wouldn't be exposed just before they wiped me out. I also brought hand sanitizer. Now I'm no germaphobe, but I knew what was at stake here. My life. I figured both of those diseases (or anything else that someone had spewing out of them) had an incubation period of about three to five days, so if I was infected on my day of harvesting, I'd be shit out of luck once they erased me. I sincerely thought this was prudent.

Every single one of the technicians asked me why I was wearing a mask. It had to have been five of them. They told me "you won't need that in here," and that "you have plenty of white cells to fight off infection." No shit. Right now I do. But what happens in four days when I have nothing, and the virus is already in me? I explained my reasoning, and they looked at me as if I was a moron. They reiterated that my immune system was fine, and I didn't need the mask. What the hell? No one saw my logic. I felt like the only sane person in the asylum. Maybe it was the other way around. Nonetheless, I stuck to my guns.

Finally, at some point, Dr. Norton (my oncology specialist) came in to visit all his patients to say hello. Not all of us in there were his, but there were three or four of us under his care. We looked like we all were in some sort of horror flick, being tethered to tables with our blood being cycled in and out of our bodies against our will, as if they were converting us into the undead or something. Surely Dr. Norton would understand my reasoning for wearing a mask.

"Hi, Marc, you don't need to wear that mask in here," were the first words out of his mouth.

Had I not been wearing a mask, he would have seen my mouth open in disbelief. I was exasperated. I didn't even bother trying to explain. I wondered how many people had crashed and burned from catching a cold from a sniffling technician unknowingly. Perhaps that's where the 2 percent came from. I don't know. All I know is that I kept the mask on, and everyone thought I was a knucklehead. At least they couldn't see my face and later identify me as that guy. I had that going for me.

There were ten of us in the room. My chair had its back to the windows with four other people lined up parallel to me. I was dead center (no pun intended, although it wouldn't be my worst), with two on my left and two on my right. Directly across from me were five others against a pale blue wall. None of us spoke to each other. We just sat there, like the zombies they were trying to make us. A few people had relatives with them. One guy had his son reading him a book on the far side diagonally to my left. I lay there by myself, under my mask, just watching the blood flow out of my neck and back in through the same port. Hour after hour went by. I really should have brought a book. I was bored out of my mind.

The machine they used looked like an old reel-to-reel tape recorder, except instead of tape running through the reels, they had tubes that the blood flowed through. There were lights, knobs, and numbers all over the thing. It was quite a piece of technology, and they had ten of them. I couldn't imagine what one of those things must cost. Dying certainly is a profitable business, that's for sure. The cost of the whole procedure was something like $100,000. I was staring at a million bucks with the poor buggers that were with me. I wondered if they did this every day or just certain days of the week. I started doing some calculations, and it was mind-blowing. It didn't matter what they paid for these suckers, they were paying for themselves in spades. So my mind wandered through senseless stuff like that.

I wondered if today was multiple myeloma day, or if they had just lined up whomever they had next on the docket for whatever disease they might have. It seemed unlikely that we all had the same thing. I started giving people diseases. The guy across from me probably had Hodgkin's lymphoma. Lucky bastard. He was in his early thirties, seemed to be fairly athletic, so he fit the bill. A young girl with blond hair to my right had to have acute lymphoblastic leukemia. Too young for anything else. But what did I know about anything? I was just bored. What kind of sick mind starts giving people diseases?

What the hell is wrong with me? I thought. I stopped after giving the guy who was being read to by his son chronic myelogenous leukemia.

I had to quit that nonsense. These were people who were in real trouble, and there I was trivializing their situation. That said, at least I was one of them. So of course my mind went even more cynical. I started wondering who would die first. Jesus, I was going crazy. I put myself back in the grandstands in my mind and started to watch some of Honey's races in my head. I'd watched videos of them plenty of times, and even the ones I didn't have I could still replay in my brain almost as if I were there. I could even remember the quarter times, the halftime splits, and the finish times.

Numbers. I can remember them for some reason. And this put me in a better place.

HONEY'A BEST WINS AS A THREE YEAR OLD IN BANGOR, MAINE.

I watched the miracle mile at Rochester. Magnificent. I was calling the race in my head as if I were the announcer. I watched her win against a horse named Repatriate, when she went off at 60–1 in the first start of her 1990 campaign against the boys. It was nothing short of brilliant. She won by a whisker in 2:00.1. I replayed her win as a two-year-old in the championship when she dusted the competition and set a new record for two-year-olds. But my thoughts wandered. I couldn't stop them. With all this cancer around, some bad juju started creeping in. I couldn't keep my mind from reliving her loss in the New England Sulky Championship as a four-year-old.

I saw her being parked out on the outside by Nicky Anderson, who was supposed to be a friend. My father had let him live on the farm for several years when he was hard up. He wouldn't let Honey get to the rail. Doug would try to pull back in behind, and he would put the brakes on and shut him off. When Doug pressed again for the top, Nicky strung him out.

The track was incredibly muddy that day, and they slugged out a half in 57.3. I'd never seen a half that fast at Foxboro, and this was in the slop. My heart started racing, I felt hot, and I was getting angry. If Nicky had been standing in front of me right then,

I could have killed him. I wanted that race back. I wanted my life back. Instead, Honey lost the race because of that scumbag, and here I was being strung out just like she was. There's a saying about life and fairness. It was never truer for me than at that moment.

How did I get there? For a few minutes, I was reliving glory, and then I just went dark. Dark enough to want to kill someone. Was this normal? This type of thinking? This rage? Did other people fantasize about bashing someone's skull in because of an incident that happened over twenty years ago? I had to let it go. Had to stay positive. Instead, I watched her lose the championship as a three-year-old. No one to blame there, other than bad luck that she was sick that day and probably shouldn't even have raced. She finished second, just beaten by a head, which if she'd won, would have capped off an undefeated season. I went pitch black.

A nurse asked me if I wanted lunch. She snapped me out of the fugue I was in. I ordered a cheeseburger and fries. I didn't care about calories at that point. I was already a load, and I wasn't about to worry about eating healthy (actually, I think it's healthfully, but who cares?). I mean seriously, I already had cancer. A cheeseburger wasn't going to kill me, that's for sure.

I scarfed down the food and realized that my anger was likely related to hunger. It's a little like the Hulk thing: "Mr. McGhee, don't make me hungry; you wouldn't like me when I'm hungry." I try not to let myself get to that point, but sitting in that bed for six hours without any food (after fasting for the previous six) had clearly put me in a state of mind that wasn't very nice.

The food had done the trick. My mood changed almost instantly. In my mind's eye, I watched Honey sweep four-wide down the stretch and win her first race. That was quite a finish. Eight lengths off with a sixteenth of a mile to go, and she just turned on the afterburners. Right then, we knew we had something special.

And just like that, I felt myself crying. But it was from the sheer joy of the incredible gift that she was and what she did for us. She was an amazing animal. The cancer didn't matter anymore. I had a great life. I had my family around me, Jen by my side. That's all I needed. If I didn't make it, I had done enough and lived enough to make my life seem worthwhile, even if it ended today. Light. Positive. I was back. Amazing what a cheeseburger can do. I think the fries helped.

My family had learned fairly early on in my adulthood that hunger was a big trigger for my anger. Many times when I started to get pissy, my father looked at me and said, "Go eat something, you're being a dink." He was right of course. And food was the answer.

One infamous night on our way back from Foxboro Raceway—I had to be about twenty years old—I was starving. It was a hectic night in the paddock, grooming three horses by myself that we had going, and I hadn't eaten anything all evening. I wanted to stop at the Red Wing restaurant, but it was late, and everyone wanted to get home straight away. Doug and I were in the back seat of our dually truck, and my mom and dad were up front with my father driving, of course. I don't think my mom ever drove the truck and trailer, but don't quote me on that.

I could feel it. The fury was building, and there was nothing to be angry about. We'd had a great night at the track and there was no reason for me to feel anything but good. But there it was. I was getting more and more agitated with each passing mile. We absolutely *had* to stop for some food. My mother said we had plenty of food at home and suggested we eat when we got there. Unacceptable! I needed to eat. And soon. The little Hulk was starting to morph. I told them we were stopping in Haverhill at the Burger Chef (some of you might remember that chain). I wasn't going to make it.

Haverhill is only twenty minutes from home. Any sane person could have waited. But the hunger made me turn. It made me a different person. We were stopping at Burger Chef. They all knew it. They had seen me before without food and had heard enough of my chirping about it for the past half hour to know they better stop. Needless to say, I won the battle, only because they didn't want to listen to me anymore. Pissy Marcopio (as Doug sometimes called me) was in full form. He had arrived.

We couldn't go by way of the drive-thru since we had the big rig, so we all got out and went inside to get our orders to go. I just assumed that as soon as we got back in the truck, we would all dig in and eat. This was when things went a bit sideways. My mother had the food up front, and she thought it would be a good idea if we just waited until we got home and ate in the house. Was she out of her mind? Just the mere suggestion of waiting made me even angrier. The whole point of stopping was so I could eat right then, not in twenty minutes. What?!

"Mom, give me my food, I want to eat it now," I said fairly sternly, trying to control my temper even though I was simmering.

"Why can't you just wait until we get home? We'll be there in a minute," she said.

"I'm starving and I want to eat now. Hand it back here," I repeated.

"Oh, Marc, just wait, we're all hungry."

At this point, Marc had left the building. The Hulk could no longer stay hidden, and a line that will live in infamy came out of my mouth.

"GIVE. ME. THE. BAG!" I stammered out loudly, in a steady one-syllable chant.

Silence followed. And the bag followed that. In seconds I was wolfing down a double cheeseburger with extra ketchup (no onions of course). It was then that I broke the silence and spoke once again, muffled by the food that was stuffed in my mouth.

"You don't mess with a man's food."

Those two phrases have plagued me for years, as I am constantly reminded of how big of an asshole I become when I'm hungry.

Couldn't wait twenty minutes. But oh, how my mood changed after that. I was all chipper and good. My mom was none too happy, though. She was sore at me for quite a while for addressing her like that.

From that day on, I've tried to make sure not to let myself get to that point of hunger, at least not when I was around other people. So a cheeseburger had once again saved me from myself.

After I finished devouring the food, I looked over at my little travel bag that had a few items in it like hand sanitizer, tissues, and a sweatshirt. Jen had also packed a bag of Pepperidge Farms goldfish for me. Really? She knew. She's the best. If only I had seen them. Oh well, at least I didn't kill anyone.

ME AND JEN

I was told that if they didn't get their six million cells that day, I would have to drive back in again the next day. Or even the day after. For some people, it took up to three days. The thought of it was making me anxious. Then I thought about how much

Neupogen had been pumped into my body and that ridiculous night of pain. I *had* to have produced enough stem cells. It felt like a trillion of them had made a break for it. Oh God, I couldn't come back at 5:30 a.m. again. Please, please, please, let them get enough. So I just sat there, waiting and hoping.

As the blood circulated in and out of my body, my right finger and thumb started going numb again. The night before, I had felt the same sensation. I had called the hospital because I thought I was having some sort of blood clot. I got the doctor who performed the catheterization in my neck, and she didn't know why I was experiencing something like that. I asked her if maybe it had something to do with the Hickman line being put in. She assured me that it was unrelated.

The night before the harvesting, when it first happened, I have to tell you, I kind of freaked out a bit. I didn't know if it was going to stay isolated in my distal extremities or start moving up my arm and then who knew where it would stop. I needed to tell Jen what was going on. I didn't yell "Hey!" down the hall, that's for sure. I got up and went down to her room and calmly apprised her of the situation. She encouraged me to call the doctor, who had been nice enough to give me her number. But like I said, she did little to ease my mind. But soon the sensation had waned to a slight tingle, so I left it at that.

But there it was again. This time, I couldn't feel either my thumb or my index finger. Nothing. I would later find out that it was called brachial neuritis or Parsonage-Turner syndrome. Guess what it's caused by? Trauma to the brachial plexus; as in when they put in the Hickman line. Come on, man. You're telling me that the doctor who put in the line never had this happen before? Come on, man. I couldn't be the first one. They had a name for it and everything. I didn't find out why for about a week. Until then, I didn't know why I couldn't feel anything with those two digits. It finally ended up going away slowly over a month or two, but at the time, it was a bit disconcerting.

Midafternoon, I swilled down the goldfish and then ordered a grilled cheese sandwich. What the heck, I was already fat. Besides, they said I would lose weight during the next three weeks when I was in the hospital, what with all the vomiting and not wanting to eat. Again, lies. I put on another ten pounds over the next month. I must have an iron stomach or something. Never got sick once, even though I struggled with nausea from time to time. Well, there was the fish and chips incident, but I'd rather not bring that up again. Literally.

The ten hours clicked by. They finally unhooked me from the super-high-tech reel-to-reel recorder and sent me on my way. Jen was waiting for me downstairs, and we drove home in yet another massive traffic jam. Same people, different direction. They told me they would get in touch with me later on that night after the geek squad counted every little cell they took from me.

At ten thirty that night, I got the phone call. I was incredibly nervous about what they might say. Did they get enough?

"Is this Marc Mitchell?" the woman on the other end of the phone asked.

"This is he," I replied.

"Can you give me your date of birth please?"

Who else would care how many cells they took from me? I gave her my birth date, but it wasn't quite enough.

"Last four digits of your social security number?" she asked.

Oh, for the love, woman, just spit it out. Did they get enough or what? I calmly yet quickly gave her my information.

"You won't need to come back tomorrow, we got enough cells," she said very matter-of-factly. There was no jubilation or congratulatory tone, just the message. I could only assume that she may have been one of the lab rats that did the counting (my apologies to all the fine lab technicians out there for calling you rodents), and she was going to be up all night tallying stem cells. She likely didn't have time for chitchat or superfluous words of encouragement. Before she could hang up on me, I just had to know how many, and asked her for the number. Like I said, I'm a numbers kind of guy.

"We counted 16.7 million cells," she replied dryly.

I thanked her for the phone call, and that was the end of our short conversation. Sixteen point seven million. Jesus, no wonder I was in so much pain that night. Damn that Neupogen. Double dose my ass. They got almost three times what they needed. The good news in all of this was twofold. One, I didn't need to go back in the next day...or the next, for that matter; and two, they would have enough for a second stem cell transplant in the future should one be needed.

They can hold the cells for something like ten years, barring some sort of power outage or "True Bloods" breaking in and stealing them. So if at some point—and they tell me that some point will come—my response to treatment becomes less than satisfactory, they could have me go through this whole bone marrow transplant again. The next time, however, I would be spared the Neupogen nightmare that I had endured just a few days back. I figured with my luck, I'd either die before that happened or I'd stay in some sort of remission for eleven years and then still have to go through it again.

The thing is, I thought I'd heard one of the doctors say that once you've gone through stem cell harvesting, you can't have it done again. If that was the case, and if the need arose and I survived past the expiration date of the stored cells, I guess they would have to perform an allogeneic transplant instead of this autologous one.

Given the last scenario, the allogenic transplant would have me out of circulation for a year, and concern about contracting graft versus host disease (GVD), which is not uncommon. GVD is about exactly what it sounds like it is. It's when your body attacks the cells they put into you. When that happens, all kinds of bad things can go wrong. First and foremost, you can die. But if you do survive, and they can give you enough steroids and other immunosuppressive drugs to thwart it off a bit, a whole boatload of bad things can ensue.

An acquaintance of mine who also had stage III multiple myeloma (I had the good fortune of meeting him while sitting next to him in one of my treatment sessions) was not as fortunate as me. He needed the allogeneic transplant after his autologous one failed. He encountered all kinds of problems. He lost vision in his left eye. He dropped about sixty pounds and is so weak he can barely walk. And just for an extra bonus, his skin peels off, leaving him red and raw all the time. That's the kind of thing GVD can do. Oh yeah, it's a real joyride for him.

I take back the part about being the unluckiest human alive. I really need to check myself. There are so many other things that could have happened to me. So many other untreatable conditions I could have come down with. Although my disease is deemed terminal, at least I can hope for a little time. On the bright side, if I ever do need such a transplant, it means I've survived eleven years, and that wouldn't be so bad.

Let's face it, life is terminal. It's just that most of us think it will happen when we're old. When you get diagnosed with cancer, it just changes the clock a little. Well, maybe a lot in some cases. But there's still no denying death. It will get you. The funny thing about cancer is that when it finally wins its fight and kills you, it loses. I wish it knew that. Maybe it wouldn't act so aggressively if it understood that its fate lay in its own hands. Stupid cancer. It really is a ball buster.

I was extremely relieved to know that they had enough cells. I could "sleep in" the next day, which meant I could toss and turn in bed until my back and neck were too stiff to stay lying down any longer. At least we didn't have to drive in that traffic again.

CHAPTER 11 – FIRST WEEK OF CAPTIVITY

Although I wasn't working full time at this point, I still got my hands dirty in the hospital doing a few surgeries and procedures while I waited for the megadose of Melphalan that would destroy my immunity. I guess with surgery, I should say I got my hands clean, but, you know, it's an expression. I performed an anastomosis on a cat's intestine (took out a chunk of bad intestine and sutured together the healthy ends) that had lymphoma. I had to chuckle a bit, wondering who would last longer, me or the cat. The surgery went well, giving me a sense of worth at a time when I felt completely useless. In a matter of days, I would be just that. Utterly useless.

Another trip to Boston. Fun stuff. This time I wouldn't be coming back for a while. My release date was set for April 3, if all went well. That is, if I didn't die and all that. (But since you're reading this, you know that didn't happen.)

Now this Melphalan stuff is pretty toxic. The nurses wear masks and double glove their hands. They take all the necessary precautions. If this drug doesn't go into the vein and somehow leaks out into your subcutaneous tissue, it acts like battery acid. Or even better, a brown recluse spider bite. Not right away; it takes a few days to work its magic. Horrible stories are out there about people sloughing off massive amounts of skin because it got outside of the vein. That's right. Bing it.

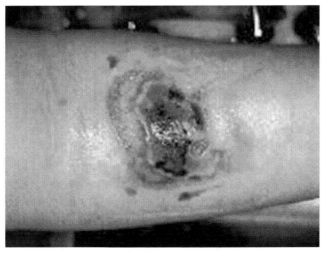

HERE IS A NICE RECLUSE SPIDER BITE PICTURE SO YOU DON'T HAVE TO LOOK IT UP.

In the past, each time I received a harsh chemotherapy drug intravenously, they always placed a catheter for similar reasons. Most of these drugs are extremely toxic outside of the vein. They want to ensure there is a secure line when they drip it in. Now here's the strange part. There I am at Dana Farber Hospital, the world-renowned cancer center, perhaps the best in the world, and they put in a butterfly catheter to give me this stuff. Basically it's just a needle on the end of a tube. It is hardly a secure line. I know, I've used them plenty. The needle is only about a half inch long and can be persnickety at best about staying in the vein. I've had quite a few of them start leaking out while giving fluids to a number of different animals. We call it blowing a vein.

Of course, some animals don't like to sit perfectly quiet sometimes, but still, those tiny needles are dicey when it comes to security. I looked at the nurse perplexedly as she whipped out this puny little butterfly catheter.

That's what you're going to use to give me this shit? I thought. *You have to be kidding me. Where's that two-inch twenty-gauge that will set in nice and deep in my vein?* This thing was a half-inch, twenty-three-gauge joke. Oddly enough, the higher the number, the smaller the gauge.

This is what they might use in a triage tent in Haiti or something. What the hell? I watched her set it in my hand and check for a flash of blood. Sure, it was in, but for the next hour, as that bag dripped into me, I didn't move an inch. Was it a cost thing? It couldn't be. They just dropped a hundred grand on me sucking my cells out. Why would they skimp here and use a second-rate catheter? It didn't make any sense. And I was too chicken shit to ask. Fortunately it didn't leak, in part because I did my best Lincoln Memorial impression and partly because she was good at setting those things. But still, I was at a loss for words.

And so began my sentence in the hospital. On the following day, they performed the same procedure with the same flimsy little catheter. This was Dana Farber! I still couldn't get over it. But it worked, so I guess they knew better than me. But would it have killed them to use a real catheter? Okay, forget it, I'll let it go.

For my second dose, they moved me into my real jail cell, where I wrote in my journal that it was my first official day of captivity, but technically it was my second. They put me up on the sixth floor of tower A, among ten or twelve other inmates who were going through some sort of bone marrow transplant for different diseases, all at various points in their time there. It was a regular carousel of patients going in and out. Some had just a few days left, and some were midway through it. As they wheeled me in, I saw one guy leaving. Man, he looked like shit: I thought, that's me in three weeks; what a comforting sight.

Jen thought it would be nice if I gave people updates now and then on how I was doing (or she could do it for me if necessary), so she set me up on a website called CaringBridge. It's a place for patients, family, and friends to chat and converse online while someone is in the hospital. At the time, I didn't think I would be able to do it. I was already feeling pretty crappy, and I knew that with each successive day I would feel worse, making writing almost an impossibility.

On day one, I made an entry, even though I was feeling horrible. I got a lot of responses of encouragement, and people seemed to have a genuine interest in how I was doing. I was shocked really. I also knew that my family would want to hear how I was doing each day, and quite frankly, I didn't have much energy and didn't feel like talking on the phone. If I could keep them updated via this site, and they could see that I was doing okay, I could put their minds at ease and not have them worry. Moreover, Harryman wasn't doing very well with his fight against his lung cancer, and the last thing I wanted was him worrying about me.

So each day, usually in the morning, I mustered up just enough strength to write something about the previous day's events or what was going to transpire on that particular day. To be honest, looking back, I don't know how I did it. It was a struggle to say the least. But with each entry, I got more responses and felt as if I had an audience I couldn't let down. After the third day or so, I was pretty much committed, and if I didn't write something, I was sure my family would think the worst and know I was doing poorly. So I wrote…every day…for seventeen days.

The segments that are in indented are directly from CaringBridge, unedited and complete. Comments on how I was really feeling are in regular text; kind of a director's commentary, if you will. In order to keep morale high at home, I tried to keep it light, but the fact remains, it was difficult to say the least.

First Day of Captivity

Mar 18, 2012 10:27am

Well, it has begun. My little vacation has started and I'm so excited! There's a beautiful view of the city from my cell. The guards keep referring to it as my room. The food is good, surprisingly. It's no Capital Grill, but it's better than McDonald's. Although they conveniently forgot to bring me salt for this morning's breakfast. Just another tactic to get me to talk.

In about thirty minutes, they start their torture techniques by giving me a drug that will wipe out my bone marrow. They are threatening me with another dose tomorrow. This should make the next four to five days a barrel of laughs.

Well, one of the "nurses" just came in. Time for my medicine. If I'm up to it, I will post again tomorrow.

Thank you all for the support!

Marc

After that first entry, I was almost certain I wouldn't write again. The drugs were doing wretched things to my body. I had already shaved my head to avoid waking up next to a cat when it all fell out, but my shave job wasn't quite perfect. There was still a little stubble left. Miniscule pieces of hair started parachuting off of my head, much like a Labrador sheds. I think I made it worse with the buzz cut. Those little bits of hair were everywhere, like tiny barbs. They poked me relentlessly for the entire stay. Plus, all the other hair on my ridiculously hairy Greek body started shedding off.

Every day, my sheets were covered in shards of hair. I would lie there not knowing which part of my body to scratch; they were everywhere. Just an added bonus to what was already a difficult time. My body ached horribly, I had diarrhea from the Melphalan, and my sleep apnea was in full throat. Pardon the pun.

Second Day of Captivity

Mar 19, 2012 8:36am

Well, it was no idle threat. They are hitting me up with another dose of toxins that they call chemotherapy. And if the chemical warfare isn't enough to break a patient, they are employing a psychological strategy as well. They are making me poop into a puny plastic cup so they can look at it. I think they are doing it to laugh at me. Who looks at someone else's waste? It's just not right. Oh, they want the urine too. I'm not sure who is being tortured there, me or them. The humiliation of going into a plastic chamber pot is one thing, but having to handle it is quite another. The thought of it makes me want to puke. Either that or the chemo is kicking in.

They have also employed some sleep deprivation techniques and wake me up every two hours or so, to keep me from being able to focus. They keep saying they want to "take" my vitals. I don't know what those are or where they imagine they're going to find them, but I don't think I want to give them up.

Today marks the final dose of the drug that tries to kill me. Tomorrow, I will receive my own stem cells to try to get me back on track.

I have watched several episodes of "Dexter" on my laptop (it's quite a good show if you haven't heard of it. Jen got me hooked a few months ago and I'm slowly catching up. I'm in the third season of six). I'm also playing a ridiculous amount of those silly games on the iPad (Words with Friends, Hanging with Friends, Scramble, and finally the newest is Draw Something). If I ever get back to work, I don't know what I'm going to do about playing anymore. I fear I will turn into the Jackie Paper of iPad games. I'll leave a bunch of Puffs waiting for me to play, and it just won't happen. Ah, poor Puff. Even today, I still feel bad for that stupid dragon.

Anyway, I need to rest up. The drugs should really start kicking my ass soon. I probably don't have to get into detail of what will happen, but let's just say that the whole hat thing could become messy. Not good.

Hope all is well out there. I will continue to update as I can, hopefully daily.

There was little to no hope of getting a night's rest. The meds they gave me were making me sweat, and just the idea of what was happening in my body gave me a sense of angst that kept me awake. I was absolutely certain that I wouldn't write again at this point. They started me on OxyContin, but that made me nauseous, so they switched me over to oxycodone. The former is a longer lasting, perhaps more potent pain killer, whereas the latter is taken every four hours for pain. Without that stuff on board, I would have been in real trouble.

Every part of my body ached. All my injuries from the past came back to harass me. My broken ankle when I was four, my wrist from 1992, the broken ribs in 1995, and my constant aching neck and back pain that I already had, all were magnified by the drug they gave me. That's about when I decided that I couldn't write anymore. It was too much. I was going to just hunker down and try to stay within myself and suck it up. But when I woke up the next morning, even though I felt like a truck ran me over, sprinkling hairs on me after it passed, I read the comments of a dozen or more people wishing me well. Oh God, I thought, I've created a monster.

I got through about three and a half seasons of the *Dexter* series and either ran out of time to continue watching or lost the ability to focus for more than ten minutes in a stretch. Either way, I never got through the six seasons I had on DVD. It's about a guy who is a serial killer, but he only kills people that "deserve" it, so he is likable in a morbid kind of way. When I was released from the hospital, I found it impossible to watch it anymore. The very thought of the show now places me back in that hospital bed and conjures up visions and sounds of that dreadful time. I think we have a little Dexter in all of us. There are a few people out there that I could imagine laying down in plastic and driving a knife into. For the record, I said I could imagine it, not do it.

Third Day of Captivity

Mar 20, 2012 9:31am

To be honest, things are no better today than they were yesterday. As a matter of fact, it's worse. The nausea is not a lot of fun, and the idea of the hat doesn't help. I convinced them yesterday that I didn't need the hat for now, because I'm a big time doctor and all. I told them that I could keep them apprised of any changes that were noteworthy.

Escape seems to be futile. I would make a run for it, but they have my jugular vein (or whatever vein they ended up using) tethered to some weird pole with a bunch of bags that contain the poisons that they feed me all day long. Besides, I'm afraid that in my weakened condition I could take a nasty spill down the stairs and subject myself to further school absences.

Last night was a rough one. My room is hotter than it should be, and after inquiring, I found out I can adjust the temp. Good to know; after three days of living in a sweat shop. There are no doors on most of the cells in here, just a privacy curtain that they insist on opening even after I close it. This allows me to hear everything that goes on just outside my room.

What's just outside my room you ask? Well, for starters, the front desk where the nurses hang out. Then there's some sort of paper roll that they pull on and tear away at deafening levels.

And finally, the piece de resistance; the ice machine. That's a real pleasure to hear them dig into that every half hour or so. You have to wonder who needs so much ice at 3:30 in the morning? I swear they're doing it on purpose. And anyone who knows me understands just how much I hate little noises like that. That's right, have a laugh at my expense…not funny. I know Harryman is getting a good chuckle right about now. It was like happy hour outside my room last night. I actually got up and asked them to keep it down. That worked for about 45 minutes, then they were back to doing Jell-O shots and keg stands.

Post time for stem cell transplant is at 4:30 today. My lab results show that despite all the toxins they have pumped into me, my kidneys and liver are doing well. My white cells are dropping but haven't bottomed out yet. Must be that rugged furry Greek blood.

So that's what's happening today. Hopefully this is as bad as I will feel. I can only hope. As always, it's great to read the comments, but that doesn't mean you have to post, it's just nice knowing I have so much support.

Marc

During the first three days, with sleep being at a premium but almost impossible, the heat in the room was unbelievable. It was set at seventy-four degrees. I had no idea that I could control the temp. The room was open to the nurse's area by a mere curtain, so I just figured the whole place was that temperature. I sweated my ass off. I couldn't believe it when I asked if they could turn the temp down out there and they told me that I had my own thermostat. Really? What the hell? That little tidbit of information would have been nice. Balls hot, I tell you. It was insufferable.

Despite the nausea, I kept on eating like a trucker at a greasy spoon. It almost seemed as if the food helped me from feeling nauseous. So I ate. And ate. With little to no exercise, the pounds just kept adding up.

The noise outside of my room was nothing short of maddening. The nurses made absolutely no effort to keep quiet. Now I understand that they have their jobs to do, but it was insanity. At one point, two of them sat directly outside of my room chatting about *Desperate Housewives*. It wouldn't have been so bad if they were talking about the Bruins or *Fletch*. At least then I could have listened with some interest. But *Desperate Housewives* (insert vomit noise)? They couldn't have been more than five feet away from me. They just kept yapping. Gabrielle. Bree Van De Kamp. Susan. Lynette. And who could forget Carlos? Oh yeah, I got quite an education.

At home, when Jen is sleeping, I do my best to slither about the house so that I don't make any loud noises to wake her up. And she does the same for me. That place was a three-ring circus of conversations and drawers being opened and shut with no concern about how hard they did it. They even had a noise meter that lit up when it detected certain decibel levels. That thing was flashing like a Christmas tree.

I wondered if these people behaved this way at home with their significant others. If so, no wonder the divorce rate is so high. They seemingly had no regard that a dozen patients who were desperately trying to get just an hour of sleep here or there were being kept awake by their incessant talking. It really bothered me. So I ate.

Fourth Day of Captivity

Mar 21, 2012 10:24am

Well, the good news is I'm not dead. The bad news, that extreme makeover bus still has its wheels on top of me.

Move the bus indeed. Better news, it was much quieter last night. I think that they may have been hung over. Tomorrow is Thursday, and that is traditionally ladies' night, so that's something to look forward to.

They gave me my stem cells yesterday around five o'clock and I had the chaplain bless the blood. They asked me beforehand if that was something that I wanted them to do. My grandmother would roll over in her grave if I refused. I'm not an overly religious person, but I figure I can use all the help I can get. Besides, I wouldn't want "someone else" to slide in and put some voodoo hex on my blood because I didn't have Him there to thwart off the evils.

Had a good night's sleep aside from a few ice stabbings that rattled me awake. Oh, and the guy next door had a meltdown and was yelling "help! help!" for about 45 minutes. He sounded exactly like an old witch crying out. Jen will get a chuckle from this…I think it's the same dude that was yelling "ow, ow, ow" when I was getting my Hickman line put in a week ago. Sounded exactly the same.

I am profoundly tired but able to nap and get rest, since there's absolutely nothing for me to do here. My room is pouring in some nice sunlight as I reminisce about those days of frolicking outside. One day, I think. One day.;)

For now, order me up a nice big brownie and another episode of Dexter.

From bed 20 on the 6th floor in A tower, this is Myeloma Marc, signing off for now.

They kept insisting that I crap into that absurd plastic container. I had flat-out refused. I guess they wanted to know if I was producing enough, or if there was blood, or whatever the hell they were looking for. I didn't care. I wasn't doing it. First off, it was just plain embarrassing. Second, it was disgusting. Third, it wasn't sanitary. There I was, with almost no immunity, and they wanted me to handle bacteria-laden excrement. Didn't seem very prudent.

Each time a nurse asked me where my sample was, I just told her that the last nurse took care of it. They obviously didn't write it down or anything, since no one caught on that I wasn't using it. So you tell me, how important could it be? Besides, if I noticed a problem in that department, I was certain I could alert them to any issues. But there *was* this one nurse that really had a thing for shit. She was furious when I didn't have any for her to inspect and was vehement that I use it and show her my waste. I think she may have been some sort of necrophiliac or something. It was just weird. Her scolding had no effect on me. I felt like the shit Nazi. "No poop for you! Insist all you want, that hat is staying pristine white."

Let's go over this whole thing about the collection process, shall we? The container they wanted me to "go" in was the size of a small soup bowl. It was no more than four inches deep, and that's being generous, and about six inches around. Now keep in mind what these drugs do to your intestinal tracts. It ravages them. By doing so, it creates some of the worst diarrhea imaginable.

I WASN'T KIDDING, THE THING WAS TINY. OBVIOUSLY, IT IS PICTURED UPSIDE DOWN HERE.

118

At the risk of being too graphic...ah, screw it, I'll be graphic. They wanted me to spray diarrhea into this tiny little plastic thimble. The force that it came out with was insane. If I placed that underneath myself, it would have been a disaster. Can you imagine what kind of a mess would ensue? I sure could. I wasn't going to be a part of that nonsense. There would have been brown slop everywhere...on my hands, on my ass, on my legs, the floor...a real shit show, if you will. They were out of their minds if they thought I was going to be a party to that fiasco waiting to happen.

When I thought about it, all I could think of was one of our horses called Sparkle Road. She experienced an episode of diarrhea that was one for the ages. Each time I looked at that little container, her incident came to mind.

Sparkle was the next foal after Honey's Best from the same mare, Honey Sparkle Way. We bred her to a nice stallion named Middle Road, and her name was produced fairly easily by combining the sire's name with the dam's. Sadly, Sparkle was the last foal out of Middle Road, as shortly after his rendezvous with Honey's mom, he freakishly impaled himself on a fence post and died. We dallied with the idea of naming her End Of The Road, but thought that was a bit morbid and perhaps a bad omen.

Sparkle turned out to be a huge filly who showed amazing potential. She clearly had more speed and stamina than even the great Honey's Best. We were more than just a little excited when she showed this on the racetrack, giving us great hope that we may have caught lightning in a bottle a second time. It seemed that there were some pretty good genes in that old mare, Honey Sparkle Way. Sparkle Road's size, however, wasn't always a good thing. It's usually easier to handle a small two-year-old that wants to be a fruit loop, rather than a monster like Sparkle was.

At one point while she was still fairly green, she reared up and came crashing down on top of my father, shattering his ankle under her enormous weight. He watched us train her from the sidelines in a wheelchair for the rest of the summer. He had to have a plate and a couple pins to put it all back together. His lower leg never healed right and stayed swollen for the rest of his life. We called it his "Flintstone" foot due to its massive size. They say time heals all wounds. I'm not sure that's entirely true.

That's not to be confused with his "Froogie" thumb. Harryman had a knack for getting injured. One day he was tacking a shoe on Frugality's front foot (Harryman was a pretty good blacksmith for having no formal training). As he banged away with his hammer and drove the nail through the hoof wall, Frugy spooked and jumped up in the air, ripping his thumb back viciously and tearing his flesh on the point of the nail. That was definitely one of his angry moments. I won't tell you what he said; well, yelled, actually. The expletives were a-flying. That thing swelled up just like in the cartoons. Blood was everywhere. Nothing a little rag and some black tape didn't fix. Good old Harryman. He never bothered going to the hospital.

His hand was never the same. He had permanent nerve damage. He couldn't lift his thumb up over his index finger. You wouldn't think that would be a big deal, but it was often the exact maneuver he needed for certain pool shots when he used his hand as a bridge. He now had to take his right hand and manually lift his thumb over and place it on top of his index finger to create a bridge.

We had built a pool room in the barn and played quite a bit together. Every time he did that little flip of his thumb to make the bridge, Doug and I would quietly chime out, "Frugy." He would just shake his head and laugh.

As a three-year-old, Sparkle matched Honey's best mile at the same age, and Doug had a choke hold on her in the win. She was shaping out to be something truly special. But as the fates would have it, she developed lameness issues in her right hind leg (in the hip area) that we never could get under control. She could never be cut loose on the racetrack, since the pain made her rough gaited and slowed her down considerably. It was discouraging to see her talents go to waste like that. If we raced her in classes that didn't force her to go all out, she could make some hay and stay in her comfort zone.

In the end, her lameness progressed, and as a five-year-old we had to retire her on the farm, and we made a brood mare out of her. She had proven her abilities and was a half-sister to Honey, so we figured she would be worth breeding. She threw a few foals for us, all with tremendous speed, but none that could sustain it for the whole mile. I guess lightning really does only strike once.

SPARKLE ROAD WINNING EASILY AT ROCHESTER FAIR.

As she grew to be a mare, she was gigantic as standardbred mares go, at least sixteen hands, and a beautiful chestnut. She had a gorgeous white blaze on her forehead and a flaxen mane and tail. She was a real looker. Her appetite for food was notorious. She was an absolute pig. She'd gobble down her grain in mere minutes, while the others in the barn took their time dining. The fact that others were still eating disturbed her, and she would nicker and kick, asking for more. I think she would have eaten until she exploded. We had to be careful with her rations, as she was getting a little fat just hanging around being a brood mare and doing nothing but lounging out in the field all day.

In the spring, the large pasture that most of the horses were turned out in got quite muddy. There was a three- or four-week period of time in late April and early May when the frost thawed and we couldn't turn horses out there. They would have utterly destroyed the paddock by churning it to pieces before the grass had a chance to grow in. A horse can put five thousand pounds of pressure on one foot when running. Imagine twelve horses in a muddy paddock frolicking around. It would be like having a dozen four-hooved rototillers out there making a complete mess of the place.

Instead, we either left them in or rotated them into the small paddocks that we didn't care as much about. Owners of horses that boarded at the farm were always anxious for us to give them the green light to let them out there in the spring. It was often quite a battle holding them off. They didn't like it when their horses didn't get turned out. But we held our ground so to speak, waiting until the grass caught and the soil firmed up enough so that we could have a pasture for the whole season and not just for a single day.

As it was, it was the day we were going to finally turn them out into the main pasture. The grass had come in beautifully and was tantalizingly plush and ready for the picking. We really should have known better. It's best to break horses into fresh forage slowly to avoid any stomach aches from overeating on the first day out. We knew this, but for some reason, it escaped us that year. Again, we should have turned them out for just a few hours to avoid any colic from such a lush buffet.

Sparkle was a complete glutton. When she got out there, she must have thought she was in heaven. She put her head down and started munching…and munching…and munching. I don't think she picked her head up once. Seriously, that's not an overstatement. She couldn't get enough. She just kept packing it in. At some point in the midafternoon, we realized our error and brought them all in. We were too late.

While the rest of the herd ate like civilized beasts, Sparkle looked like she was pregnant with triplets. Her belly was making sounds that you could hear from forty feet away. It's called borborygmus, that gurgling in the stomach. It's one of the more underused words in our vocabulary, but a good one. She was clearly uncomfortable. Who wouldn't be with the amount of roughage she ate? She started pacing the stall. She got down on the ground and rolled. Yup, we had ourselves a gen-u-ine gas colic on our hands. We gave her medicine to dull the pain, which put her somewhat at ease. What followed was nothing short of a blowout of biblical proportions.

When the disgusting amount of ruminating digesta finally made it to her distal colon, it was truly incredible to watch the explosion. Green diarrhea started shooting out of her in projectile fashion. She literally coated the walls. It was everywhere. After a few hours of emitting a dark, pine-colored ooze, not only were the walls completely covered in it, so was she. Her once flaxen tail was sopping wet and dripping with green goo. Her body no longer was its brilliant dappled chestnut; rather, it looked as if someone had taken a brush and thrown green paint all over her. She had swished her tail countless times in distress and sprayed it everywhere. Even her mane was covered. It was unbelievable. Poor Sparkle. The expression on her face when it was over was priceless. She just stood there in relief, with a look that said, "Holy crap, that was brutal."

When I looked into that little plastic cup, that's all I could think of. I wasn't going to be a Sparkle Road. I was certainly eating like she was, and my intestines were grumbling just as badly.

The thought of having to clean up after such a mess was as displeasing a thought as I could envision. So no, I was not going to use the hat. No way, no how. Granted, I couldn't have produced the quantity that she blew out that day, but the mental picture of it was all I needed to make me stand firm.

Fifth Day of Captivity

Mar 22, 2012 8:42am

I would love to report that I am feeling much better, but I don't want to lie. It's a horror show trying to sleep in this asylum. It's a broken symphony of trash bags crinkling, sharps container tops being slammed shut, ice cubes being slayed, and muffled conversations. I'm waiting for Mr. Marbles to come into my room and molest me. The nausea is a wave that keeps coming and going. At times, I'm really not sure if I'm hungry or sick to my stomach. It's odd. But we press on and keep tearing off the days of the calendar.

They drew blood at five o'clock this morning...again. I guess it's so pressing they have to do it at five. Can't wait till say 8am when normal people are up. And if any of you think that getting up at 5am is normal, then just go to Facebook and unfriend me right now. It ain't. Let's just say I'm not a morning person. The blood will hopefully show that my white cells are completely wiped out (I know that sounds weird to be hopeful of that). After that, we watch and wait for them to come back slowly. That is why I have to be here so long, as we watch the counts come back up to a level that is compatible with fighting disease outside isolation.

Digressing off the topic, I just want to address a comment that my dear and beloved Aunt Aphy made earlier in the week.

And I quote, "wishing you a speedy recovery so I can make that wonderful coconut cake that you love." Let's just dispel any misconceptions right now. I hate coconut cake. She was being facetious. I had to laugh, though. For many, many years, she would make me a coconut cake at Easter or my birthday (they often coincided) and thought for some reason that it was my favorite. At some point as a very young lad, and very shy (hard to believe, I know), when asked if I liked the cake that was handed to me, I must have said yes. And she remembered.

From then on, it was coconut cake every year. And I hated it. The first couple years, I thought it was just that everyone else liked it, so she made it. Imagine my disbelief when I found out she was specifically making it for me! Oh no, what was I supposed to do? It was too late to tell her. It's like when someone has food in their teeth. You better tell them right away when you have the chance, because if you wait too long, the opportunity passes and then it's just awkward. So the years rolled along, and I kept my silence...and forced down coconut cake. It wasn't until I was in my late twenties that I mustered enough courage to tell her the truth. I'm not sure who felt worse. Anyway, we can laugh about it now. So despite what you may have read, no coconut cake please.

That's about it for now. Bruins are on tonight at 10:30. Right in my wheel house for all you early risers. I won't be sleeping even if I wanted to.

They are starting to insist that the hat make a return, but I am holding strong. We'll see how long I can go just refusing to use it. If I don't recognize its existence, it really isn't there, right? For now, I am gratefully hatless and hope it stays that way.

We are now on a white cell watch. I will keep you posted.

Marc

I didn't mention the whole oral hygiene routine in any of my posts. At least I don't think I did. They wouldn't allow me to have a toothbrush or dental floss. What they did permit me to have was some crappy little plastic sticks with sponges on them and some horrible-tasting paste that I was supposed to "brush" my teeth with. It didn't do anything for taking off the sweaters that were forming on my enamel. It was like trying to scrape ice off your windshield with a raw hotdog. Useless.

Don't tell anyone, but I smuggled in a toothbrush, toothpaste… and dental floss. Shhhh. I know it probably wasn't the smartest move if any of you doctors out there are reading this. The whole reason they didn't want you using a toothbrush or floss was because they didn't want any of the oral bacteria entering your bloodstream should you break even a tiny vessel in your mouth. Yeah, yeah, I got it. But the food in my teeth was killing me. Psychologically I mean. Knowing that there would be a piece of pizza stuck between my molars for three weeks was just unbearable. It had to be some sort of torture technique. I couldn't take it, I tell you.

They had warned me beforehand about this whole dental hygiene denial thing, so I was privy to their shenanigans. There was no chance I was going three weeks without brushing. No chance. I thought it out logically. I normally brush my teeth a minimum of twice a day and floss nearly every time I eat. My gums are like leather. They never bleed when I brush or floss. I figured if I was very careful and just brushed my teeth and stayed clear of my gums, I'd be fine. As far as the flossing, I slid that sucker in oh so gently, and then pulled out any remnants of food that were hiding in the tough spots. Man, would they have been pissed. I did it every single day, bad shoulder and all (you'll hear about the shoulder debacle shortly).

I hid my contraband in the bathroom, high up on the top shelf of a cabinet, all the way in the back. I felt like I was hiding dirty magazines from my parents. No one would ever look there. I needed to pull in a chair and step way up to reach it. It was no easy task, doing it with a fluid pole and cords hanging off my neck, but it was worth it. And guess what? It didn't kill me. Besides, had I gotten mouth sores the way they anticipated, wouldn't that be worse than brushing? Those would be open wounds that bled on their own and would have allowed a complete onslaught of oral flora to penetrate my system.

Their reasoning seemed unreasonable. Besides, these were the same people who wanted me to handle a bacterial soup in an oversized coffee mug. Also the same people who told me not to wear a mask four days before they dropped "Fat Boy" on my bone marrow. I chose to brush. Each day, I put that awful paste on the sponges and scrubbed the counter with them to make it look like I used them, just in case they got suspicious. Oh yeah, I could be a real cagey bugger if need be.

I know I took a big risk doing what I did. Some people might call me a pompous idiot and that my arrogance could have killed me. They're probably right. I admit it. I was stupid and irresponsible and I certainly don't condone anyone else doing this. My father would often tell me when I acted foolishly, "for a smart guy, you're pretty stupid." He was a wise man.

But I followed just about all of their other rules. I didn't use deodorant. They made me wash my mouth out with this God-awful-tasting yellow paste twice a day, which I did, albeit reluctantly. I drank six glasses of water every day. I took all the medications they shoved in front of me. I didn't shave. Well, I didn't have to, since all of my hair was gone and nothing was growing anywhere. Strangely enough, the hair on the side of my calves never fell out. They clung on for dear life. Not sure how they dodged the bombs, but they really hung in there. In my defense, I didn't shave that either. So there.

Sixth Day of Captivity

Mar 23, 2012 9:23am

The sleep deprivation techniques continue to haunt me. I swear they were having a party early this morning. My new nurse may be a double agent and perhaps an ally, since she got them to quiet down for an hour or two after reprimanding them. That was nice. So from 5-7am, I got some sleep. Haleh-freakin-luyah!

Mulling over the whole coconut cake scenario, and not being able to tell when someone is writing in a sarcastic style, I am proposing to start something that could forever change the grammatical landscape of the English language. I suggest that if you are going to write anything sarcastically, those comments should be contained by the following two symbols, < and >. Much like you would use parentheses. So, as an example...<I'm so glad she made me coconut cake again, it's my favorite.> Right away, you know that the sentence requires a sarcastic tone and should be read as such. No mistakes, no having to say that I am saying this sarcastically, or he said sarcastically. Just throw in those little carrots and we're good to go. I'm telling you, this could catch on and become global. You'll see. <You guys are behind me 100% I'm sure of it.>

But I digress...

I know I've only been here for five days, but to me, it feels like nine weeks and five days. The first day seemed like a week. And the second day seemed like five days. And the third day seemed like a week again. But the fourth day, you went to see your mother, and that seemed just like a day... wait a second, I think that's from the movie "The Jerk." Well, you get the point. The days are dragging along. And the Bruins lost last night. Bleck.

Had a funny incident last night when a fairly large Jamaican nurse came in singing, "Doctor, doctor, give me the news, I got a bad case of lovin' you." The other white nurse chimed in and they laughed. The Jamaican woman looked at me and asked if I noticed her moves (apparently she thought they were dance moves) she was displaying while singing. So I looked at her and said, "Yeah, I saw 'em, but for a minute I thought you were white, then I looked up and saw your face." She nearly lost it and burst into laughter and squeaked out, "I think I just peed myself." So at least we all had a good laugh.

Those tough hairy Greek white cells are clinging to life and don't want to be sent off just yet. My counts are at 2.4, down from 4.5 yesterday with normal being 2-3 times higher than that. They're telling me that they may not bottom out until Sunday. Yay. My red cells are not faring so well and my hematocrit is at 24. Any lower and it's transfusion time. Yay, #2. In the meantime, I should expect to have pretty fun diarrhea as the villi in the intestines die out (they too are of the rapidly dividing cell line, like blood and hair that die out after chemo). So I have that to look forward to. The nurse then threatened the shat hat once again, so they can make sure they know how much fluid I've lost. I may become the first chemo patient to never get diarrhea. At least that's what I'm going to tell them. Can you imagine what kind of literal backlash one could expect whilst going into a four-inch-deep container? Hell no. That ain't happenin'.

Status quo otherwise. I hear you guys had temps in the 80s and enjoyed a wonderful day outside. <Good for you. So happy you could enjoy.>

Marc

Chapter 12 – Things Remembered

Seventh Day of Captivity

Mar 24, 2012 11:14am

Well, I've been here a week and this sucks. I would like to get off this train, Mr. Conductor. But alas, there are no stops on this ride. We either make it to the station or we don't. My mood has darkened considerably, but I'm not without hope. Seriously, it can't get much worse.

For some reason, I have lost some of the function in my right index finger and thumb. I have no strength flexing it. <This should have little impact on my ability to perform surgery.> It is quite worrisome, so I had a physical therapist look at it for me. He had no clue what was going on. They asked for an occupational therapist to come in next week. I'm not sure what the difference is between an occupational therapist and a physical therapist, but the name is longer so it must be more important. The physical therapist gave me some advice. He said I should do some body exercises while I can, before my platelets drop and it is not wise for me to do them. You know, keep my muscles active. So I did. The result of this was me in a whole lot of muscle pain. It was so bad that at one point I was curled up in the futile position. That's when you try every position possible but cannot get relief from the pain. It was a rough night.

The war of the hat continues, but I am winning the battle. I just act like it doesn't exist, and so far no one has called me on it. The smell coming from the bathroom after a hat-required session is nothing short of chemical warfare. You know how they say people don't mind the smell of their own? I have now disproven that theory.

Not only has the chemo affected that part of my body, it has made me nauseous and is now threatening to completely take away my ability to taste. My father would contend, however, that I never had a sense of taste. Because of this, I have been endlessly teased throughout my life that I am not a true Greek. Harryman would always say that I sit on my taste. While this may be true, I would argue that there is a considerable difference between having a poor sense of taste and not having the ability to taste.

My white counts are still dropping and are now at 1.9. Once again, they need to get to zero before we start going back in the right direction. The good news is my hematocrit is holding steady at 24, so I don't need another transfusion yet.

That is all for now. If my physical strength weakens any more, and I can't imagine that's possible, you may not hear from me tomorrow. I thank you all for your support and warm thoughts and constant positive energy. It is for sure helping me get through this.

Marc

That sixth night was probably the worst night I had. It was nothing short of a living hell. I should have known better than to exercise at that point of my treatment. After the therapist told me I should use my muscles to keep them active, I did ten standing squats to get my blood pumping. Just this act alone was difficult with the weakness I was experiencing and from the anemia. I was left exhausted and gasping for air. It was just ten squats...with no weights!

The result was disastrous. Since I had no white cells left, my muscles couldn't deal with the toxins that they produced. There's a condition that racehorses get when their lactic acid builds up rapidly during a race, and they go into a full body muscle spasm and can't move. It's called "tying up." That night, I got to know exactly how some of those horses I treated have felt.

Every muscle in my body was in pain. Well, not entirely true, my tongue was okay. As a vet, I should have known that my body couldn't handle any kind of stress at that particular juncture. You know the expression "if someone told you to jump off a bridge, would you do it"? Well, the therapist basically told me to jump, and like a donkey, I dove in head first. I don't blame him, he was only trying to help. He just chose the exact wrong day to give me the advice.

The pain was merciless. My hands were curled closed, my feet were contracted, and my legs felt like steel beams. My back? Oh, that was status quo; loose as a goose…in rigor mortis. What a dope I was. It was during that night that I won't say I welcomed death, but if he came along to take me, I would have followed him. I know, I know; play till you hear the whistle. But there comes a time that your mind can't fight it anymore, and it's not so much that you don't *want* to fight, you just can't. That's the state I was in. It was horrific. My entries didn't convey this, because again, I didn't want people to worry about me. But I was in big trouble.

They had to up my dose of oxycodone to two pills every four hours. I lay in bed, wide awake, watching the clock tick away until the next four hours were up, waiting for my next dose. I felt like a heroin addict in a back alley searching for his next hit. That night, at exactly four o'clock in the morning, I was due for another dose, and there wasn't a nurse within earshot. I didn't wait ten seconds past four. I hit the little red button on my bed to summon someone for my drugs. I might have hit it twice. Okay, it was three times. I was that desperate. It took them three minutes to get my prescription filled and bring it to me. Felt like an hour. I don't think I slept more than twenty or thirty minutes.

It rivaled the night the stem cells made a break for it out of my bone marrow. Except in this case, I was feeling the effects of the drugs and the anemia that went along with it. I had bottomed out mentally. I felt tears stream down my face from pain and anxiety, but I wasn't audibly crying. I thought, if I'm going to die from this whole thing, this would be the time for it to happen. I had just about given up at that point and desperately wanted out. I truly believed that those types of thoughts would never cross my mind. Don't give up, don't ever give up. That's always been my mantra; but I couldn't hear it anymore. They were just words. It was a scary feeling, not wanting to fight anymore. It's just not how I'm wired. But there I was, raising the white flag and surrendering to death. I just wanted the pain to go away.

As I stated in that last post, the drugs had taken away my sense of taste. This was a real bummer. It would last for the next three months. I wasn't sure if it was ever going to return. It wasn't as if I couldn't taste *anything*, it's just that everything tasted the same. Everything tasted like a stale cracker. It reminded me of the crackers we used to feed the pigs back in the late seventies and early eighties.

During the Cuban missile crisis in 1962, the government was almost certain we were going into a nuclear war. Or, as President Bush would say, "a *nuke-u-lar* war." You're the president, man, learn how to say it correctly. It's just like some of our clinicians in vet school in Ohio who would pronounce *larynx*, "lair-nix." It's "lar-ingks." Say it with me now..."LAR-INGKS!" You're a friggin' doctor, say it right!

Sorry, I got sidetracked. Don't axe me how that happened. Anyway, they built bunkers all over the place and made large quantities of rations in case we were attacked. They made two sources of food to sustain the general population in case of such an event. They made crackers and candy. They all came in shiny silver tins packed in cardboard boxes. They were rectangular, taller than they were wide; about the size of a small microwave on its end.

The candies came in two flavors: lemon and raspberry. The crackers were just plain crackers, like a water cracker, with no salt and no flavor. Strictly carbohydrates for survival and nothing more. They stored these massive quantities of rations in various locations, mostly along the Eastern Seaboard. One of those locations was at the Phillips Exeter Academy just down the road from us. Our friend Ron Jennings was a security guard there and knew about these boxes, because he had seen them on his nightly tours of the place. They had hundreds upon hundreds of them. Maybe thousands. They had been sitting there for fifteen years or more. Incredibly, they were still edible. Well, at least they wouldn't kill you.

The government told the academy to get rid of them, and the academy was going to just throw them all away. When they opened the rooms that held them and started removing them, Ron and Harryman went down there with a pickup truck and started hauling truckload after truckload of these things out of there. We were going to use them to supplement the feed for our pigs. They had to do it secretly, as the government wanted the crackers destroyed. As the late night security guard, Ron was able to gain access to the "vault," and he and Harryman wheeled them out of there under the cover of nightfall. They brought home at least two hundred boxes of each, making five or six trips back and forth to the farm. There were so many left behind, I don't think anyone noticed. Each box contained two tins. The crackers were fairly light, but the candies had to weigh about twenty-five pounds a box. It was quite a night's work.

The pigs loved them! We made a trough out of an old acetylene tank cut in half. We had to cut open the crackers with metal shears. I'm sure the government had issued some sort of instrument to get them open more easily than our crude shear technique, but it's what we had. You had to be careful of some extremely jagged edges when you snipped those tins. They were pretty thick and dangerously sharp after you opened them.

We filled the trough up with crackers and added water, and the pigs dug in like it was a Thanksgiving feast. We all tried eating the crackers ourselves. Disgusting. They were as bland and stale as you could imagine a cracker would be after nearly two decades. If you were hungry enough, you could have eaten them, but they tasted musty, if that's conceivable.

The candies, on the other hand, were quite good. They were sugar coated and very tasty. They came in screw tops instead of the vacuum-sealed cracker tins. They were much easier to open. Let's face it, sugar really doesn't "go bad." Sure, it can get contaminated with bacteria if you introduce them, but those containers were capped off good and tight. All the people in the barn sucked on those things for years after that. We had so many. But we mostly fed them to our four-legged garbage disposals.

When the pigs heard you opening up one of the candy lids, they started squealing with anticipation. They would catch them in their mouths if you threw them at them. Just like a dog. When the tin was finally empty of candies (there were hundreds of them in each tin), the bottom of the container was full of sugar that had fallen off the outside candy coating. We'd pour that right into the trough as well. Pigs certainly have a sweet tooth…and a meat tooth…and a fat tooth…Let's just say they'd eat just about anything. They're pigs. Although they're not particularly fond of brussels sprouts.

They had smuggled in three years' worth of pig feeding. Don't get me wrong, that's not all we fed them. They got all kinds of other things. They got pig chow from the Agway down the street. Ron Jennings also brought home a bunch of scraps from the dining hall in five-gallon buckets every night. Those pigs ate well. Oh man, the sounds they made; it still makes me smile. The slurping, the smacking, the muffled squeals of delight; they made that slop sound incredibly appealing.

Usually one or two of them would stand facing the doorway if you watched them eat. After four or five smacks, one of them would stop abruptly, pick his head up out of the trough, stand perfectly still, and stare directly at you. He'd give a little grunt to let you know he didn't particularly like being watched, or that you weren't welcome to join in the feast. No matter their reasoning, it was just fun to watch them dig into a meal. The pig could very well be the coolest farm animal there is. It's kind of a shame we had to do what we did with them, which was probably why we usually didn't give them names.

In my hospital bed, back up on the sixth floor of tower A, it didn't matter what I ordered—a turkey club, pizza, cheeseburger, even Oreos. They all tasted like those survival crackers. Although the taste was gone, it did bring me back to a nicer time. I was back in the barn looking at the pigs, tossing them candies and watching them snatch them out of the air. It's amazing what a single taste or smell can do. It can mentally teleport you back to another time and keep you there, although in this case, it was the lack of taste that did it.

I tried adding salt. The salt was bitter. So it seemed I hadn't lost all of my taste buds, just the good ones. So each meal was the same, just a different texture or temperature. In my head, I so looked forward to having a pepperoni pizza, and I could smell it, almost taste it with my mind. But when I put it in my mouth, it was a pig cracker. It made me angry. So I ate.

Eighth Day of Captivity

Mar 25, 2012 9:10am

What a difference a day makes. So many positives compared to yesterday. First off, the Bruins won. Tim Thomas had to stand on his head for the last five minutes of the game, but they got the job done. Last night, I got four and a half hours of straight sleep until they woke me up to draw blood, so it could've been longer. That's the longest night's sleep I've had in over seven months. My sleep started to be disrupted long before I was diagnosed due to night sweats that would have me up three and four times a night to change sheets. Then, when I got diagnosed, the treatments stopped the night sweats, but I developed sleep apnea from the chemo and the steroids. As you can see from recent pictures, I look like a puffer fish. That's from all the drugs. That thickness is also in my throat, which makes the apnea so much worse. But last night, with the combination of being crazy tired, narcotics for pain, and Ativan, I was placed into a mini-coma and actually slept through the night (at least what I now consider sleeping through the night).

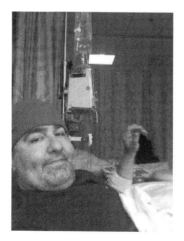

I HADN'T HIT MY HIGHEST WEIGHT YET, BUT YOU CAN STILL SEE
WHAT WONDERS STEROIDS CAN DO. JUST LOVELY.

They are moving me to another room just down the hall. It has its own shower. Up until now, I've had to wait for the community shower (one stall) to be available, and then traipse down the hall and use that one. So on any given day,

I had no idea what time it would be ready. A couple days ago, it wasn't until like 3pm, and I ended up opting not to take one. Not only does this room have a shower, but it has a door! A door, I tell you! Well bless my stem cells and slap me silly. Can you believe it? It will help filter out the noises that have overpowered my flimsy little curtain. This is big news. That happens around 1pm today. Can't wait.

My white cells are at 0.66. So close to the bottom of the pit. Tomorrow will likely see them all but gone. <They are starting me on that wonderful drug called Neupogen.> It's a subcutaneous injection that will stimulate the bone marrow to start cranking out cells, so that I will once again have some cells to fight infection and to produce red cells to carry oxygen. The drug is amazing, but it has some not so desirable side effects. There's so many, I won't even start to list them.

I took my morning walk today. The ward is set up in a three-quarter circle, with the rooms on the perimeter. The front desk is at the center and curves around the hallway that separates it from the rooms. I walk back and forth around the almost full circle but can't complete the circle because the doors to enter at either end are closed for isolation. Each hallway walk is 33 steps. I do 30 passes up and down the hallway. At three feet a step, 33 steps, 30 passes...let's see, multiply by 30, carry the three...about 2970 feet...give or take a few feet. It takes me at least an hour.

Today, I could smell the all too familiar smell of DMSO that we used in liniments when we raced horses (incorrectly pronounced DSMO instead of DMSO by almost all horsemen). It acts as a pretty good preservative for stem cells, and they actually mix it in the bag of cells you get when they transplant them. So for a couple days, I smelled like a horse. Fairly appropriate given my history.

That's about it for today. Excited about the move down the hall, the fact that I can sleep, and that my white cells are just about gone and ready to be revived. We are just keeping our fingers crossed, and praying that they bounce back the way they are supposed to. I have faith. My blood is strong like bull, smart like tractor.

Marc

The smell of the DMSO also brought back a lot of memories. As I stated earlier, we used that stuff as liniment on the horses' legs. Industrially, it's used as some sort of solvent. It did wonders for healing and decreasing inflammation in tendons in horses. I dare mention that my father (as well as other trainers in the barn) would apply it on himself at times when he had aches and pains. He said it helped, but I never tried it. At least I know *that's* not what caused my cancer. I have that going for me.

The strange thing is that some trainers, who shall remain nameless, gave the drug intravenously to their animals. Yes, you heard me correctly, intravenously. Why they did this is still a mystery, but its safety is questionable at best. Due to the fact that they were giving it to me in the vein made me feel a little better about it, I guess. But these guys would use far more than what was used in that little bag of stem cells they hung on me. Rumor had it that they would plug something like 60 cc's right into the jugular. Maybe more, I never asked.

I suppose their reasoning was that if it helped inflammation externally, then it would help kill pain in the joints and muscles of their horses if given internally. I have no clue, but I know they used it.

The smell brought me back to the paddock in Lewiston, Maine, where Honey lost her heartbreaking three-year-old finals race. The paddock there was more like an aircraft hangar, at least two hundred feet long and with stalls on either side. It could hold twelve races of eight horses, so it had at least sixty stalls on one side facing sixty on the other. The floor was made of cement, and horses urinated and defecated on it all the time. The smell was overpowering. After a few hours, you kind of got used to it. They call it olfactory fatigue, but it clung to your clothes, and the next day you could smell it all over again.

The huge double doors were never closed, even when it was ten below outside, and on some of those cold nights, the DMSO must have been used at its highest levels, because the place reeked of it. Huge trails of steam would blow out of the nostrils of the horses in their stalls and blast you with an odor that can only be described as a mix of garlic and rotting oysters. Horrendous. You could pick them out of a lineup with your eyes closed. You would think that someone would have tested for the drug, but they didn't, because it went on for as long as I can remember.

When they gave me those stem cells, and that smell wafted through the room, I was mentally back in the paddock in Lewiston. It was kind of nice. My mind didn't go to the loss that Honey suffered. It went to a better place; probably because I had just downed an entire cheese pizza. I remembered the camaraderie of our family and how we would handle four and five horses with just the three of us in the paddock. We were quite an efficient unit. Some nights, my buddy Jim or Scott would come along and help out, but they usually only joined us at the more southern venue of Scarborough Downs.

On the bitter cold nights, I must say there were more than a few times Doug was noticeably absent, as he spent a fair amount of time up in the driver's lounge above the paddock that overlooked the backstretch. It was the only place that was heated. Can't say that I blame him. Being out on the track on some of those frigid nights was just ridiculous. It was an absolute necessity for him to go up there and thaw out. I suffered the cold consistently but tolerably. Meanwhile, he would suffer intermittently, and almost to the point of hypothermia. No guts, no glory, I guess. Being a lowly groom like me had its perks.

For nearly a day, I was able to reminisce about the old times by just taking a good whiff of the air that filled my room. It was a nice distraction from what was going on. Those days of racing were some of the best times of my life. And of course they were some of the worst times when things went bad. But when I think back on the "good old days," I often block out the bad stuff and focus on the positive. It's just kind of how my mind works. Unless I'm hungry that is. That's when I start to think about the two-and-a-half-hour drive back and forth, the losses that should have been wins, the nights we made the trip with four horses and didn't even pick up a check, the ever-permeating smell of urine and horse manure, and of course how my feet and back ached after a five-hour night walking on pavement. Even with all that, though, the good far outweighed the bad.

Back in the ward at the hospital, the shower scenario was a joke. I had no idea when it would be available, and to be honest, I didn't care if I showered or not. They had to unhook me from the IV drip and then paste this huge square sheet of plastic over the Hickman line so it wouldn't get wet. The whole process took about twenty minutes. Some days, it just didn't seem worth it. I wasn't using deodorant, so for a few days there, I was fairly ripe. I didn't care. My will to do much of anything had been all but removed. I think I went three days without showering. When I finally couldn't stand the smell of myself, I forced the issue.

The kitchen was closed after eight o'clock at night. In order to get food at that time required leaving my room on my own or summoning someone to get it for me. Getting up and fetching food myself was no easy task.

The rooms were set up with a one-way circulation system. Air came in from some megafilter somewhere in the building on the window side of the room and blew across toward the doorway.

Above each doorway was a long rectangular fan that spanned the entire entrance and blew outwardly. This prevented airborne pathogens from entering. The nurses who came in were required to wear gloves and masks at all times.

Instead of getting up myself, I decided to buzz someone to get me a snack. A male nurse poked his maskless face over the threshold and asked me what I wanted. It was right when my white cells were at their lowest. I couldn't believe he was doing that. I called him out on it right away. This was my life at stake, and I didn't like him sticking his bacterial-laden breath into my room like that.

"How about putting a mask on?" I said sternly.

I certainly could have been nicer, I admit it. But you know what? I didn't care. The guy was breaking protocol, and I didn't want to die. They had this procedure set up for a reason. He was none too pleased with me. After all, he was checking in to see what I wanted. But then he scurried backward, realizing his error, put a mask on, and came back in. I told him I was all set. I was officially on his shit list. Oh well, he could go shit in his hat. On second thought, he could use mine. I certainly wasn't going to use it.

In order for me to leave my cell, I had to put on special socks, a mask, and gloves, and wheel the pole along with me that had the fluids that constantly dripped into my veins. It was a whole ordeal just to get up for those Oreos. That's what I wanted when I buzzed him, but since I knew I had pissed him off, I thought it best to get them myself. It took me about five minutes to finally get out to the snack area and return to my confinement. Five minutes to travel thirty feet. I was pathetic. I sat back in my bed expecting to enjoy the beautiful flavor of chocolate and cream. Instead, I ate a pig cracker.

CHAPTER 13 – SECOND WEEK OF CAPTIVITY

Ninth Day of Captivity

Mar 26, 2012 8:26am

The new room is a huge improvement. Huge. It's like a sensory deprivation chamber in here compared to the last room. I had a very nice young good-looking blond nurse last night. Today, I get a dude. There really is something to this whole yin yang thing, isn't there?

Last week, I heard you guys had temps up in the 80s, and it looked like summer was going to come early. I wouldn't know firsthand, being in lockdown and all, but I have sources on the inside that give me "information" when I ask for it. It might cost me a few Oreos or a fruit punch drink, but I get the 411. And now I hear it's miserably cold and gray. <That's a shame.> Hopefully spring will have arrived in its true form when I finally make my escape in about 10 days.

Sleep was tough last night because of the whole-body muscle aches that I still have from the exercise debacle. I can't believe I did that to myself. Actually, I can't believe such little exercise would cause such an absurd reaction in my muscles. I can only attribute the problem to the low white cell count and the fact that I have no soldiers around to remove the toxins from my muscle tissue. So they just sit there creating pain. Lucky me. I tried to go the whole night without any pain medication (just to reduce the drugs in my body). I made it a span of ten hours and broke down and asked for them. I don't think I'll try that again.

The occupational therapist came in yesterday to look at the finger thing. (I hope I didn't offend any PTs or OTs out there with my earlier comment, but it just shows my ignorance.) At first I wasn't sure if she knew what she was doing. After all was done, it seems it was just a lack of confidence that I was detecting, rather than a lack of knowledge. I think she made the diagnosis after performing an exam and then doing some online research. It looks like we have a tentative diagnosis of brachial neuritis or Parsonage-Turner syndrome. It's extremely rare, of course, perhaps triggered by the placing of the Hickman line in my jugular. Multiple myeloma and Parsonage-Turner syndrome. I wonder what that perfecta payout would be? The treatment for it is controversial, of course. They say that antivirals can be helpful, and luckily I am already on them. The other treatment is high doses of corticosteroid…you know, the drug that made my face puff up. Dear God, no more steroids. Any more, and I'll look like the Snoopy balloon in the Macy's parade.

My white counts continue to drop and are now at 0.42. Stubborn little suckers, clinging to life. I think tomorrow could be the day. I'm not holding my breath, though. They tell me they are where they should be. My thought is that they should be at zero now, but that's just my impatience. The waiting is killing me. I just want to start going the other way. Soon, though.

Other than the muscle pain, I feel pretty good. My spirits are good, even if John is my nurse. I once again thank you all for the incredible support. I am not alone in this fight. Strength in numbers. This thing doesn't stand a chance against us.

Marc

What I failed to relay in that last post was that somehow I slept on my left shoulder in such a way as to cause agonizing pain every time I tried to move it. When I sleep, I always eventually fall asleep on my left side. Some people sleep on their backs, others face-down, and the rest of us usually choose one side or the other. For me, it's been the left for a long time. I used to sleep on my back, but the snoring that it produced kept Jen up most of the night, so I converted to a side sleeper. She says I still snore anyway, just not as badly.

When I try to sleep on my right side, it's odd, but I can feel my heart beating. It seems as if it's dangling down in my chest cavity, and I can physically feel it moving. When I lie on my left side, that sensation isn't there. It's too bad, really, because my body is more relaxed when I lie on my right side. Go figure. Most nights, I start on my back, flip to the right, thinking that this will be the night that I can convert over, but when all is said and done, I have to sleep on my left side. Always.

It seems that somehow, while contorted with my muscle pain, I pinched a nerve in my shoulder and basically denervated one of my muscles just above my scapula. The ensuing pain was hor-rible. At least it took my mind off of my legs and back. Three weeks later, the muscle atrophy was profound. It looked like a shark took a bite out of my upper back, and I couldn't lift my hand above my waist. Most days, it just hung by my side like a dead fish. If I tried to move it, it hurt like hell. I told you I was lucky. Who pinches a nerve and completely kills it while sleep-ing? Seriously.

From that day forward, I became a right-sided sleeper. Heart-beat be damned. It's now a psychological thing. I can't take a chance on that happening again, although I know the odds are that it won't. When I think about the pain I had, I just can't seem to get myself to put my body back in that position. Too risky. I never want to go through that again. I suppose it's entirely possible that it could happen to my right side, but that's the chance I have to take.

Tenth Day of Captivity

Mar 27, 2012 7:46am

Pretty good night last night. It was typical in that I was up just about every hour with a rare little burst of two and a half hours from 2:30am to 5:00am. That's when they woke me up for the wonderful vitals check. Am I breathing? Good enough. Leave me be. I was pleasantly surprised to see the time on the clock. When I woke up (well, when the nurse woke me up), I expected it to be around 4:15am. Ah, the little things I get joy from in this place. Tried to watch the Celtics, but couldn't muster the energy to watch the last quarter. Fourth quarters in basketball can take forever. It seems like they take about thirty time-outs in the last two minutes. They won anyway. Bruins play tonight against the Lightning. I just have to do nothing for ten more hours. Gah, this is boring.

The muscle pain is letting up. Tried to do the moonwalk (don't scoff, I can do the moonwalk) on the slippery floor in the hall...the hammies would have nothing of it. Way too tight still. I'm better, but clearly not ready for Michael Jackson. That's the only move I know from him, so don't expect to see any YouTube videos of me dancing anytime soon. Not one of my fortes.

My cells have unofficially bottomed out! They are at 0.04. Close enough. We can now officially start thinking about watching for regrowth. Should take a few days to see anything significant, but let's hope something happens. This is crunch time. No cell growth? Well, I think you know what happens. Visiting is probably off limits today and tomorrow, but if the counts go up and I have some semblance of an immune system, then we can talk about it. Although I should be getting sprung from this joint soon enough, so not sure I would waste my time coming into Boston (but that's me).

Even better news...no John today. I drew Emily and Amanda. They're certainly no Jen Raaf, that's for sure, but who is really? It just nice not having an extra "Y" chromosome hanging around. No offense to male nurses. When you're sick, at least something nice to look at helps. Oink. That's right, we're all just pigs.

Had one of the lady nurses try to work out some of the kinks in the muscle of my shoulder. First off, she had daggers for fingernails and drove those babies into my skin. That was no help at all. Second, she lacked the strength to do deep tissue massage. I kept telling her that she could push harder, but it never happened. It felt like three rats doing the river dance on my back. That was a complete bust. And then she says at the end, "Whoooh, I have to stop and give my arms a rest, they're tired." You would have been proud...I bit my lip and said nothing.

Getting ready for rounds. That's when the "team" of doctors looks at me for about two minutes and then dashes off to the next patient. The nurses really are the real deal. They do EVERYTHING. The doctors, sure, they do their thing, but it's the nurses that deserve all the credit in the world. Well, except John. Nah, he was fine. Just not very good eye candy. Should have had *him* do the massage.

Well, that's it for now. We are turning the corner and staying positive. Blood will continue to be drawn daily to watch the counts (hopefully) go up. I have all the faith in the world that they will. Way too many prayers out there for it not to happen. Thank you again, and see you tomorrow.

Marc

During the Melphalan injection, they encouraged patients to chew on ice. The reasoning behind this is to cause the blood vessels in your gums to constrict and not allow much of the drug to have its splendid effects on the mucous membranes of your mouth. Remember, this drug likes to wipe out rapidly dividing cells. Well, your mouth is one of those places. Now there's nothing they can do for the effects on the intestine; you can't very well swallow a block of ice and hope it freezes your bowel lining. But you *can* help with the mouth.

When they said chew on ice, they didn't really say what they meant. What they meant was, get your gums and tongue as cold as possible to vasoconstrict the blood vessels. If you just sat there chewing on ice and didn't let it chill your entire mouth, it wouldn't do all that much to help. I made my mouth completely numb. I stuffed ice into my cheeks like a squirrel hoarding nuts and held it there until it melted. Then I poured in another batch. For the record, it wasn't pleasant. But I knew that the repercussions for not being aggressive at that moment would likely be terrible mouth sores and bleeding gums.

Because of this, the doctors were surprised to see that I didn't have any internal oral lesions whatsoever during my stay. They would ask me to open my mouth, and they would shine in their little light and say something like, "Huh, looks pretty good in there." I'm pretty sure they were expecting to see something bloody and nasty. Part of me thinks they were disheartened that they didn't have something cool to look at.

What I failed to do, however, was ice my lips. Big mistake. Around day ten, my bottom left lip swelled up like a grape. Then it started oozing blood. I was a real sight to see. Fat face, pale, bald, and a big, swollen, raw lower lip. Oh yeah, I was a real lady killer. So earlier, when I said I bit my lip, that was definitely an expression. I didn't need to. It was already bleeding.

I ALMOST COULDN'T RECOGNIZE MYSELF WHEN I LOOKED IN THE MIRROR.

Eleventh Day of Captivity

Mar 28, 2012 9:44am

I'm having a bit of a rough morning to tell the truth. My arms are still very painful from the muscle thing, and now it seems I slept on them oddly and the pain is worse. PT is going to come and perhaps give me a sling to wear on the sorest arm to prevent further damage. I am also pretty severely anemic now (to be expected), but it is bad enough to require a transfusion that I am receiving as I write this. I think the blood may have been from a chef, because suddenly my sense of smell is like that of a basset hound. Could there be onions in my future? Perhaps even coconut?

The Bruins won last night. Finally playing like a playoff-bound team. They had me a little concerned for a while there. It would have been a crappy recovery at home without them on TV to watch. Ever since some friends gave me a signed picture of big "Z" (um, that's Zdeno Chara, people, work with me here) for my room, they haven't lost. GO BIG "Z"!

Well, I wish I could write more, but I feel like crap and am so very tired. I will be better in a little bit, but right now it's a tough to stay focused and awake. No worries, this is how it's supposed to be. Gotta crawl before you can walk. Soon enough, my cells will push through and I will be stronger than ever.

Marc

I was getting stir crazy at that point, as you might tell from my ramblings. I was in bad shape. There was still fuzz on my head that continued to shed each night. The first nine days or so, I obsessively tried to pluck those little hairs from my skull. In hindsight, I shouldn't have shaved my dome. The hair would have come out in clumps, leaving me perfectly bald. But those tiny hairs had no weight for them to fall off easily. So they would only come out when I rubbed my head on the pillow or sheets. They were incredibly itchy once they made landfall. I wanted them out, but realistically there was no way I could get them all. They came out when I pulled on them simple enough, but damn it, they just wouldn't fall out altogether. So I plucked and plucked and plucked. When Jen visited me, she was shocked to see my head all spotted from the areas I had been grabbing at. She said I looked like I had mange.

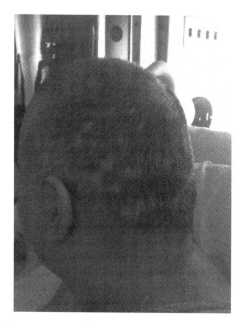

Jen was right, I did look like I had mange.

After I got Parsonage-Turner syndrome, I couldn't use my right hand because I had no feeling in my thumb and index finger. Well, after I crimped my left shoulder by sleeping on it wrong, I couldn't lift my left arm to my head. This ended the plucking. That's right; I could no longer go pluck myself.

Twelfth Day of Captivity

Mar 29, 2012 9:02am

Good morning everyone. It seems my anemia continues to be a problem. It is slightly worse (22.5 today, normal is 40-50) today than yesterday, but that's why they have transfusions available. They haven't hung the blood up on the pole yet, so I am still feeling the effects and am very tired. But I will press on.

I slept well, when people weren't coming into my room to give me medications or checking my vital signs. At 5:30am, one of the assistants came in, woke me up unceremoniously, and told me that my calcium pill was ready to be taken. One calcium pill? Seriously? That couldn't wait until 7am when my next vitals were done? Wow. If I had any strength at the time, I would have told her that her hair didn't look good. That would have been something, huh? Instead, I just sat there, angrily awake and in disbelief. In an act of defiance, and to prove a personal point, I waited until 7am to take the pill. Take that, establishment!

The muscle pain has improved, largely in part due to the advice of the occupational therapist that saw me yesterday and taught me positions to sleep in that would aid my muscles. After one night, I must say, it has helped. Whether or not they were improving anyway is still a possibility, but I think the positioning helped. It certainly made the pain less while I was in bed. The real question will be, how do I feel at the end of today?

In one of the response posts that I have omitted since there were so many, one of my friends mentioned that we used to hunt rats down in the barn. I, of course, completely denied these allegations. I didn't want to offend anyone, being a vet and all. This next post was in response to that.

Okay, okay, we killed rats. I'm not proud of it, but we did it. It was a different time. It was a dark time for us. Rats hadn't tried to become recognized as one of the farm animals. They were rats. They were dirty. And they were eating our grain. And these weren't just ordinary rats, no sir. They were like nuclear or something. Huge. Biggest rats you'll ever see outside the Seabrook power plant. And they were cocky too. They would walk across the rafters above and stare you down. When your eyes met, they stopped, squared you off, and gave a look that said, "What's your problem?" I kid you not. That's what they did. They weren't so arrogant when we were going after them with pitchforks, but before the attack, they were pretty puffy.

So we eradicated the rats. Sue us. Today things are different. There are movies about rats making them heroes. *Charlotte's Web* didn't do enough for rats with Templeton, but movies that followed, like *American Tail* and *Ratatouille*, have made them folk heroes. We don't dare talk about pitchforks and ice choppers for fear of persecution. Today we talk about have-a-heart traps and relocation projects. They're still rats, people. Rats.

No real change in the white cell line, although the report today shows it at 0.09 from 0.03. Yes, it seems to be going up (that's what we want), but it's a day too soon to get excited. Could just be a statistically accepted anomaly, which means it may be 0.06 tomorrow and we all let out a "Whaaaaaaat?" Tomorrow's blood will be a much better indication of which direction we are going in. Hopefully up. Soon, the powers that be will come in my room and do their rounds and I will ask them about said values. I'm sure they will parrot exactly what I just wrote. They will never go out on a limb and say for sure it is going up. I wouldn't either, I suppose.

So, for the most part, I am feeling better, but due to the anemia, still very, very tired. I already went for my morning walk, and it nearly killed me. Felt like I ran a half marathon. That's it for today, hope all is well in the real world, and looking forward to entering it soon.

Go F*** yourself Multiple Myeloma,

Marc

The weakness was debilitating. With only half of what I needed for red cells swirling around in my bloodstream, I was out of breath from just minimal movements. In all, I think I got four transfusions over the course of a week. I still had the pain in the shoulder that was sharp at times, especially when I forgot about it and tried to use it like an idiot.

Then there was the worry. Worry that my cells wouldn't respond. That number 2 percent kept kicking around in my head. Now who would be unlucky enough to fall into that 2 percent category? I didn't want to answer that question. I knew I was a candidate. But I tried to stay positive and not dwell on what could happen. I just had to assure myself that my body was strong and that it would recover. The alternative was too bleak to imagine. Although I did anyway.

I'm not sure why I walked every day. I don't think it did much to help my conditioning. In fact, it could have just made me weaker. I guess I felt that any kind of exercise at that point might help my muscles not completely break down. As it was, they were melting off of me. I could see that my chest had shrunk down considerably, and my arms felt as if I could floss with them. It had been only two weeks of down time, but it had a profound effect on my muscle mass. All those years of lifting weights and getting stronger were erased in just thirteen days. Amazing.

I think I was the only person who walked each day. I never bumped into anyone in the hallway, nor did I ever see anyone pass by my room trolling along a fluid pole. I certainly understood why. It was hard work. It took every bit of mental fortitude to force myself out of bed and wander the halls like an apparition. During each of these walks, one of the nurses would stop me and ask me to get on the scale. They made it a habit of writing it down every day. And every day, my weight went up. Even with the loss of muscle, which weighs more than fat, I got heavier. I think my highest "off the record," when the nurses weren't looking, was 220, but on their sheets, I topped out at 218. What a blob. I was disgusted with myself. Just a few months ago, I was in perhaps the best shape of my life, at a fighting weight of 180. All gone. It was depressing and aggravating. So I ate some more.

Thirteenth Day of Captivity

Mar 30, 2012 8:43am

Hello out there!
Very long night of very little sleep. Combine a little fever with a couple of very painful muscles and some ridiculous dreams, and you get a recipe for disaster. No sleep at all. I thought once the Bruins went to OT, my night would go swimmingly. But they lost in the shootout, and it went downhill from there.

The dreams were about aliens coming to take me away, and I would move quickly, sending a shockwave of pain just in one particular spot in my left leg. Really weird. This happened like four times. Same dream, same result. Finally, the nurse outside my room heard one of my f-bombs when I was waking and took me for a walk to break the cycle. Thank God she did that, or it could've have been a sequence loop that just kept repeating.

I'll throw this out there just in case there is one or two of you that remember it. It was an episode of *Land of the Lost* with the Sleazstacks, and the crew kept seeing themselves perish over a waterfall with the words from one of the kids being, "Daddy, do something…AAAAHHHHHHHHHHHH!" and they all plummeted to their deaths. It was played in a loop over and over again and was quite annoying. When I was dreaming, that's what was going through my head. Now tell me someone out there remembers that episode!

I was able to put headphones on and listen to music to stop my mind. It was the only thing that would get me out of the funk. So this morning, I am exhausted. Not to mention that fact that I am still anemic (HCT = 23.9) and my platelets are at 7. If that sounds low, then you are correct. It should be over 150. I can't do any exercises today for fear of bleeding. They are giving me whole blood and platelets as I write this, so I should be better soon. But because of the fatigue, I will be signing off quickly.

I will now interject and enter one of the many inspiring posts made by my family and friends.

***

It's the end of round 10 of the World's Boxing Championship, and things are not looking good. Marvelous Marc (his nickname) has been losing rounds like trees lose their leaves in the fall. Big C, his opponent, is an ugly rat-like brute; fat, bulgy, hairy, slimy, like a hunk of purple mucous. He glowers and slobbers and thumps his chest. But MM has dealt with rats before. The arena is packed with thousands upon thousands of loyal supporters, chanting, "You can do it, Marc; you can do it!" Everyone in the crowd is wearing a distinctive white plastic, wide-brimmed hat—Modell's, Sport's Depot, and Olympia Sports have been sold out for months. MM slumps in his corner, almost too weak to text. His face is puffy from the beating he's been getting. His arms are heavy and ache badly; his hammies hurt. His corner man, "Pierre-au-foire" (in English, "Point-o-Four"), a puny Frenchman, a bit light on his feet, keeps slapping his face with a wet sponge. His manager, Ms. J, whispers sweet nothings in his ear to arouse his spirits.

She has trained him for years, even back when he was a famous football player, and had discovered long ago the power of a soft whisper in Marc's ear. MM is down, but the faithful know he is not out. At the end of every round, no matter the blows he has received, before he returns to his corner, he tells the crowd a string of one-liners. "A horse walked into a bar, and..." Round 11.

The referee, Hickory Dickory, enters the ring, wearing a long white smock, a stethoscope around his neck, and thick, dark-rimmed glasses. They call him "Doc" for short. He is in charge of the fight and in charge of "making rounds" (groan). He rings the bell and both contenders rise. But something is different. MM rises more quickly than before. Maybe it was the band of seven lithe blondes, dressed in short white dresses doing the can-can during the break. Maybe it was the wet sponge, or the whispers, or the secret powers of the white hat he wore.

The white hat gives him confidence but is a bit problematic as it tends to fall off at inopportune moments during the fight. This time, there is a new energy in MM's stance, a quirky half-smile on his lips and a twinkle in his eye. Everyone feels it. He gives Ms. J a light noogie, and she slaps him on the ass. Round 12, 13, 14…MM begins pounding the crap out of Big C; a 1-2 to the gut, an uppercut to the jaw, a roundhouse to his left eye, and a specialty two-fisted punch MM named "the pitchfork" to his nose. 15, 16, 17… (It's a long fight, but time goes by quickly.) MM is punching like a mad man, and his footwork is amazing! (Big C finds the moonwalk especially disorienting.) Rounds 18, 19, 20… Big C fades. MM has him against the ropes and the crowd of millions goes berserk.

There is no mercy for Big C. He is a very bad dude and deserves everything MM hands him. Round 30 and Big C is gone. Literally. There is nothing left of him but a purple puddle on the canvas. The crowd erupts, screaming and dancing. They throw their hats high in the air (which is a mistake, because they come down hard) and begin slapping each other in ecstatic joy. Hickory Dickory (Doc) leads MM to the center of the ring, lifts his right arm into the air, asks him to turn his head and cough. "The new Wide World Boxing Champion of the Whole Wide World (WWBCWWW)," he announces. Ms. J joins him, and after a fist bump, they embrace. The crowd becomes hushed, and slowly, one by one, the billions of supporters, with tears of joy running down their cheeks, begin to sing, "Glory, Glory Hallelujah...Glory, Glory, Hallelujah..." MM steps to the mic and says in a soft yet assured voice, "A priest, rabbi, and a minister go into a bar, and..."

***

These were the types of entries that kept me going. Nine hundred and sixty-three to be exact. It was incredibly uplifting to hear from people every day. It is why I couldn't stop writing every morning. My apologies to all the others who posted that I haven't included in this book. If I did, it would be an entire book all by itself. Thank you all for the positive impact you had on me.

The good news in all this is that I am planning on escaping on Monday! Thaaaaaaat's right. I'm outta here on Monday. Crazy, it's almost here. So thankful. All your support has made it so much easier. Thank you all again. I look forward to tomorrow, when I feel good enough to really write again. But for now, I'm starting the countdown. Yeeeeehawww!

Marc

P.S. My white blood cells are up to 1.5. We're headed in the right direction.

It's hard to put into words how long those nights were. The noises, the pain, the interruptions, the weakness, the itching, the anxiety; it was all too much. You would think that at some point the exhaustion would finally overcome you and sleep would prevail. It never did. I only watched TV when the Bruins or the Celtics were on. I wasn't interested in any movies or sitcoms or anything. I stopped watching *Dexter*. My mind couldn't handle thinking on any level. I was in complete shutdown. I watched the clock as it slowly wound its way through the early hours of the morning. I watched and waited until my four hours were up, and I could get my next dose of pain meds. I was pathetic. I would have been absolutely miserable without them.

No one ever questioned me about taking them, so I assumed that the pain was par for the course. Sometimes they were a few minutes early, and they would tell me not to say anything because the rules state you *have* to wait the four hours. We were talking about a six-minute jump start, not an hour. Um, no, I won't tell them you give me my meds six minutes early. Would they really get in trouble for that? Geez. Pretty strict. I had to weigh it out in my head, though. If I took them even a touch early, it meant that it would be four hours and six minutes before my next dose. I was in such bad shape that I didn't want to be in trouble for those last several clicks of the clock when the drugs wore off. If by chance they were early, I would wait until exactly four in the morning to take the dose so that it wouldn't wear out before 8:00 a.m.

You can't get a true sense of my desperation from the CaringBridge entries, but it was no picnic. The whole point of the journal was to keep morale up at home. If I told it like it was, I'm certain my family would have been more worried than they needed to be. I only wanted positive vibes. There is power in positive thinking. It probably would have gone a whole lot easier if I never did those damn squats or got my shoulder all jammed up, but such is how it went down. I'm just a lucky bastard.

Chapter 14 – Making the Escape

Fourteenth Day of Captivity

Mar 31, 2012 8:24am

My white cells are overachievers! I have surpassed the magic number of 5.0 that they wanted me to reach by Monday. It's Saturday morning, and my level is at 6.0. That Neupogen really works. They want me to inject myself again this afternoon. My bones are already killing me from that stuff, and my values are higher than expected. I got news for them; that injection might have an unfortunate incident with the bedspread. There is no way on God's green earth that stuff is finding its way into my body today. Okay, maybe I'll take it. My red cells are still lagging (Neupogen doesn't help the red cells so much). I will be receiving another pint of blood this morning, hopefully the last one necessary. I am weak because of this, but each day I feel stronger. Getting sleep is still an issue, but I'm dealing with it. Just a few more days, and it won't be a problem anymore.

Now I know the "hat" has received its fair share of exposure on this website. Perhaps it has even been overdone on my part. However, to me, it has become more than just the source of a funny sidebar. It has become a source of strength. I have taken a stand against this ridiculousness and have stood firmly by my convictions. I have contended from the beginning that the sanitary issues of using such a stupid device outweighs its usefulness of monitoring for problems. I have told them that if I have an issue, I will notify them of any problem, and we do not need to collect every sample for this to happen. For thirteen days, I have been successful. For thirteen days, I have ducked and weaved, and weaseled my way out of using it.

Mind you, there is a nurse's aide that really has a problem with me not using it, and gets quite irritated when it's empty at the end of a night. She once called me out after she smelled something coming from the bathroom. When she entered the bathroom...the hat was empty. "Did you move your bowels?!" she asked angrily.

"Yes I did," I calmly replied.

"You're supposed to use the hat!" she exclaimed. She was not happy that she didn't have something in her little trap she had set.

"Oh yeah," I answered. "I forgot."

"You need to use it! We need to see every one!" And she left in a huff.

She has been a bit of a problem, but I have found ways to avoid the issue even if she is working. I always tell her that I just went to the bathroom when she comes on her shift and that the other nurse saw what I donated. Each time she gives me a glare, as if to say she knows what I am up to and that she isn't happy about it. For some reason, this girl wants to see my stuff. And I'm not giving her the satisfaction. Like I said, this hat thing has given me a source of strength and power. It's me against them, and I'm going to try to outplay, outlast, and outshit the whole collection scenario. For thirteen days, I have succeeded. The three pronged technique of 1) ignore, 2) ignore, and 3) ignore has worked beautifully. It has been quite amusing to watch the looks on their faces when the hat isn't where it should be. Other than the one particular nurse's aide, none of them have had the cojones to call me out. For thirteen days, that is.

Last night it happened. A nurse, who shall remain nameless (Kelly), decided she wanted to do battle with me. The previous shift nurse warned me about her, saying she has been in the business for over twenty-five years, and she knew everything. What she meant to tell me was that she was a know-it-all. Big difference between knowing a lot and being a know-it-all. She reminds me of the Eugene Levy character in the movie *Serendipity*. He worked in a department store selling men's clothing. He was very particular about his station and let everyone know how important he was. "You can't cross that line, sir! Sir, you must buy a minimum amount in this store in order to make a purchase! Sir, the line!"

This woman had her protocol, and no one was going to tell her otherwise. I knew there was going to be a problem when she went into the bathroom and I heard her shuffling for the "hat" that has been in hiding for nearly two weeks. So she starts in on me.

"You need to use the hat every time you go," she says very matter-of-factly.

"Yeah, that's not going to happen," I said right back to her.

I couldn't believe how easy it came out of me. It was like I was in a movie, and I was the hero, and everyone in the theater was just begging for me to make a stand and tell this lady to give it a rest already. It felt so good. The words just oozed out of me without any hesitation. She was quite taken by my frankness and started back in on me.

"It is very important that we document eve—"

"It's not going to happen," I quickly interrupted her.

I felt empowered. I was saying what anyone would actually want to say but usually don't muster the fortitude to do it. I was in the middle of it, and I was standing strong. I didn't let her start back in, and continued to talk in a very calm, yet purposeful voice.

"The whole hat thing…it isn't going to happen. I refuse to use something that could ultimately be more harmful to me than good. I assure you, that if there's a problem with my bowels, I will report it to you, and that will be that."

She took a moment to ruminate on what I had just said. I have to think that in twenty-five years, not many have stood up to her like that. I was quite proud of myself. I knew it wasn't quite over. She couldn't just let it go. There had to be one more rebuttal coming.

"The reason we like to have you—" and I cut her off one more time.

"Not happening. We can talk about why you want me to do it, but it will not change the fact that I am not going to."

And that was the end of the discussion. The hat is dead. Victory is mine. And it feels tremendous!

Later on, she asked if I wanted anything. I told her that a Gatorade would be nice...any flavor except lemon lime. You guessed it. She brought me lemon lime. Well played, madam. Touché. I said nothing. Sometimes the battle isn't worth it. Sure she won that little skirmish, but I won the war.

Monday is still the tentative day of release, unless my anemia continues. Keep those prayers a comin'!!!!!

Marc "The Hatless"

I told you earlier, in so many words, that I'm an agnostic, yet I'm certainly not against the idea of prayers. As I said, I'm not certain there isn't a God, just as much as I'm not certain there *is* one. But, if there is, anything would help. Besides, I am a huge believer in positive energy, and if prayers are the source, then pray your ass off. I am grateful for any help that I might have received. It certainly was inspirational to hear that so many people out there were pulling for me.

As far as the hat goes, it was dead after I told that lady off. I was probably wrong and shouldn't have done it, and I'm sure I'm now on *her* crappola list. First the maskless wonder, then her. Oh well. Now I know they have their reasons, however insane they may be, for me showing them my excrement, and I should have followed protocol.

The thing is, I couldn't. It was repulsive. Besides, I had gone nearly two weeks without an issue and was being released in just a few days. I didn't need the lecture at that point. That shit had sailed. And yes, I could have been nicer about it, but her condescending tone when she spoke to me hit a nerve. Not the one in my shoulder as I couldn't feel that one; more of a metaphorical nerve. I wasn't going to be scolded by some holier-than-thou nurse who just showed up for the first time ever in my room. I'm surprised she didn't report me to the Feces Police, but she didn't. So ended the hat discussion forever.

Looking back at that moment is just one of the many reflections of myself as someone I never was. There's an expression, "don't be that guy." Well, I was that guy. What an asshole. But the drugs, the pain, the illness, and the solitude all changed me. I had become the worst version of myself that I could imagine. This woman was only trying to do her job and I snapped on her. It was so out of character. The fact that in my journal entry I mention how proud I was of my actions is probably the most appalling part of it. Shame is what I feel now. Oh well, I can't undo what's been done, but I can learn from it and try to be a better person if I ever get put in that mental condition again.

Fifteenth Day of Captivity

Apr 1, 2012 8:17am

I watched Honey's miracle mile win this morning on DVD just to give me that last bit of determination to beat this thing. She was, and still is, a great source of inspiration to me; I think more than people really know. When I get out of here, I will post a few more of her wins on the Internet.

This will be for my benefit more than anything, but if anyone wants to watch them, they will be available. Her "Miracle Mile" can be viewed at *http://youtu.be/B9sgRi1gy_4.*

My total white cells are continuing to rise and we are still waiting on the complete differential (the breakdown of the different types of whites cells in the total count) to be complete this morning before they give me the ultimate green light to get out of here. What they don't understand is that I have already planned the escape, soooooo...not sure if it matters really. I suppose if they don't untether my jugular, I will have to stay. I like my chances. Doctors are saying that it's really just a formality at this point, but they have to be sure.

I had a very good night's sleep last night. When they did wake me up for my vitals or blood draw, I was able to immediately fall asleep. That's something that I haven't been able to do in months. It felt so good. I just knew I was going to fall back to sleep without counting ceiling tiles. Spectacular. Not sure if it's because my body is becoming more normal or the sleep deprivation is catching up to me. I think the former. I will know for real once I'm home. Man that sounds good...once I'm home.

It feels like I'm back in senior year of high school and there's just a couple days left of school. You don't listen to anything they tell you, you don't go to class. All you can think about is going to the beach, kicking back and not ever going to school again! Of course, in many of our lives, that wasn't completely true. We would only have the summer off, and then go back to school in the fall to college or find a job. Eerily, that holds true again. I have for now kicked this disease square in the face, and it is reeling. Hopefully my summer lasts forever. But at some point, I will likely have to go back to school and face this thing again. For now though, I am going to enjoy the hell out of my summer, for as long as it lasts, and embrace life with all of you. Thank you again for everything. It has meant the world to me that you have been with me through this.

For the second to last time from the sixth floor of Tower A, I am signing off. Thank you for all your support!

Marc

The wait for my white cells to bounce back was more than a bit angst ridden. It's all I thought about before they started going up. I just kept thinking about the number 2 percent. Now I'm not sure if all those people died or they just had to stay in the hospital for a lot longer waiting for them to come back. They never really told me, and I never asked. I just heard the number. I can only assume it means they died, but it might be a poor assumption. Either way, I waited anxiously each time they drew the blood to hear what my counts were.

The first couple draws were only slightly encouraging. When I heard they hit 6.0, I knew I was going to be okay, at least for the time being. It meant my life wouldn't end in the bed I was lying in. It was a giant relief. It turned out that later on my bone marrow really stalled. My white cells dropped down again to 2.5 and hovered there for a month or two. They had to put me on twice a week Neupogen for eight weeks. Oh yeah, just another lucky break. Ah, but I'm still here, so I'm not complaining...much.

There is something that I will mention to illustrate how dark my mind could go when I was in the hospital. A few days previously, when I was feeling near my worst, one of the nurses came in to give me my meds. I was in really rough shape. She asked how I was doing, and I basically told her that I was in hell. Her response was, "This too shall pass." I think she thought she was trying to be helpful and placate me.

I don't know why, but that made me incensed. It seemed pretty easy to say when she was on the other side of the fence and not worried about dying. She said it as if I was going through a breakup with a girlfriend. Very dismissive. It felt as if she was implying that I should just suck it up and stop complaining. *I* might pass. Did she think of that? I was obviously in a vulnerable state of mind and overreacting. The fact that such a benign comment could send me into a rage worried me. Clearly she was just trying to help, yet it angered me anyway. Yup, you know it. I ate some more.

Sixteenth Day of Captivity

Apr 2, 2012 8:09am

I thought this would be my last post, but unfortunately it won't be. They just informed me that my white cells dipped a little bit to 800 from 1100 yesterday. Very disappointing. This means I stay at least another night.

AHHHHHHHHHHHHHHH! I needed to get that off my chest. That was certainly not what I wanted to hear from them this morning. I had my little meltdown after they told me, and told Jen it was my fifteen minutes of shame. It was just tough to wrap my head around staying here another night. I was so mentally checked out.

It's worse than when you go to a restaurant and you're dead set on getting the prime rib. The guy right next to you gets the most beautiful piece of meat, and you are just moments away from sinking your teeth into a similar portion. Then the waitress tells you that that dude next to you got the last piece and that they are all out. As a matter of fact, they're completely out of steak altogether. Chicken too. She says she has a day-old hot dog she might be able to wrestle from the trash if that would be something you're interested in. No. No hot dog. You'll just have to come back tomorrow and hope that the prime rib is still available when you come in. Ugh.

Man, oh man, oh man, oh man. This sucks. Not only that, but they didn't have the Bruins on the TV in this joint last night. They were on one of the secondary NBC networks, which doesn't come in here. Double Ugh. I had to find them on the Internet (audio only). At least they won!

So, here we go. My escape was thwarted. I will continue to plot another one for tomorrow and see what happens. The biggest question in everyone's mind right now is probably "Why?" Good question. There probably isn't a good answer. I don't get too upset trying to figure it out. So please, no questions asking why. Just press forward with treatment and wait for the counts to be at a level they are comfortable sending me home with. If not tomorrow, the next day, or even the day after that. Triple Ugh. Like Fat Sam said in the movie *Fletch*...When it comes, it comes.

Once again posting for the second to last time; quadruple Ugh...

Marc

That really was a kick in the groin. I had already mentally checked out, and they decided to keep me another day. As you can tell, I didn't want people on the CaringBridge to start asking questions about why I wasn't being released, because I was too depressed to address anyone. It was a dark day indeed. My white cells were fluctuating downward, and they were concerned I was crashing. That too was on my mind. *Was* I crashing? What did it mean? Needless to say, it was a troubling twenty-four hours, waiting to see if my counts would bounce back up. Staying positive can be difficult when you are staring down the barrel of negatives. I did the best I could to stay focused on the good and not go dark. It wasn't easy. The entries on the CaringBridge each day from friends and family were a huge source of inspiration.

Seventeenth Day of Captivity – The Escape

Apr 3, 2012 8:15am

Have been waiting on my bloodwork all morning. The initial results came in and were very promising. They went from 1100 on Sunday to 800 on Monday, and now they are at 4000. The doctors have the final say on whether or not I can get out of here. They just left my room a couple of minutes ago.

Jen, my love, if you are reading this...come get me, I'm coming home.

I will steal the words of a great man and say, "Free at last, free at last, thank God Almighty, free at last!"

I will be updating this journal every Monday for quite a while to keep people informed as to what's going on. Otherwise, it would be very difficult to let all my support staff know how things are progressing. It will be quite a while before I can really go out in public, but the golf game should be coming along within a month.

They don't put many restrictions on being outside except for not mowing the lawn and kicking up dust and such. All you members of the Kingston Golf League, you heard it, I get free lifts out of ALL sand traps. I wouldn't want to put my health at risk.

Only fitting that it's the 17th day of captivity that sees me getting out of here, since my number for sports and good fortune has always been seventeen. I'm just glad that this leg of the journey is over. Sure, it's just another phase, but I can tell you without much hesitation that this was tough. Without all of you guys out there, I'm not sure I would have made it through so easily. Thanks to Mom, Dad, and Gooch for being with me every step of the way. They are the best family anyone could ask for. And a final ridiculous thank you to my wife, best friend, and confidante, Jen, for being my rock throughout this ordeal. She is amazing.

Hope to see many of you soon, perhaps though a mask at first, but slowly I will weasel my way back into society. From the 6th floor in Tower A, I am signing off for the last time from captivity,

Love,
Marc

When I wrote that last post, I was crying. The relief was over-whelming. I had made it through to the other side. I'm not sure why I was so emotional, but it did hit me pretty hard—the idea that I was going home. It was only eighteen days, but they were the longest days of my life. Each night, being woken up by a nurse to take my blood pressure, even making me get out of bed to take it while standing each time. Each night, being woken up from a brief period of sleep by someone getting ice from the machine directly outside of my room. Each night, listening to the nurses cackle like chickens in a hen house. No more. It was over. I broke down. I had held on long enough. It was time to let it out and be free of it all.

It made me wonder how POWs could ever be the same again after any type of *real* captivity. Mine was at least finite, and for a purpose. The mental and physical abuse that they must have endured is not something I like to think about. Perhaps I was a bit dramatic calling my stay there hell. War is hell. I was more like in the waiting room to purgatory.

Fresh air for the first time in almost three weeks. Fresh diesel smoke, cigarette-filled, pungent Boston air. It was great. It lasted only fifteen seconds as I quickly got into Jen's car and she whisked us away toward New Hampshire. It was an unceremonious depar-ture. No hugs with the nurses, no hearty handshakes from the doctors. Just a signature, an instruction sheet on what not to do, what not to eat, and so forth, and an appointment for my next visit in a month. A balloon would have been nice. Nothing. Here's your hat, what's your hurry? They could keep the hat, I didn't use it anyway.

It was a moment I had been looking forward to not just for three weeks but for months. This date, the rebirth of my new life, had been circled on my mental calendar ever since the day they told me I needed the transplant. From the very beginning, I just wanted it to be over. And finally that day had arrived. I was so completely exhausted and weak. I struggled to stay awake on the way home. My anemia would be a problem for months to come, and my muscles were atrophied more than I could have imagined.

Chapter 15 – A Horse Called Romaleen

On the way home, I started to think about all of the people in the transplant ward who had treated me. So many of them were extremely kind and generous. I know, all you heard about were the ones who drove me crazy with the noise and the insistence of me using the "hat." But for the most part, they were really good people.

Let's face it, they saved my life, and all I did was bitch and moan about it. I will be forever grateful for their efforts and kindness. Dana Farber is an amazing place, perhaps the best there is.

I began wondering if I would ever see them again. In one respect, I hoped I wouldn't, because that would mean I would be sick again. The chance of me running into them in public was fairly unlikely. If I ever did need another bone marrow transplant, it would probably be years from now, and those who were there for mine wouldn't be there any longer. My mind drifted back to a little horse called Romaleen. She was a horse we owned briefly, and although she never won a race for us, I still think about her from time to time and wonder what happened to her.

***

When Honey's Best (nicknamed 'The Beast') hit the ground in the fall of 1983, none of us knew that we had struck gold. We had been mining for years, but never really found anything along the way that was worth much to speak of. It would take two years before we realized how big a nugget we had miraculously uncovered. She sparkled like no other horse we had ever owned. And she carried weight; a true precious metal. We had searched and searched through countless pans of sand, and we finally stumbled upon what we had always been searching for. But we couldn't ever sell her. She was priceless.

BABY BEAST AND HER MOM HONEY SPARKLE WAY

Before that find, we were gypsies really. We had enough to be happy, healthy, and content, but in the racing game, there was always the dream of owning a champion. Not just for wealth (because in New England you weren't really ever going to get rich) but for pride. Sometimes we would buy horses that were low claimers that we thought we could improve, and for the most part, we did. We were pretty good at finding the diamonds in the rough, polishing them up a bit, and for a little while making them shine.

A couple of times a year, either at Lewiston or Scarborough, they held a weanling/yearling sale that attracted a lot of action from potential buyers in the state looking for that special something to develop, just like all of us dreamers. Most of the young horses at the sales were sired in the state of Maine, but some were higher-classed New York- and New Jersey-bred stock that usually brought in a little more money. Depending on the sire and dam, the price of the foals could range anywhere from $500 to $10,000. Most of them brought in under $5,000, but there were some exceptions. Needless to say, we weren't there for those.

As a good gold miner, you have to have some sort of understanding of the land. You need to know where the main vein ran years and years ago. You need to know which rivers have simply been overmined and which ones still have potential. The big money miners use excavators, heavy machinery, and sophisticated machines to locate metals and such. We had a few pans and a screen for sifting. At the Lewiston sale in the spring of 1984, we were panning for gold once again.

Romaleen was HIP number 350. I can remember that because it took three days for it to fall off of her left hip. I don't think any of us had the heart to rip it off. They must have used some sort of high-tech superglue to put those things on.

She was a two-year-old at the time, but she looked like a yearling. She was out of Romano Hanover, a Maine stud who had thrown some nice stock, but her mom was just a pauper. Her dam had raced the Maine circuit for a few years until she was retired, and the owners bred her out to see if they too could find some magic. Her slight build and poor early potential landed her at the sale.

I think we bought her for $650. Funny, I can remember the irrelevant HIP number, but not what we paid for her. Probably because I didn't fork the money over myself. I'm quite certain it was less than $1,000. She was tiny. At that time, I wasn't acutely aware of horses' sizes in hands as I am today, but thinking back, she couldn't have been more than fourteen hands. She really was a midget. Sorry, a little equine. She was a beautiful light bay with fine highlights and dapples that really jumped out during midsummer.

She was also supermodel thin. She almost looked like a cardboard cutout of a horse. From the side she looked normal, no ribs showing, with a nice coat. But from the front, she couldn't have been two feet across. She was like a huge wedge of bay cheddar. From a narrow point at her nose, she slowly filled out as you cast your gaze to her rump. In the fall, there was no chance of turning her out in the back forty with the others to graze. She looked so much like a deer, there was little doubt she would have been picked off by a myopic hunter thinking he had stumbled upon the biggest doe of his life.

She really was a sweet little horse. Very calm. Very willing. At the sale, they labeled her as "green-broke," a classification of how much she had been handled and to indicate if she had any experience with a harness. That term is fairly well used by horsemen, but it doesn't give you any more information than seeing a car in the classifieds that says "runs good, needs work." It could mean it runs good, but it doesn't have any tires and the body is completely rusted out. It could also mean it runs good if you set it at the top of a hill, throw it in neutral, and jump in without ever so much as starting the engine. It's relative to the seller.

True green-broke horses should have been handled quite often with a halter and have no issues with leading and grooming. It also should mean they have had at least a harness on their backs at some point (more than just once to say you did it would be nice). It can also imply that someone had tried to put some sort of jog cart behind them to let them get the feel of the wooden shafts on their flanks. That's not to say that the yearling was jogged or asked to pull someone around, but just enough work was done so that the idea of a jog cart was not a foreign one.

Romaleen knew how to lead, and that was about it. The previous owner had taken the time to make her calm and easy to work with, so all was not lost. No one had put any kind of leather on her back, that's for sure. To her credit, she wasn't like some of the orangutans we had tried to break in the past. She had a real pleasant demeanor and a willingness to learn that was refreshing.

We knew she would never be a large, strapping mare when we first saw her, but her pedigree was good, and let's face it, we got her on the cheap. We also knew she wouldn't be one of those power-house fillies that took the world by storm, any more than I knew I would never be an Olympic athlete. But that never stopped me from trying to be the best I could, even after that realization was reached.

Back in the summer of 1976, my cousin Chuck Pappas (Harryman's sister's oldest son) came to live with us and work on the farm to get away from the suburbs and expand his horizons. You know, just like those after-school specials where the kid goes away for the summer and becomes transformed and all that good stuff. But Chuck wasn't a bad kid, he just wanted to give the farm a try for a few months and get out of the house in which a seventeen-year-old didn't want to be confined to anymore. He moved in upstairs, at the end of the hall from my room and my brother Doug's, and worked with us the entire summer.

After a long day of work and play, we always had a sit-down dinner in the kitchen that my mother prepared. It was often a Norman Rockwellesque scene, with all of us talking and laughing at the table and enjoying a meal. Some nights, it was just spaghetti or hot dogs, but other times, Mama Pajama (my mom's nickname) would prepare some serious kick-ass meals in true Greek style, with three or four different sides to go with a nice lamb or roast. It didn't matter what was served, really. Looking back, it was more about being together and enjoying that time for what it was. Time together.

During some stretch in July and August, the games of the XXII Olympiad played on our modest little TV in the family room downstairs. And that's what we watched. Every single night. It seemed like all summer to me, but it was only about three weeks. Nadia Comaneci was dazzling in gymnastics. The men's swim team won almost every event they entered. And of course there was Bruce Jenner, winning the decathlon and setting a world record for points.

It was patriotism at its best in America, or at least our little slice of it at the farm. It was my first real feeling of a heartfelt connection to our country. I saw some of our athletes on the gold medal platform listening to the national anthem. I watched the emotion of the scene carry them away to a place they had only dreamed of being during all of their years of training. I found myself transformed onto that stage and felt that pride, and for a moment, I *was* that person. In my mind, I had just won the medal for the country and could feel the love for and of a nation. It was overwhelming.

It wasn't just me. We all felt it. It inspired all of us. The seed was planted. We were going to be Olympic athletes. Training would start the next day. And you know what? It did. The three of us—my brother, my cousin, and me. We were going to be Olympic athletes. So our training started, as it did for Romaleen.

ME AND MY BROTHER DOUG (GOOCH). WE NEVER DID MAKE IT TO THE OLYMPICS.

Looking around the farm, we didn't have much in the way of equipment necessary to train for many of the games of the summer Olympics. We didn't have a high jump, no parallel bars, no rings, no pommel horse, and certainly no pole vault. Money was limited, so acquiring any of the said equipment was out of the question.

Ah, but we did have a track. And since none of us was graced with the gift of speed, long distance running became our specialty. Perhaps the 10,000 meter would suit us. It didn't matter. We started running. The little filly would need a bit more preparation than just throwing on a pair of shoes and getting to it. She would first need to be broke to the harness.

The process of breaking a young filly or colt is never a simple endeavor. We were no strangers to breaking weanlings to drive, so Romaleen was just another project that lay before us. We had two things in our favor from the start. First, she was small, and the damage a young horse can do is usually in proportion to its size. Second, she was a filly, and generally speaking, they are easier to deal with than colts. However, these two points are blanket statements, and anyone who has dealt with enough young horses knows there are exceptions.

Romaleen was sweet. That's not to say breaking her was easy. She had her issues, just as they all do. Romaleen's biggest problem was the croup. Most mares don't like the croup. I know that sounds sexist, but in my experience, it's the truth. The croup is a loop of leather that goes under the tail and attaches to the main harness, which prevents the harness from sliding forward. If you somehow pinch some of the short tail hairs under that leather strap, young horses didn't take too kindly to it. Neither did the older ones, for that matter. I think the term getting a "hair across your ass" may actually come from this piece of equipment. You had to be sure all hairs were clear of the leather before setting the tail back down over it. Very important.

Breaking horses is painstakingly slow. In the movies, they do it in an hour. Sure it's sexy, but it sure ain't the way it happens. In reality, it takes months. If you wanted to, you could try doing it the old-fashioned way and manhandle them, but that meant you wouldn't have spent any time with that filly or colt prior to that. That isn't realistic. And you know what? Someone is probably going to get hurt. The breaking process happens over time. Much like someone learns to speak a new language. You don't learn it in a single day. You pick it up slowly until it finally sinks in.

When we finally broke Romaleen to the cart, she was fun to jog. She willingly did her four or five miles, enjoyed her shower afterward, and never once soured to the idea of work. Although she put all of the required work in, she never developed any real muscle in her chest, and she lacked speed. We couldn't do much about the speed, but my dad thought we could muscle her up. He thought up a plan that was a little outside the box.

He decided to attach the screen drag that we usually pulled behind the truck to smooth the track surface of the hoofprints that were made jogging. Hitting those little potholes with the wheels of jogcart was an act of cruelty to the kidneys and man parts. So we used a piece of chain link fence to smooth out the sand after four or five horses were jogged to make it tolerable to be out there. Instead of a truck, Romaleen would do the pulling. Harryman figured it was a win-win scenario. She would strengthen up her chest and drag the track at the same time.

Jogging her after that was even more pleasant. Not a single hoofprint existed with each pass around the track. She simply erased them as we went. The little filly didn't seem to mind, although she lathered up quite a sweat with the increased workload. And she got stronger. The problem was, she didn't get faster. Her stamina was great, but her speed was mediocre at best. She raced once or twice, but never made it to the winner's circle. Like the three of us in training for the Olympics, she was never destined for athletic greatness.

No photos of her exist. Since she didn't win, we never had a win picture of her either. The only image I have of her is in my head. She even erased any evidence that she ever existed by smoothing out her own hoofprints in the sand when she jogged. It's as if she was never there. Somewhere on the wall, where the old harnesses used to be, you can barely make out her name in purple. We sold her as a riding horse to some people in Connecticut.

I often think about her and what might have happened. How she was one of the kindest horses we ever owned but never turned out to be a racehorse. I wonder if she ever thought about the farm and pulling that screen behind her. I wonder if she thought about us. Would she recognize me if we ever met again? I know she was only a horse, but animals will surprise you sometimes. As it happened, we never did cross paths again.

Looking out the window of the car on the way home from Dana Farber, I wondered the same about the kind people who had helped me. All of the Romaleens I had met in the hospital. The Jamaican nurse who peed her pants laughing. Emily and Amada. The nurse who made the hens quiet down for a few hours. Even John. There were so many who touched me in a positive way. I would probably never see them again. I wondered if they would ever think of me, or was I just another patient among the vast numbers who ran through there? Would they remember me if we met again? I have no pictures of them, nothing other than what's in my head. As we drove away, it felt as if we were pulling a giant screen drag behind us, wiping out any trail that I had ever been there. In a way, it was a bittersweet moment.

Chapter 16 – Many Shades of Cancer

When we got home, the air was cleaner and crisper. It was the day before my birthday. Happy birthday to me. I was alive, and I was home. I could barely make it up the back stairs of the house from the weakness. I had to use the handrail, and by the time I made it to the top, I was out of breath. I collapsed on the bed and fell into the deepest sleep I had experienced in months.

I dreamt I was back in vet school. I was in my junior rotation in surgery and hadn't studied for anything I was about to be thrown into. This actually happened in real life (a story for another time perhaps). But in this dream, it was a bit different. I was in the equine ward, assisting on a colic surgery on a horse. I had to identify all the names of the different intestines that were opened up in front of me. *I should know this*, I thought. This was my thing. Transverse colon, that's in there somewhere. The pelvic flexure? I couldn't find it. Everything was fuzzy. Then we found the reason for the colic. There was a giant tumor wrapped around the descending duodenum. Nonsurgical. The horse would have to be euthanized on the table.

The odd thing about it was that the death of the horse didn't bother me in the least. What was freaking me out was that I still had another two years to go in vet school. I had already made it, hadn't I? Why was I here? There was no possible way I was mentally prepared to go through two more years of this. I remembered how hard it was, and my dreaming mind was struggling with the idea of studying for the next two years…again.

When I woke up, I realized that I *was* indeed a vet. Almost twenty years removed. A sense of great relief came over me. Thank God that was just a dream. I rolled over, and the pain in my left shoulder screamed at me. My mind whirled back into consciousness.

The dream would have been a better scenario. How ironic that the nightmare was better than the reality. I would have given anything to go back there now. Start over. Be me again.

The days that followed were tough for all of us. Jen had to work *and* wait on me, and my family had to worry about both me and Harryman. He was doing what he could with the poor prognosis that he had been given. He followed all of their instructions, took all the meds they asked him to take. Nothing was working for him. But every morning, he brought me my coffee.

Sometimes it was more like noon, since both of us felt so crappy, but he would drive himself to the convenience store, get his white Styrofoam cups with no brand name on them, and make his way over to my house. He would come up the back stairs, and we would sit in the living room instead of my office. We had our talks. We commiserated about how we felt since we both were going through chemo, both bald, and both depressed about our fate. We kept it light and made a lot of jokes about how bad we both looked, both of us sensing that neither of us likely had a lot of time left.

I cherished those moments with him. Not everyone has the chance to spend time with their dad as I did every day. Some people don't even know their fathers, while others have lost them way too young. I was blessed with having him for forty-six years, and for that I am forever grateful. Even so, I wanted more. I didn't want to see him go. He was the centerpiece of the family, the rudder that steered the ship. We wouldn't necessarily be lost at sea without him, but we would be off course, wandering.

The thing about cancer is that in most cases, no one can really tell how long you have. At least not until the very end. There are plenty of people who have beaten the odds, somehow defeated the beast, even against doctors' predictions. Some have even been cured of incurable diseases. There are all kinds of stories out there. Take this berry, take this herb, see this guy, drink this veggie drink, and you too can be cancer free. If it worked all the time, we wouldn't need oncology wards. What you *don't* hear are the 492 people who did in fact take that herb but died anyway. What you *do* hear is about the one guy it helped, and you hear it a thousand times, through the voice of a megaphone.

The thing is no two cancers are alike. What works on one person might not work on another. A person who has a 90 percent cure rate dies in six months. Another guy gets six months to live and is still kicking after ten years. It gives people both hope and angst. One thing that continues to bother me is when someone says something like "my uncle has the same thing you have." *No one* has the same thing I have. Let's just be clear. Every form of cancer is different. Sure, they can be named the same, but I assure you that every case is different in one form or another.

My form of multiple myeloma is stage III. It is the highest-risk stage there is. I'm not saying that to hear violins playing for me. I'm stating the facts. It holds the highest death rate. Stage I is called smoldering myeloma. It can be left untreated for decades, and the patient can live a long and prosperous life, notwithstanding some aches and pains. If it changes over to stage II, treatment can be initiated, as long as it is monitored closely. Stage II is the form that hasn't spread to the bones and other organs but has remained in the bloodstream and bone marrow proper. This too is fairly treatable for a fairly long time, although if it becomes more aggressive and is later classified as stage III, the treatment changes.

Now in between these are a multitude of stages (at least in my opinion). For simplification, let's just say there might be stage I (A, B, and C), stage II (A, B, and C), and stage III (A, B, and C). I have taken some liberties here since no staging system like this exists. I am trying to illustrate an idea. There could be ten or twenty different variations of each stage given any single patient's condition. My point is that every case is different.

I know that mine, even though it is stage III, is different than others' because my kidneys didn't fail and my calcium was never off the charts. This gives me a little hope that maybe mine isn't as bad as it could be. Maybe I'm a stage III, type A. Who knows? Up until now, this disease has been relatively unstudied, but for some reason, it is becoming more and more common in the population. Perhaps you have heard that Tom Brokaw is one of its latest victims. It's become almost hip, a real disease du jour. Reasons? Probably environmental, perhaps food related. They might figure it out at some point.

For me, the *why* doesn't matter. I have it. I can't turn back time and not develop a thousand x-rays in a nonventilated processing room and see if I don't get it. Again, it doesn't matter to me. It *will* matter for the next person that might be able to dodge it from happening to them. It would be helpful if they found a cause so that people could avoid whatever it is that triggers it.

My point in all this rambling is that people with cancer don't want to be told that someone they know has the same thing you do. The fact that Aunt Betty was diagnosed with the "same thing" and has had it for twenty years doesn't help my situation. Perhaps they want to give me hope because someone with the "same thing" has lived for so long, but that's because they don't have the facts. I will say it again. No one has the same cancer. Similar? Absolutely. It might have the same name, but it's always a slightly different game.

And who knows, maybe I'll get lucky and outlive all the healthy people. The odds are against this, but there is no way of knowing for certain. I am not looking for sympathy or pity; I just don't want to be told what I have by someone who has limited knowledge of what he or she is talking about. There are men out there right now dying from prostate cancer, but Cousin Jimmy had the "same thing" and he's cured. There are women dying from breast cancer who watch others on *The View* tell survival stories. It just isn't fair to compare. Not to get preachy, but if you want to help, just say you're sorry that the person has it. Wow, that was preachy.

Okay, climbing off of my soapbox now. I look at old people differently today. I get a little jealous. I look at them and get the sinking feeling that I will never *be* one of them. I won't grow old with my wife. It can be depressing if you let it, but I try to live each day now, in the moment. Every day really is a gift. This disease has given me a perspective that I never had. I worked six days a week for seventeen years straight and never really saw life for the majesty that it is.

Every now and then, I see people on TV, maybe on the *Tonight Show* or the evening news, celebrating their one hundredth birthday. Invariably, the host will ask them what their secret to living so long has been. Then they always get a cute little answer like, "I eat chocolate every day," or "I make sure I laugh at something every day." I can tell you one very big secret that will help you live to a hundred.

Don't get cancer. That would help tremendously. Don't get hit head on by a drunk driver. Also helpful. Don't get sucked into a sinkhole while sitting in your bedroom. Or how about don't be an innocent child in a classroom when a madman comes in with a loaded assault weapon. Secret to living a long life. Please. There is no *secret*. It's called luck. Or maybe it's genetics. Or fate, or whatever else you want to call it. It's not chocolate, I can tell you that.

I was discussing life and how delicate it is with a friend. He tried to understand what I was going through and made the comment that none of us know when our time is up. "I could get hit by a bus tomorrow," he said. While this is true and seems logical enough to the person without cancer, here is the truth. Those without cancer are walking on the sidewalk. Those with cancer are dancing in the traffic, and it's only a matter of time before the bus does hit you. To be honest, it doesn't bother me that people think that way. In fact, I had the same reasoning before I got sick when I saw others with similar plights as my own. It's just a perspective change.

Chapter 17 – Cool Bad Harry

The days that followed the transplant were painstakingly slow. I hadn't anticipated being so weak. I thought that as soon as I got out of the hospital, I could start exercising again, eating better, lose the weight, and get back in shape. I figured in four weeks, I could be right back to where I was. Man, was I off base.

The first day I got home, I could only lie in bed. I slept the whole day. I got up to eat around 9:00 p.m., and then went back to bed again. I didn't get out of bed until noon the next day. I was so feeble that I took home one of those urine collection containers and kept it by my side so I didn't have to get up to walk all the way down the hall to the bathroom. It was really pitiful.

I was slowly regaining feeling in my right hand, but my shoulder was killing me. It was a chore just to lift my arm past my hip. It was impossible to lift it up above my head. Oddly enough, it didn't hurt if I tried to do push-ups. Before my ordeal, I was working out quite a bit and did maybe two or three sets of thirty push-ups a night to stay in shape. A few sit-ups, some planking thrown in, and an occasional run on the treadmill was the norm. I decided that push-ups were a good place to start.

I got myself on the floor and prepared for maybe a set of ten, setting what I thought was a realistic goal. When I tried to lift off the floor, my body shook, my arms trembled, and you maybe could have slid a piece of paper under my belly. Nothing. Couldn't even do one. Hell, I didn't even do a quarter of one. It was devastating. I collapsed on my stomach, panting from the "workout," and just lay there. I should have had one of those medic alert buttons. I've fallen, and I can't get up!

I was about as strong as a toddler. Hold on a second. Don't toddlers have, like, a kung fu grip? Then scratch that; I was weaker than a toddler. Somewhere between an infant and a toddler. I'm sure there's a name for that age, but I don't have kids, so I'm not privy to such things. For argument's sake, let's just say I was junk.

I was truly winded from the effort. I was disgusted with myself and, for the first time, angry at the cancer. I never went through the five stages of grief when I learned of my illness. I jumped right to acceptance. The first is denial. Well, when I saw the x-ray on the screen, as a doctor, it was hard denying that I indeed had a monster inside of me. Check that off the list. The second is anger. I've had a lot of anger in my life and have learned how to deal with it on most days. My father taught me a lot about that.

He was about the coolest cat you'll ever come across. He lost his temper about once every presidential administration. And when he did, he exploded for about ten seconds, and then it was over. He was right back to being Harryman again, smiling and doing his thing. He was wired differently. I, on the other hand, dealt with anger within me. I'm not sure where that rage comes from, but when I was younger, it showed its ugliness quite a bit. But along the way came lessons. Hardwood Bret was maybe the final straw that taught me how to harness it up. I learned that it's okay to get angry, but you can't let it consume you. I devoted a whole chapter in my first book to that horse, that's how much impact he had on me.

I was a different person after we failed to get that horse back. That was a long day. My father and I traveled three and a half hours up to Skowhegan, Maine, to buy back Hardwood Bret, a horse that had been claimed from us a few months prior. When things went sour, and the deal broke down because of a clerical snafu, I lost it. I went completely out of my mind. I had a real meltdown. And there was my father, who should have been just as pissed off as me, calm as always, telling me that everything would be all right.

My fury lasted the whole ride home. Finally my dad told me to let it go, he was sick of listening to me. And that's when it hit me. It was only a horse. There were so many worse things that could have happened. What would I do if something really bad went down?

If this was how I handled something so trivial, I had no chance of making it when it mattered. Something in me clicked that night. I guess you could call it an epiphany. Maybe I just needed some perspective. Watching how he acted, and seeing how I acted, was really the eye-opener. There was an adult in the driver's seat and a child sitting next to him. It was time to step up and be a man.

Back in the eighties, when we were racing ten to fifteen head of horses, my friend Jim came up with a nickname for my father because of his level-headedness and toughness. He called him Cool Bad Harry. We shortened it and just called him CBH. The name fit him perfectly and stuck for many years until the Harryman moniker took over. His calm demeanor was truly remarkable.

It may sound like a terrible thing to do, but my father's coolness was so sickening to both my brother and me that we would occasionally try to get him upset by pushing his buttons. It almost never worked. There was one time, however, that I was able to rattle him, even if it was for just a minute.

It was back in the day when the Nextel phones had just come out, and they were promoting the walkie-talkie feature. Harryman absolutely loved that option, He would chirp any one of us three (my mom, Doug, or me) at any given time just to use it. I think he just liked playing with it rather than wanting to actually talk. I had to tell him to lay off the thing while I was working because it went off every time I was with a client. There would be a loud chirp, and then his voice would boom out in the exam room, "Hey, Cope, you coming over for dinner tonight?" If I didn't respond in a timely fashion, he just chirped that sucker again and so on. At some point, I just left it in my office. He couldn't help himself.

One day, the whole family went to the Back Bay of Boston for a birthday party. Jen and I drove separately and planned to meet up with the rest of them there. Since I had no idea where I was going, and driving in Boston is a daunting task, I decided to chirp him on the way to get directions. As we got closer, the directions got more difficult, and he was trying to use landmarks to help me out. At one point, my Nextel made its annoying beep-beep, and Harryman was on the other end.

"You will see a castle on the left pretty soon. Do not take a left at the castle. Stay straight."

Harryman was like a frozen beehive. You really had to heat him up to release even a few yellow jackets. I thought then that I had the ideal scenario to maybe light a little fire and see what happened. What a horrible son, I know, but he was just too damn laid back. Someone had to shake him up now and then. I answered him back.

"Okay, take a left at the castle."

He quickly clicked back. He probably figured the message he sent got garbled, as those phones were known to do.

"Do not take a left at the castle," he replied calmly.

"Got it," I said. "Left at the castle."

This time his answer was a little more intense, and the hive stirred.

"Listen to me. Do *not* take a left at the castle. Go straight."

I knew I had him. He couldn't hear me laughing on the other end since my finger wasn't on the button. I had to control myself, get my voice steady, and once more fan the flames.

"Yup, I see it, I'm coming up on it. So I take a left at the castle."

His next reply was something none of us will ever forget. He actually got angry. So agitated in fact, he slipped into a Greek accent. He didn't speak English for the first six years of his life, but there wasn't a hint of an accent in his voice as an adult. But when he chimed back at me, his anger had somehow regressed him slightly back into his first language.

"*Noooh!* Do *not* take a left at de castle!"

Jen and I were laughing almost to tears. I really am a bad person. When I composed myself, he could hear me giggling as I let him off the hook.

"I know, I'm just messing with you. I already went straight."

"You bastard," he clicked back. And then I heard him laugh.

In a way, I felt terrible, but I got him good. The significance of that moment was echoed by the many times we brought it up in the future. He just plain didn't get mad very often. I might not have released a swarm out of him, but I was able to wake up a few hornets. I can still hear him laughing about it today. He was a good sport about things like that.

Chapter 18 – The Scorpion

So when the verdict came down and they told me I had multiple myeloma, I didn't get angry. I've said it before. I didn't ask why. More specifically, I asked why not? There are so many diseases out there, it would seem impossible not to get one of them at some point in time. I figured it was just my time. Granted, I wasn't happy about it, but the rage wasn't there.

Getting back to number one for a moment. Denial. I have to admit that I did have some denial at first. But it wasn't about *having* cancer. It was about the *type* of cancer they told me I had. I had done all the research on my alleged condition, and none of the parameters fit. As I said before, at the time, the average age for a multiple myeloma patient was seventy. High calcium was apparent in almost all cases, and kidney failure was common in many of the stage III patients. I fit none of these criteria, so yes, there was denial. I thought I had a different *type* of cancer. But I did not deny the fact that I was likely dying.

Third is bargaining. I had no chips to bargain with. If only I— what? Saw the doctor sooner? It didn't matter, it was still there. Ask God to help me? Nice try. If he was there for me in the first place, he wouldn't have let me get it. My feeling about the whole God thing in all this is simple. He doesn't give anyone a disease, nor does he cure them. I'm pretty certain he didn't look down and say, "Hey, there's that doubter, Marc Mitchell, let's give him cancer." In my most humble opinion, he is only there to help you through it, if you so choose his help. I know there are thousands, nay millions, of people that disagree with this way of thinking, and that's fine by me. As I said, I never claimed to be right. We all have to choose a belief. That's just mine.

What's number four on our countdown, Casey Kasem? It's depression. This was not an option for me. Depression is a killer.

It may be worse than the disease itself. It's what the cancer wants, a weakness, a chink in the armor. I wasn't going to let that happen. Positive thinking was my only hope if I was to try and win the battle. I might lose the war in the end, but depression was not going to be the ammunition used against me.

That's not to say I don't have bad days and feel depressed. But when I think of depression, I think of it as a shadowy place where your mind goes, and it sucks you down into it. It's a cavern of darkness and despair. If you let yourself go there, it can be hard to climb out. That was not going to happen.

And finally, rounding out the top five: acceptance. That's what I did. I had cancer. For me, there was no other choice. It was staring me in the face. Either accept it and push forward or start with number one and deny it. By denying it, you can't start to fight it. That whole five-step process was just too laborious for my logical mind. From that grave day when I hoped I was looking at someone else's x-ray on the screen, I accepted my fate. Game on.

So there I was, facedown on my maroon berber carpet, unable to do a single friggin' push-up. You're goddamn right I was angry. I was losing. And there's nothing more I dislike than losing. Well, that's not entirely true. I dislike the cancer more. My whole life has been about winning. Winning in hockey, winning horse races, winning pool tournaments, winning a chance to go to vet school. It is ingrained in my DNA.

Today I see kids playing little league, and the adults don't keep score. They don't want a winner or a loser. They think that these kids are too mentally fragile to handle losing a silly game of baseball. Horseshit. There is always a winner, and there is always a loser. Yeah, I know, there can be a tie. Those suck. I'd almost rather lose than have a tie. My will to win started at a young age, when we kept score for everything.

I worry about the kids of today. When faced with the real challenges of winning and losing in life, they may face some hard obstacles should they fail if they haven't experienced losing in the first place. You have to feel the pain of a loss so you can motivate yourself to win the next time. It's what we are as human beings. We want to win. We are the scorpion; it's in our nature. Just for kicks, ask the kids who in fact won the game that "wasn't being scored" who won. I bet every one of them knows, and they know the actual score. The losers? There aren't any! Hooray for them!

If you don't know the story of the scorpion, I will tell it to you now. It's one of my favorite fables that my father told me as a kid. It can be told with either a turtle or a frog, but I prefer the turtle. One day, a scorpion and a turtle are at the bank of a river, and both want to cross. The scorpion, who obviously can't swim, asks the turtle if he wouldn't mind carrying him across to the opposite side.

"But you're a scorpion. We will get halfway across, and you will sting me with your tail and kill me," replied the turtle,

"Don't be silly," said the scorpion. "That would mean we would both drown. I would never be so irresponsible and do such a thing."

The turtle thought long and hard. He didn't trust this scorpion, or any other scorpion for that matter. He didn't like the thought of dying, and once again he spoke.

"I do not wish to carry you across. No offense, but I do not trust you, as you are a scorpion, and you will surely kill me as I carry you over there."

The scorpion argued his case. He promised he wouldn't sting him. It wouldn't be very practical to kill his only means of getting across the river.

After several minutes, and much pleading on the side of the scorpion, the turtle reluctantly agreed to let the scorpion on his back and take him to the other side. So the scorpion hopped on his back, and the turtle started swimming through the current. When they got about halfway across the river, the scorpion raised his mighty tail and lashed the turtle under the shell and penetrated his flesh.

"What have you done!?" the turtle cried out in anguish. "Why did you do that? Now we will both surely perish!"

The scorpion replied very coldly, "It's in my nature."

I am the scorpion in a sense. I want to win. It's in my nature. This disease has a fight on its hands. But I am also the turtle. I didn't willingly let it on my back, but it's there nonetheless, and I have to try to swim to the other side. I will fight this thing until it kills me. If it doesn't, I win. If it does, I will go down swinging.

But first, I had to get off that stupid rug. Couldn't even do a single push-up. Oh boy, this was going to be one hell of a comeback. I had spotted my opponent something like twenty points already, and there I was, down on the mat. Literally. I thought back to that floor hockey game, where we came back from 6–3 with just over a minute left and won in overtime. Okay, Marc, get up. This isn't over. I could hear Paul's words. Another level.

I learned the story of the scorpion at a very young age. We had a horse called Mini Mitch that was not very nice, to say the least. I asked my father one day why she was so angry and difficult to break. That's when he told me about the scorpion.

Mini Mitch was one of those exceptions to the rule when we talk about size and sex being in your favor. She was a little black filly that had a serious mean streak. She was as sour as they come, and she never was given a reason to be that way. She was just plain mean. It made breaking her to the cart or even the harness very dangerous. It took three men each day just to get a saddle pad on, without her having a tantrum and destroying the shed row. One man stood on each side of her head with a lead to keep her from going up in the air or spinning around, while the third did his best to ease the harness over her back. She would have nothing of it for days. Kick, buck, rear, bite, spin, jump. You name it. She did it. Man, she was just a sour thing.

Howie Miller was watching my father struggle with her from the bench behind the barn. We called it the "Knocker's Bench," so named because trainers who sat there almost always had something degrading to say about horses they were watching on the track from that vantage point. It was usually in good fun, but sometimes they really slung it.

After a few weeks of finally getting a harness over her back and seeing how poorly she was coming along, Howie thought he could be the one to tame this little demon. Howie was a good horseman and figured Harryman was going about things the wrong way. Typical New Englander who thought he could do better than the next guy. He spoke in a nasal tone that only Howie had. It was as if he held his nose closed when he spoke. When he talked, there was no way you could mistake his voice for anyone else's.

One day he yelled over to my father as the little filly reared up in the air, "Hey, Harry, let me have that son of a bitch for a couple weeks. I'll show her how it's done." Most of Howie's sentences ended with some sort of expletive. Usually it was something like "son of a bitch" or "son of a whore." There were much worse, but you get the point.

My father had just about enough of her shenanigans and didn't think twice about giving Howie a shot with her. If Mini Mitch didn't respect my father's booming voice when he reprimanded her, I feared that Howie's trumpeted whimper wouldn't carry much weight. It turned out I was right.

He took Mini Mitch out to a small paddock with her harness on and started to longe (pronounced "lunge") her on a long rope to get her tired before making a move to the track. Then he said we should help him put some sort of jog cart near her for the first try, or maybe some wooden poles, just to give her the idea before we let her destroy even the makeshift jog cart used to teach with.

He led this little filly out to the paddock and brought a longe whip with him. The process of longing (pronounced "lunge-ing") is fairly simple. You stand in the center of the paddock or round pen, and the horse is extended at the end of a twenty- to thirty-foot rope. The horse is then asked to jog in a circle around the center by the horseman, coaxing the animal with voice commands or the light snapping of the whip. The whip is rarely used to touch the animal; it's just intended to make noise and keep a lazy horse moving. Most horses get the hang of it very quickly and have no issues learning how to do it. But Mini Mitch was an exception.

Howie got in the center of the ring and extended the little filly with her harness to the outside of the paddock, and gave the whip a slight crack to get her attention. The look on her face was one that said, "Do that again, and you and I are going to have issues." She went up in the air, bucked wildly, and started off at a gallop counterclockwise in the paddock. She went twice around in a bit of a frenzy, then stopped abruptly on the far side and froze. She was done. But Howie wasn't.

Although he had been warned by a not so subtle stare in the beginning, our unsuspecting trainer raised his whip once again to start the petite monster on her circumferential route. As he raised it to make it snap, the black-hooved little devil turned and faced him squarely. He might as well have been holding a red cape, as she made her best impression of a bull fighting a matador at center stage. In a blink, she was running straight toward him, and this time the look in her eyes was one of pure evil. Ears pinned, head down, she came full bore at poor Howie. He had a twenty-foot head start because of the length of the lead, and it was just fifteen feet to the outside fence. For a portly man in his forties, he moved pretty darn quickly. He dove through the split rail fence just as she tracked him down and nearly killed him. Fortunately she stopped and didn't crash through after him, but I think she thought about it. Oh, the verbal obscenities that followed that scene! All uttered in a nasal, comedic explosion. Well, it was funny to me anyway.

No one could get near her for the rest of the day. She wouldn't let anyone back in the paddock. She was one pissed-off filly, and she was holding a grudge. She paced the paddock wearing her harness and dragging the lead around for hours in disgust. Just around dusk, she got hungry and was finally coaxed in with a bucket of grain. Her tack was removed, and it was a long and difficult process to get her broke over the course of the summer. She raced only once, and finished last, swishing her tail the entire mile in an act of defiance. A colossal waste of time.

This was when I asked my father why she was such a difficult horse to break.

"Why is she so sour?" I asked.

"It's in her nature," he replied. He then went on to tell me the story of the scorpion.

It was clear that I wouldn't be able to will myself back into shape. I needed to start with baby steps and very slowly make my way back. I had to set realistic goals that could be achieved. I started walking every day. It was early April in New England and fairly chilly. The snow had melted and the track at the farm was clear for walking. And so I started.

CHAPTER 19 – THE ROAD BACK TO THE FARM

The farm was only a couple miles away. Driving there wasn't too difficult, although I hadn't driven a car since October 10, when I passed out behind the wheel and almost killed myself. Later on, in early May, I had my court date and brought my friend Keith Dias with me, who went to law school in his forties and got his degree just a few years back. He served as my counsel for the reckless driving charges. I was certain that if I went in alone, I would lose the case. In a matter of two minutes, after Keith spoke to the little weasel of a prosecutor, I was cleared of all charges.

I feel very comfortable calling him a weasel since I had spoken to him at length before my hearing about my condition and the incidents leading up to the accident. I thought he might be reasonable when I explained to him that I was not being reckless since I didn't realize what my body was going through. I tried to persuade him not to charge me. He was extremely smug and wasn't even listening. I even sent a letter to the Chief of Police. They still wanted to prosecute me to the fullest extent. I don't know what Keith said to him, because they spoke to the side in hushed tones, but it didn't take long at all. They dropped all charges. Amazing, I won a court case. Alert the media.

For the first time back in the driver's seat in six months, I made sure my mind was clear and that I wasn't feeling lightheaded. I drove myself over without incident and started my way back to being human again.

Although my house is in Brentwood behind the veterinary clinic, I still call the farm in Kingston my home. It is always comforting just to be there. It is sixty-five acres of pasture and woodland. We wouldn't sell it at any price. There are too many memories there. It defines who we are. We are farmers. It made us tough. It made us sensitive. It molded us into what we've become. If I close my eyes, I can see every acre. As kids, we explored everything, everywhere. There isn't a square foot of soil my brother and I haven't walked on or ridden across on horses or dirt bikes (off-road motorcycles). We even mucked through the swampland in the back just for kicks.

FRONT VIEW OF THE BARN.

The barn is sky blue and rambles along for about a hundred and forty feet in length. The first half is the "old barn" and watches over the road. It stands forty feet at the peak, with a very sharp pitch to the adjoining roofs below, which then sprawl out in either direction for fifty feet. The lower ridges have long, slightly pitched roofs that mimic a bird's wings. In the center of the A-framed old barn is a hayloft door that opens up into a vast space that can easily hold six thousand bales of hay. I know this, because each summer we would fill it ourselves. We would cut it, tether it, bale it, drive it home in pickup trucks, and then stack it in there. All with a three- or four-man crew.

Back in the day, Doug and I occasionally climbed to the very top and just sat there watching over the horses and the splendor of it all. It just might be the most peaceful place in the world. At least it was to us.

A few feet under the very peak of the barn are three little holes; two are diamond in shape, and one is circular, that make a triangle as a cluster. Barn swallows are able to use these as a gateway into the hayloft. On summer days, you can see them darting in and out, making their nests and doing their thing. Just below those holes are three floodlights that were installed somewhere around 1978. They hold 150-watt bulbs and light up the whole paved area out-side the front of the barn.

We used them all the time. We played street hockey under the lights, basketball, Frisbee, or whatever else we wanted to do out there when night fell and we didn't want to call it a day. We also used them every time we came home from the races when we unloaded the horses. The point being those lights got a lot of use. And you won't believe me when I tell you this: the same bulbs are still work-ing today. Not a single one of them has burned out. That has to be some sort of record. Thirty-five years of use, and they're still burn-ing as bright as the day they were put in. And you know what? I don't know who would change them. They are sickeningly high up and impossible to get to without a seriously long ladder. If they ever need to be changed, it won't be me going up there. It certainly would be ironic, not dying from cancer but from falling from that peak. We all still marvel that they continue to work. Now that I've said it, I'm sure the jinx is on. My guess is that in a few weeks, they all go out.

The old farmhouse that Doug lives in is painted the same sky blue as the barn and stands to its left. It is a standard colonial with a small addition on the right side with a nearly flat roof that we call the family room. It's where we did nearly everything as a family, so it was aptly named. We played games of Monopoly, watched TV, made houses out of cards as high as we could (the record stands at thirteen), warmed our feet by the woodstove after playing hockey for hours down on the pond, listened to Doug and my father play folk songs, and just sat around talking about life and horses. We didn't have much back then, but we had each other, and that was enough.

AN AERIAL SHOT OF THE FARM. THE POND IS IN THE UPPER LEFT CORNER, SURROUNDED BY THE LARGE TRACK. THE BARN IS AT THE BOTTOM OF THE PICTURE IN THE CENTER. THE FARM HOUSE IS TO THE LEFT OF THE BARN. THE PASTURE FOR THE 'SIDEWINDERS' IS TO THE LEFT OF THE BARN. THE FIVE SMALL PADDOCKS ARE ON THE RIGHT. THE CIRCLE ON THE BOTTOM RIGHT OF THE PICTURE IS THE ROUND-PEN USED FOR LONGEING HORSES. IF YOU LOOK CLOSELY, THERE ARE TWO HORSES BEING RIDDEN ON THE TRACK AT THE TOP OF THE STRETCH NEAR THE POND.

The "new barn" is connected to the "old barn" and is long and narrow, stretching out behind it, and much lower in profile. It has two shed rows. The main one on the right has stalls on either side. In the middle of the barn is a small corridor that connects to the other shed row, which only has stalls on the side that adjoins the main aisle. The side of the shed row to the left is lined with small windows and overlooks the thirty-acre pasture that most of the horses get turned out into. The "new barn" is in essence a very long H. The little cut through has always been referred to as simply "the H." That's where the old black phone with the rotary dial and old bell ringer is mounted on the wall. It still works today.

It's also where all of the harnesses were hung for each horse, with their names etched in different colored chalk above it. When a horse left, we would simply put a line through the name and write a new one above it. None of them ever got erased. Those names are still there. The ghosts of hundreds of horses are inscribed there. Some are so faded that they are almost illegible and would be to those who didn't know their names, but *we* can still make them out. Beau Mite Win, I Blu By U, Spirit Special, Hardwood Bret, Ben Dover, and of course Honey's Best, just to name a few. They're all still there; on the wall and in our hearts.

Since the shed row on the left has a side door that opens up to the large pasture, the horses that go out there are affectionately called the "sidewinders." Uncooperative horses that don't work and play well with others are turned out in smaller pastures on the other side of the barn. There are five smaller pastures over there that are maybe a half acre to an acre apiece. It's more than enough room for those horses to romp and play, albeit by themselves, since they insist on hurting others or getting hurt if they get turned out with the herd.

THE PASTURE FOR THE "SIDEWINDERS".

Behind the barn is where the track is laid out. It is made entirely of sand and was constructed in the early seventies with some major movement of land from one part of the farm over to lay the new track. It is elevated on the far side by about twenty feet above the wetlands behind it. To its left is the large paddock for the sidewinders. The track is a third of a mile long and is almost a perfect oval. The near turn is slightly tighter, making it just a bit oblong.

On the inner part of the far end of the track that faces the woods is a small pond that was dredged out to fill in some low-lands by my father the first year we moved there. It's shaped like a half moon, with its outer border lining the entire far turn. The hours we spent down there as kids are countless. We either swam, fished, or played hockey on it. It was one of the best assets we had growing up. You couldn't have paid us to have a swimming pool. The pond was our holy grail for fun. We could have done without the water snakes and leeches, but if we left them alone, they usually did the same. My fear of serpents stems from a day when I tried to catch one and he sprang up and almost bit me in the face. Can't say I blamed the little bugger, as I did have him trapped under a bucket. Like I said, if you just leave them alone, they will return the favor.

The large track has another smaller track on the inside of it. Its far border lines the near side of the pond. It is about a fifth of a mile long. We used the little track for breaking young horses (no issues with going over the steep banking as was the case on the big track) and for jogging while other horses were training on the larger oval. What I mean by training is going speeds similar to racing. Jogging is just getting miles under the horses to get them legged up.

The word "training" is reserved for going the right way on the track to simulate a race. The "right way," as horsemen refer to it, is counterclockwise, which is how they race (at least here in North America). Conversely, the "wrong way" is clockwise. So horses are jogged clockwise and trained counterclockwise. In this manner, a horse knows when he will be asked for speed.

My father usually told one of us that he wanted us to jog a horse a couple miles and then turn him the "right way" and give him a trip. A trip is just lingo for a mile prepping for a real race. The horses all knew what it meant to get turned the "right way." Most of them got racy as soon as they faced that direction. The reins would tighten, the ears pricked up, and they were all business. Not all of them. Some of them were slackers and had to be coaxed into getting revved up, but the good ones always knew.

Some of the ones without a lot of gray matter between their ears didn't know the difference. Or they didn't care. I think the former. They pulled hard on the reins no matter which direction you went. They were a real pain in the ass to jog. You had to hold them back for the entire four miles (which was our standard regimen). By the end of the session, your forearms and back ached from pulling on them so much, and your fingers were stuck clenched together for three or four minutes afterward. It was good for a workout, that's for sure, but no one wanted to jog horses like Synek or Sky High

Skipper. They just wore you out. When you did turn them to go, you were just a passenger.

Most days when I walked, my brother Doug joined me, as well as my mother. Harryman was too weak to do it and watched by sitting on the "Knocker's Bench" out behind the barn. My father was struggling. It was hard to see him there, but I knew he took solace in the fact that I was on the road to recovery. On the first day out, with my left arm hanging limp by my side, I started walking.

I don't know if you remember those old Carol Burnett shows, but Tim Conway used to play the character of an old man. One time he played a butcher behind the counter as Harvey Korman's character ordered sausages. He walked at a painstakingly slow pace, from one station to the other, as Korman waited impatiently for his meat. Even though Korman did his best to show agitation, he couldn't stop himself from laughing at his counterpart's actions. Tim Conway was the best. He just shuffled along with a deliberate languor, and every move he made was in slow motion. If you get a chance, you really should watch some of those old clips. They're comedy gold.

On the track, I was Tim Conway in the butcher shop, lumbering about. I was also Korman, extremely irritated by my ineptitude but laughing at myself at how ridiculous I was. I just shuffled along. It took me nearly fifteen minutes to make one lap around the one-third-mile track. That was it. I was done. Breathless and in pain, I had to stop. But I had begun. My journey back had started.

The next day, I did another lap, this time just a little faster. When I say faster, it means I was almost walking slowly, more like a zombie than the tortoise I was the day before. On the third day, I did two laps. Finally I walked a full mile. My shoulder was feeling a little better and didn't shoot pain through me with every step anymore. It was now just a constant dull ache. I was making progress. I walked every day that April, no matter what the weather. My brother and I walked together every time, and sometimes my mom sat on the bench with my dad, but we walked. Two miles a day. I was getting stronger.

During this time, I kept posting every Monday on the CaringBridge. I had a pretty good following, and people were genuinely interested in how I was doing. After seven or eight straight weeks of posting, and as my father's condition started to get worse, my posts became more infrequent. I posted on holidays, or just because I had something to say.

I've intermittently thrown a few of those entries in here, although there's some redundancy in what I said, since what I wrote here does coincide with many of my posts, so I apologize if you read similar passages. As before, these are indented to indicate a journal entry.

Home – Day 13

Apr 16, 2012 10:05am
Hard to believe it's Monday again. Things are going well. Walking every day. Trying to eat right every day. Complaining to Jen every day. You know, the normal stuff. I don't know how she puts up with me really. She's probably secretly thinking she had it better when I was in the hospital. Sort of like a nice pair of dress shoes that you really love. They are stuffed away in the closet, but you can see them whenever you want. When you finally want to wear them, they're right there and they go perfectly with anything you hang with them. But after about four hours, your toes start to hurt, and after eight hours, a blister starts forming at your heel. They still look good, but man, they need to come off and get back in that closet. That's okay, I'll break in. Sooner or later, she won't even know I'm on her feet.

Not much has really transpired over the course of one week since I sit on my ass and pretty much do nothing all day. I can't go out to public places due to having almost no white cells. I can't eat any restaurant food yet because of doctor's orders. I can't do yard work because of the dust (well, that's not such a negative). And I can't play any sports like golf or hockey because I am so weak. I am bored out of my mind. The only thing I can do is play on the computer and do little exercises to start back in.

Speaking of computers and playing on them, I have an iPad that Jen got me a little while ago (when she upgraded and didn't need this old one anymore). I play Words with Friends, Hanging with Friends, and other nonsense to pass the time. There is one other game that I have been playing for quite some time now and maybe there is someone else out there that plays it as well, but it's not a popular one like Farmville (which I have never been able to even consider playing. I lived it. Now I'm supposed to play it?). Anyway, it's called Mystery Manor. It's pretty silly really. The object is to find items in rooms, in an allotted amount of time, with various distractions. It's a lot like the "Find it" pictures in *Highlights* magazine. The items are regular everyday items hiding in plain sight and you have to locate them. It's more of a sleep aid for me. I usually play it for 10-15 minutes just before sleeping to clear my mind. It works quite well.

To get to the point, I have been playing this stupid game for months and have reached level 28. Doesn't mean much to a person who hasn't played, but believe me, it's quite a feat considering I did it without purchasing any help. That's how they get you. They give you a certain amount of "power" to play each day, and if you run out (which you do in about 20 minutes of normal play), you can purchase more power and get to the next levels quicker. Well, I have done it the hard way, my friends. Okay, the cheap way. Whatever. I have done it with just the piddly little power they give you each day. I have tediously climbed to level 28 and have almost amassed enough coins to enter the Hallway. Gives me chills just thinking about it.

Two days ago, my IT guy shows up to upgrade the computers in the clinic. Harmless enough. Oh, but wait, for some reason my computer in the house doesn't play my songs that were copied from the old computer. Maybe he could find the actual songs and get them to play. That would be nice. So that's what he does. And it works! How about that? In the process, however, he also tweaked my iPad. And in that process deleted my precious little game, Mystery Manor. I downloaded it again last night. I'm at level 1. Oh goody. Level 1. Isn't that just wonderful? Level 1. Hahahahhahaha. Does anyone else see the humor in this? All my "work." Gonzo! Level 1. Where a baby could find the items. How nice. The Mystery Manor is closed, my friends. I will never enter the Manor again. It's just too painful. I wonder what was in the Hallway? Where did it lead to? I bet it was cool. Ah, but I will never know. I will always be haunted by what could have been.

But I am hardened. It is not as bad as the time I plugged in my new Nano to the computer and it synced with my iTunes library. I remember the little box popped up and asked, "Would you like to transfer songs between your iPod and your iTunes library. All files will be erased if you do?" Of course, thinking that this is a brand new iPod, it must mean transfer the iTunes library and erase anything on the iPod right? Why would it erase my hard drive? It wouldn't. Right? That wouldn't make any sense. And in one fateful click of the mouse, I hit "yes" and wiped out over 1200 songs that I had painstakingly downloaded over two years. Poof. Gone. I frantically looked around for them. They had to be somewhere. Nope. Gone. Now, if one of you computer geniuses suggests that I should have backed them up, well, just don't. I didn't. They were gone forever. After having a near mental blowout, I slowly started downloading songs again. One at a time. It took me nearly a year to get those songs back. And now I am back up to over 1600 songs.

I say all this because this is where I am now. Four weeks ago, the doctors hit the "yes" button when they were asked if they wanted to wipe out my entire immune system and it felt like they were trying to kill me. But I survived. And I'm still here. And I'm downloading songs every day. Soon I will be stronger and better than I ever was. Inch by inch. Cell by cell, I will get there. But I can tell you this, if they ever ask me again if they want to wipe out every song I've ever down-loaded, I would have to think long and hard about hitting that "yes" button.

I thank you all again for being there for me. I love all of you. From the serenity of my home,

Marc

Chapter 20 – Walks and Memories

As we walked the track each day, memories of years gone by flooded over us. We had traveled that track for tens of thousands of miles over the years being pulled by horses. Hundreds of miles on our motorcycles and go-karts. We had mishaps and incidents at every turn, every stretch. We would talk about each one as we passed by a particular spot. We talked about the old judge's stand that used to overlook the backside when we had pony races back in the eighties. Later on, we converted it into a "waterproof" fort that invariably always leaked. We talked about the old hub rail that used to line the inside of the main track and how we used to try to walk on the one-inch surface all the way around. We never made it.

Mitchell Raceway was short lived for racing ponies. It lasted maybe two or three years before interest just died out. The judge's stand that overlooked the backstretch where the finish line used to be (we later moved the finish line to the front of the barn for training) stood on stilts made of four by fours. It looked like a miniature beach house. It had four-foot walls and no roof, and was about twelve feet square. It was perfect for converting into a fort.

We didn't use the whole expanse of the thing. We used the front third of it and built a back wall and roof out of any spare scraps of wood we found lying around on the farm. Much of the hub rail that we dismantled came to good use. We also used the old cardboard ceiling tiles that the barn used to have before we took them all out. Those dropped ceiling tiles made the barn feel small, and they were a good hiding spot for rats, so we got rid of them. They were pretty flimsy and molded quite quickly when they got wet, but we used them anyway. Nothing went to waste.

At the time, our friend Charlie Ferrara's dad worked in the carpet business. He gave us a bunch of old sample carpets that were two feet square in size. There wasn't a matching pair in the lot. We had berber, shag, plush, and even that firm industrial crap that was more like a piece of wood. We had dozens of pieces, maybe a hundred. Most of them were colors that no one would ever want to use, which was probably why we got them. Green and white shag, hot pink, puke green, mustard yellow, zebra print, and so many more. When we say we had wall-to-wall carpeting, we had it in the literal sense. We had it on the floors and the walls. We even had it on the ceiling. We tacked them all up in a quiltlike tapestry and were quite proud of ourselves.

We used a tarp to cover the roof for rain, but for some reason, it always leaked. Water finds a way. It always does. On the front wall that faced the track, we cut out two tiny rectangular openings that we called windows, even though there was no glass. They were about two feet long and six inches tall. We put them on hinges, and they folded downward to the outside. With them open, we could at least get a little air in the place, as with six kids jammed in there, it got quite stuffy. From the outside, it looked like the fort had eyes. If we opened just one window, it looked like it was winking at you. Because of this, we nailed a piece of garden hose in the shape of a smile under the windows to complete the look that the fort was indeed a face, watching over the farm. We never put a nose on. I'm not sure why, but if we had, it would have been able to smell the stench of mold, mildew, and the frequent flatulence of a bunch of ten-year-olds.

We slept out there once or twice a summer. It rained nearly every time. We stocked up on all junk food and soda. We had everything: Funyuns, Devil Dogs, Doritos, Hostess Cupcakes, Charleston Chews, Good & Plenty, Ding Dongs, Oreos, Funny Bones, and anything else we could think of. It was the only time our parents let us go crazy with snack foods like that. We had six different kinds of soda, all full of sugar, and none of us brought a toothbrush. It was a dentist's nightmare.

We told ghost stories and talked about girls. We even had a little trapdoor (covered in carpet, of course) that we used as the entrance from underneath the judge's stand since it was elevated. We had a set of three stairs that led up to it, but you really didn't need to use it; you could easily just hoist yourself in there. The stairs were for the dogs. Boots and Haystack loved to join us out there. They would hover around, waiting for a Cheez Doodle to drop or for someone to sneak them a piece of popcorn. At some point in the night, I would walk them back to the house for safe-keeping and then come back to join the party.

Boots was our very first dog. My father gave him to us for Christmas during our first winter on the farm. He was a border collie mix that loved being with us kids. He was black and white, and he was named due to the white "boots" he sported on all four feet. His speed was legendary. He could keep up with any go-kart at speeds exceeding thirty-five miles an hour. He had two favorite pastimes: killing woodchucks and ripping the hat off of your head. We had no issues with him hunting the gophers, and one year he caught fifty-two in a single summer. He was a machine. Some days we could barely hear him barking out in a clearing we called "woodchuck field" since that was his favorite hunting ground. He usually had one cornered in a hole or had treed one.

Yes, woodchucks can climb trees. Doug and I would go out there and make sure he got the little rodent by poking him out of a hiding spot or shaking him down from a sapling. He wouldn't come home otherwise. He would sit there and bark at it all day long if he had to. And he did if we didn't listen for him. He was a tenacious little sucker.

The hat thing we could have done without. During the winter, if your head got lower than three feet to the ground, it was off your head and in his mouth. When we sledded on the pasture, no one had a hat by the end of the day. He wouldn't give it back either. He thought it was just a hilarious game of keep away. Ultimately, he would tear off your pom-pom (it was the seventies; all winter hats had pom-poms) and then leave the drool-ridden rag on the ground. He lived to be fourteen, spending my entire childhood, adolescence, and early manhood by my side. To this day, he is still the best dog I have ever owned. Often the first one you have is the best.

Haystack was a little shepherd mix that showed up on the farm one day. He had long hair and was brown and black with stunning light brown eyebrows. We held him in a stall for three days giving him food, water, and a name. When no one came looking for him, we kept him. He became a barn dog and lived out there his entire life. Sure, he came in the house during the day, but each night he was put in the barn to watch over the horses. It was where he felt at home. If we heard him barking, we knew something was wrong out there. He was quite the little sentry.

HAYSTACK AND BOOTS

One night in the fort, he came up the stairs through the trap-door with muddy paws from the track. I was lying on my back, sucking down a sugar high, and we were all joking around and laughing. As I lay there with my mouth open in a full, bellowing laugh from the fun of the night, he stepped directly into my mouth with his back foot. I felt his toenail scrape the back of my throat. As he did so, he deposited what seemed like a tablespoon of dirt in the back of my pharynx (not "phar-nix"). My mood changed instantly. Everyone else was still laughing. It was so dark in there, no one knew what had happened. I gagged and gagged and tried to pull out whatever nasty dog hair and track slop was back there. I'm pretty sure I tasted manure. It was disgusting, not to mention painful, thanks to his dagger of a toenail lashing my tonsils. I tried my best to gut it out, but in the end, I was too nauseous to continue. Like a little wimp, I bailed and went home, leaving all my friends and all that uneaten food behind. It was supposed to be one of the best nights of the summer but turned into one of the worst in a single moment.

That instant in time reminded me of the moment I realized I had cancer. I was leading a great life. I had a beautiful wife, a great family, a fun job, and just like that, my x-ray was on the screen, and I had to bail and run home. It's really crazy how fast things can change. One second you're on top of the world, and in the next, the world is crashing down upon you. That fateful night in the fort didn't stop me from sleeping out there again. It was just a bad moment.

That's how I felt about my diagnosis. It wasn't going to stop me from living. I may have had a huge paw slammed down my throat, and it made me want to puke, but I was going to keep pushing on and keep living life as long as I possibly could. There were still plenty of good times left, plenty of nights left to sleep in the fort, even if it did leak on me when it rained.

***

While walking the track, we passed the screen house at the top of the stretch. It was a little shack we had built overlooking the pond. The four of us often sat down there on a summer afternoon and just talked. It stood about fifty feet away from the charred circle of earth that was once the location of our annual bonfire. For twenty-seven years, we hosted a huge party that featured crazy events for people to compete against each other for a cash prize and bragging rights. We called it the Survivor Games. People would pay two dollars to compete in preliminary games to become eligible for the final sixteen that pitted two teams of eight against each other. Ultimately it became an individual battle, with the winner becoming the Lone Survivor. I spent months every year setting up for it.

THE SCREENHOUSE BY THE POND.

The spring before I was diagnosed, I just didn't have the strength to do it anymore. The thought of all the preparation for the event was daunting. I should have known something was wrong even then. I attributed it to age and rationalized that the party had run its course. Little did I know at the time the real reason why I decided to call it quits. There would be no twenty-eighth annual "Bonfire by the Pond."

It was a circle-the-date-on-the-calendar type of party. We held it on July 3 every year, rain or shine. In twenty-seven years, it rained once. People still came. We sent out invitations to at least a hundred and fifty people in some sort of humorous flyer. The attendance was staggering. One year the fire was so enormous that we thought the whole farm was going to burn down. It was a real conflagration. The heat was so intense that people retreated all the way back to the barn, nearly 200 feet away.

The party got so big that there were people in attendance I had never met before in my life. Word got out. Everyone in town knew that on July 3, the Mitchells were having a party. It kind of got out of control. Cars would be parked all the way around the entire big track and on the side lawn. I'm not kidding, it was insane. It was a lawsuit just waiting to happen, but somehow we never had a major incident to create one.

The fact that I couldn't physically bring myself to orchestrate it was a harbinger of things to come. Clearly the cancer was already there; it just hadn't reared its ugly head enough for me to know. All good things must come to an end, I guess. I just wish it had been on my terms instead of because of the monster lurking inside of me.

SOME YEARS THE FIRE WAS A LITTLE OUT OF CONTROL.

On our walks around the track, we often ended up talking about Honey. We knew she was special even as a yearling. She just had that "it" factor. She learned easily, and her speed was apparent even at a young age. As a two-year-old, before she started racing, she was hanging with the big boys in the stable when we trained them together. We always allowed her to win each training mile to show her that winning was the ultimate goal, even if it meant putting the brakes on the horse in front to let her blow by. It gave her the confidence that she could get up at the wire. The lessons were worth it. She figured it out in a hurry. It wasn't long before she couldn't be beat, even against the best stock we threw at her.

Back then, the "Honey Era" was a time of great hope, great beginnings, and an amazing bridge to our emergence as a real stable. It was also the start of Doug's career as a professional driver. She alone put him on the map. With each win, more trainers began using him on their horses. With each win, we had a little more money for me to be able to go to college. She put us on her back, and she carried us. If not for her, so many things would have been different—and certainly for the worse. She took a gypsy stable and made us relevant. One horse. Just one horse. She changed our lives forever. To walk the track and not bring her up was nearly impossible.

On the far turn, where the willow trees overhang the banking of the track, we brought up Orcma M. He was named after a childhood nickname of mine, but that's a story for another day. He was our first horse to win a stakes race. Our second, and last, would be Honey. Orc, as we called him, was a dark bay, almost black, little colt that had crazy gate speed. Every single line on his program showed him going to the top. He was nearly uncontrollable off the gate. He could throw some wicked three-quarter times, but would struggle coming home. Sometimes he could hold on and win, and other times he would fade in the stretch. He won his only stakes race up in Hinsdale, New Hampshire, with my father driving.

He was plagued with a bad left front ankle. The year was 1980, and hyaluronic acid hadn't been discovered for use in helping to lubricate joints. Most horses that had joint problems were not long for racing. They would eventually get arthritis and then have to be retired. You could keep them going with pain meds for only so long. It was just about that time that they started making this stuff called "rooster juice." Vets were importing this drug from overseas and injecting it into joints as a lubricant. It was so named because it was extracted from the cockles of roosters. It was the precursor to the synthetic hyaluronic acids that are used ubiquitously today in horses and people. The new stuff is basically synovial fluid (what your joint makes to lubricate it) in a synthetic form.

This "rooster juice," was pretty expensive. Very few horses were "worthy" of spending that kind of money on to inject their joints. Most trainers asked vets to inject corticosteroids instead, which certainly killed the pain, but did nothing to help improve the health of the joint. In fact, in the long run, it made the joint worse. Orc was one of the first horses in the world to get the drug. Mind you, hundreds of others elsewhere in the country were getting it for the first time, but he was certainly one of the guinea pigs. It worked great, but we couldn't afford to give it to him once a month as prescribed, so he got it here and there.

As an alternative, Harryman decided that the impact of jogging and training on the track was not helping our little colt. He once again thought outside the box, and we started swimming him in the pond. We used two very long ropes. Doug would lead him in on one shore with one rope, and I would stand on the other side with mine. We would guide him through the center of the pond by steering him using our leads, running along the banks as he swam. When he got to other the shore, we turned him around, and then Doug and I would switch sides and go it in the other direction. I think Orc enjoyed it. He would jump in playfully and do it all over again. After about ten passes, he was pretty winded, and that was enough. So instead of his ankle taking a pounding on the track, he swam. I think it made him last years longer than he would have otherwise.

We talked about where Greg went over the rail and almost into the pond with Sparkle Road. That was always good for a laugh. We talked about how Mike steered his horse right over the huge banking into the swampland while checking his stopwatch and rolled into the mud, both getting stuck there for over an hour. We reminisced about accidents and close calls. We filled in the gopher holes that were always popping up on the inside of the far turn. We joked that they wouldn't be there if Boots were still around. We walked clear of the manure, left there from the horses that still used the track. The memories and stories we had created on that oval were so pleasing to revisit. They were some of the best days of our lives.

After about a week of walking, I got back down on the floor and readied myself for another disastrous try at performing a push-up. With great effort, I managed to lift myself off the floor and lock my arms. One small push-up for man, one giant leap for me. Each day I tried again. And each day I got a little stronger. By the end of April, I could do seven push-ups. It was a far cry from where I was before, but inch by inch, I was getting there.

Chapter 21 – A Long Summer

Summer came, and we had hope that we could enjoy at least one more good one as a family. My father's cancer wasn't improving despite the heavy chemo they were giving him. He was getting weaker each day. On our walks, we wondered how long we would have him around and just hoped that it would be a few more years. We weren't ready. He was too big a part of the family to let go. He *couldn't* go. He was the foundation of everything we had worked for. The farm, Doug's music, my education, my writing, my mother's best friend; he was everything the farm and family embodied.

Home – Day 27

Apr 30, 2012 6:03pm

These weeks seem to be flying by. And yet they are dragging. My body is slowly getting stronger, but there are some physical issues that are still a problem. I haven't completely recovered from that damn shoulder neuropathy that hit me while I was incarcerated at the hospital. This makes it difficult to lift my arm over my head. If I had hair, I wouldn't be able to comb it with my left hand. It is slowly improving but it's a real pain. Funny, if it weren't for that freaky thing, I would be doing extremely well. My red cells are almost back to normal, and my white cells (although low) are making a comeback. People get pneumonia in the hospital. They get bed sores. They get flesh-eating bacteria. Not me. I get a friggin' neuropathy. Doctors say that they haven't seen that in a stem cell patient before. No shit? Really? I wouldn't have guessed that. I'm the only one? Of course I am. Perfect. It's better than the flesh-eating thing, so I shouldn't complain.

I have been able to hit golf balls to some extent last week. The problem is my muscles are junk, and I think they forgot how to swing. Either that, or they never knew. One way or the other, I suck right now. Again, not a big stretch from where I was before the diagnosis. Now I have to get the muscles back in shape, and it's taking what seems to be forever to recover from even though it's only been four weeks. No one has ever pegged me as patient, so it's not a big surprise.

Haven't shaved since April 4th. I feel like I'm sixteen again. Actually, I didn't start shaving until I was almost eighteen. I was a late bloomer as they say. It's kinda nice really. There are a few nuclear whiskers that are stubbornly poking through on my face. There seem to be eight or nine tough little buggers that survived the H-bomb from the chemo and are making an appearance from the bunker they were hiding in. I kind of look like a cat. A bald, puffy, big-nosed cat. I can think of worse things I could look like. Not a lot, but a few.

I am sure that at this point, my updates are probably not necessary since I am pretty much out of the woods from the whole "this stem cell thing is serious and I could die from the treatment." I do appreciate all the support, and it is unbelievable how inspirational it has been to have everyone pulling for me. It is humbling to say the least. You have all brought me down from arrogant to just cocky. But seriously, it has been awesome. You guys are great, and you helped pull me through my worst hours while I was in the hospital with your positive thoughts and prayers. I can't thank you all enough. I will continue to give updates as things change (perhaps I will continue on a Monday basis for a little while longer). Soon, however, I will be back out in society, and many of you will see me in person and get the scoop right from the horse's mouth.

Marc

June rolled around, and I was still wearing a mask if I went out in public, but at the farm I could take it off and breathe the fresh air of summer. We continued walking at least two miles a day. Every once in a while, I would jog a few steps and then stop to catch my breath, still struggling with anemia and neuropathy in my legs. I hoped to one day get back on the floor hockey rink and play again. It seemed impossible. My shoulder was junk, my legs felt like noodles, and I had no wind. But in the back of my mind, I just had to believe it was attainable. I pressed on.

They put me on a nice variety of drugs, none of them appealing. I took Acyclovir three times a day for the next year to thwart off shingles. Since they wiped out all of my immunity for chicken pox, the likelihood of getting shingles was extremely high, since the virus was still in me. The antiviral would help to prevent such an occurrence. I often wondered why they called it chicken pox, so I decided to look it up. There is no definitive answer anywhere, although some say it's because the vesicles look like chickpeas. Another source says it's because it looks like chicken pecks. I'm not sure I believe either of those explanations, but that's what I found.

They put me on two antibiotics, Sulfamethoxazole/Trimethoprim (SMZ-TMP) and another one called Mepron. The SMZ-TMP is the same drug I've used on horses for years. In fact, the pills they gave me were the exact same ones, although the horses took ten of them while I took only one. Big, white, chalky, and hard to swallow, but not a big deal. The other one, though, that Mepron stuff, was an oral cruelty. It came in a two-inch-square sealed packet and was pure liquid hate. It was almost a fluorescent orange color and tasted as if you were drinking a fart that they tried to mask with a hint of artificial flavoring. Fortunately it was only once a day, but it took everything I had to get that thing squeezed out of the packet and into my mouth. I chased it down with orange juice as quickly as possible; sort of the bite-the-lemon-after-the-tequila-shot trick. But the taste lingered. Oh, did it linger.

I had to take that one for forty-five days. Its purpose, other than creating a mouth that tasted like ass, was to fight off *Pneumocystis carinii*, the same fungus that AIDS patients and other immunosuppressed people have to worry about.

Home – Day 62

Jun 4, 2012 4:35pm

What a difference a week makes. Last weekend, the weather was priceless. This weekend?? You couldn't have sold it on eBay for a buck with free shipping.

Still got out and hit a few golf balls between some raindrops, despite my family telling me I'm overdoing it. Not Jen. She encourages me to get out of the house and move around. Not for the exercise; just to get me out of the house. It was still a good weekend. You know, being alive and all. Tried to walk the track, but it started raining late in the day. Got two laps in before it downpoured. Better than nothing I guess. It looks like today is just as much of a bust with the weather as the weekend was. The treadmill may be calling my name. To be honest, I don't feel like doing much today. Probably the weather.

It looks like Harryman may be eligible for a new clinical trial for his condition since the chemo only made him feel crappy and didn't do any good with the tumor. We are hoping he can get some help down in Boston. I must say, since they stopped toxifying his body with the drugs, he's looking pretty good. His hair is growing back, and his appetite is improving.

I was supposed to start physical therapy today but forgot about my appointment. My next one is on Wednesday. I'm only telling you this because it will help me remember if I write it down. I know, put it on a calendar or as a reminder in my iPhone. Don't start with me. I forget stuff. It's what

I do. I am a man, you know. It's in our DNA to screw up. Messing with that would be like snubbing God himself. I am not about to snub God. Not in my physical condition. I may need to lean on him at some point down the road and don't need him having some sort of vendetta.

I just got a call from Dr. Norton at Dana Farber. He confirmed that they took me out of the tandem stem cell transplant. Umm, no kidding. I guess now I'm officially out of it. That's good. He also gave me a report on my bloodwork that I had done last Friday. Everything looks great. One of the markers of multiple myeloma is called the M-protein. In my case, it was very high when I was first diagnosed, which put me in the high risk category (high risk of death, I guess, they never really clarified what that meant). On Friday, the M-protein was undetectable. High risk this. So for now, I am in good shape. Can't say what the future holds, but I'll take it. Waaaaaay better than the other phone call saying, "We're concerned because your M-proteins are higher than we like to see following a stem cell transplant." I know someone who got just that phone call. Not good. Undetectable. Phew.

On the flip side, my white cells are still pretty low. Not sure why that is, but if you ask my family, it's of course because I'm doing too much. Maybe they're right. Nah. Can't let myself believe that. I have been down for seven months. It's time to start living again. That's not to say I should throw caution to the wind, but I might spit into it. Let's face it, we all have a limited amount of summers in this life. I want to enjoy this one as much as possible. Who knows how many I have left? Or any of us have left. I know I have this one, though. And that's cool. Unfortunately, if my white cells stay on the low side, it may slow down my reinsertion into society. The plan was to get back to "normal" by July, but that seems to be slightly unrealistic at this point. More

Neupogen injections, more time, and perhaps a little less physical activity (just appeasing the family there), and hopefully I will be back to hanging with you bacteria-ridden folk.

That's about it for now. Here's hoping the sun comes out tomorrow.

Marc.

Home – Day 69

Jun 11, 2012 8:09pm

Another Monday has rolled around again. Summers tend to fly by. Have to enjoy it while it lasts. I remember as a kid, summers seemed to last forever. They say that time flies when you're having fun, but for some reason, it didn't back then even though we were having a blast. Probably because we never had to actually punch a clock and go to work during the week. Every day was a true day off so to speak. Sure, we worked the farm, but it was hardly the equivalent of "going to work." We lived each day to its absolute fullest. We never wore watches and never had a cell phone to have anyone check in on us. When we were hungry, we came home. When it was dark, we came home. Otherwise, we were out and about. People talk about the good old days. Those were them. But it doesn't have to be just then. It can be now. They weren't the good old days because of any time period. They were good because of the time we had and what we did with it. Today, there are so many obligations, commitments, schedules, and organized events that most of us don't have any time…just to kill time.

Since my bone marrow transplant, I have had the "luxury" of not working, and for the first time in a very long time, I can relax. It's really refreshing to be able to sleep in until 9 or 10 o'clock if

I'm tired. If I'm not tired, hell, I can still sleep in. I kind of feel like a kid again…when summers were forever, and the only worry was when the sun was going to go down. When someone got beaned in the face with a whiffle ball because darkness blinded us, it was time to quit. Now I'm not saying I enjoy being sick, and all the rehab that I have had to put myself through to get back among the living, but there has been a new perspective put on how I will approach the way I do things in the future.

Gone is the sixty-hour week. Gone is the year that goes by without a vacation. Gone is working six days a week just to enjoy the crap out of one day. Gone is the use of my left shoulder. Oh, wait. That's a bad thing. Well, we can't have it all. It took something horrible to see I wasn't living my life the way I was supposed to. More like when we were kids. When summers mattered. Well, they certainly matter now. And again, that's not saying I haven't had fun. I have had fun. And lots of it. But now I see I can have more.

Enough philosophy. How about those Celtics? Go Red Sox? Oh boy, well, I think I got my wish. The way the Sox are playing, it's going to be a hell of a long summer, and that suits me just fine.

Harryman looks like he will be starting a clinical trial soon. There have been several major disappointments with Dana Farber and the way things have been handled, but hopefully in the long run they will help him. It turns out that he really should have started the trial at least four weeks ago, but the biopsy went poorly, and he has to go back in for yet another one because of a failure to get enough tissue.

I know these things can happen. I've done biopsies on lymph nodes and such on dogs and not submitted enough tissue. But instead of informing us of this immediately, it took them nearly three weeks to let us know, and now it will be another week before they do another one and then get the results. It's maddening. But we press on. Getting mad doesn't solve anything, it just gets you mad.

We went out and test drove golf carts this weekend. No, not for me; for Harryman. He and Mama want to have a little cart to drive around the track and down to the pond...or just to get the mail. It's quite a walk for all of those things, and in his current condition, it can be difficult to make it that far. So we checked some out and, after careful consideration, got him a nice gas-powered cart with a roof. He will be tooling around the farm as soon as we have time to go pick it up. Should be able to get it tomorrow.

That's it for another week. Hope you can all enjoy this fantastic weather. Here's to the good old days. And that's right now.

Marc

Meanwhile, my father's condition wasn't improving at all. His x-rays, which were taken at a real hospital, showed absolutely no decrease in the size of his tumor. His malignancy was clearly aggressive. His CAT scan was clean for metastasis, so at least it hadn't spread. There was some good news in all of this. The doctors said he was an ideal candidate for a new trial drug that his condition fit perfectly. We were all very encouraged. They just needed to take another biopsy in order for them to get him in the trial. As painful as those are, he more than willingly agreed to do it. Always hopeful.

So once again they stabbed into his chest and took several samples of the diseased tissue. Once they had that, he would be clear to start treatment. They said that they were having a success rate of about 80 percent in reducing the cancer and even putting it into remission. We were all pretty excited even though the recent news was fairly bleak.

Three weeks went by and we hadn't heard anything about the biopsy or the trial. Finally, after many frustrating attempts to find out why they hadn't started him on the new drugs, we were informed that they didn't get a big enough sample on the second biopsy attempt. It was infuriating. He wasn't getting any chemo at all, and we just let three weeks go by for nothing. And now they said he would have to go through the whole battery of tests again to make sure he was still eligible for the trial. Needless to say, we were fairly upset.

If they hadn't gotten enough tissue, why did it take so long to tell us? They should have known in four or five days. They made some lame excuses, but the reality of it was that he was lost in the system. They just forgot about him. No apologies, no treatment, and he was getting worse. So they sent him up for another biopsy in a week, and another MRI...in two weeks. We were beside ourselves. As a vet, I knew that we were in trouble. An aggressive cancer, going untreated for so long, would certainly be loving life. It would be growing and spreading as fast as it could.

I was right. When they finally got around to doing the scan and getting us the results another week later, it showed metastasis to his brain. He was scrubbed from the trial. His fate was essentially sealed. They talked about how they could use other chemotherapy agents on him, but since the first big gun had failed, the others would likely be rendered ineffective against what was now a more formidable opponent. His cancer had nearly two months to get stronger and nastier since he wasn't getting any treatment whatsoever to slow it down. Cancer won't give you a mulligan. You play the ball where it lies. Harryman's was deep in the woods to the right. He was in a bad spot.

While he was off of the drugs for that six-week period, he had a bit of a reprieve and was actually stronger. We were really hopeful that he could fight this thing. We were all in denial and thought he was going to get better. It was evident in my post as late as mid-July. Hope. That's all any of us want. A fighting chance. To just say it's over is so hard to wrap your head around. Because he was off the chemo, he in fact was feeling better, but in reality, the cancer was winning. You will see by my next post that we were still very hopeful about the clinical trial, and we had no idea that he was not going to be eligible.

Home – Day 105

Jul 16, 2012 8:39pm

Daaaaaamn. Another Monday. Amazing how fast these weeks are running by. So much better than the ridiculously painfully slow days that I spent in the hospital. It really is a joy to be living life again. Although I've only been "down" for 8-9 months, I have become acutely aware of how great it is to be alive and functioning at what I would consider now to be fairly normally. Sure, I have my limitations physically, but not nearly as bad as I was. It makes me empathize with people who have conditions worse than me, that have to struggle every day, without a lot of hope of getting back to what they used to be. Did I get a bad rap? Sure. But it could be so much worse. I won't mention other conditions that would be considered tougher to deal with, because I don't want to offend or depress anyone living with those circumstances, but mostly I don't want to jinx myself and have fate stick me with one of them just to get a good laugh. Don't mess with karma. She can be a bitch. Crap, that comment might just cost me an ingrown toenail or something.

I am truly blessed to be surrounded by good people. On second thought, I should say great people. The friends that I have cultivated in my years here are really what life is all about. Family and friends. That's life in a nutshell. Cars, houses, nice golf clubs (one day I will clean mine and they will be nice), and even vacations are just material things. They are, in the long run, just things. It's who rides with you in that car, who you invite over to dinner at that house, who lets you cheat and not care in golf, and who you get drunk with in Aruba is what matters. Without the people that you care about, those "things" mean nothing. There is a saying that goes, "he who dies with the most toys wins." But I think there is a much more appropriate saying. "He who dies with the most toys is still nonetheless dead."

So in the light of what I just said, I will say that we had a fantastic weekend hanging out with our good friends, and even took a short ride off the coast in a boat and enjoyed a sunset cruise. It was really special. Afterward, we went out to Stripers (no, not Strippers) restaurant and, as luck would have it, ran into good friends Paul (street hockey Paul) and Lynn in the lobby. Mind you, this is the first time Jen and I have stepped foot into that restaurant, and we run into them. Coincidence? A buddy of mine recently assured me that there are no coincidences. I am beginning to wonder. Of all the gin joints, in all the towns, in all the world. You feel me? I mean seriously, what are the odds? I am hoping we can find time to spend with all of our other great friends that are out there.

And tonight, I visited my parents to see how Harryman was doing. We had a great discussion about how you pronounce "hummus" and "gyro." For those of you that don't know, we set the record straight tonight. Hummus is pronounced hooooo-mus, not hum-mus. And although the English language has bastardized the pronunciation of gyro as ji-roh, it absolutely and most positively is supposed to be pronounced yih-ro, with of course a slight roll of the "r" in the middle of the word. Trust me, it's Greek. So that's all I have to say about that. How about this weather? Has it been crazy hooomid or what?

I am happy to say that my father is improving, now that he isn't being blasted with radiation. He has regained his appetite and is starting to get some strength back. He has a lot of rehab-bing to do if he wants to throw around fifty-pound grain bags again, but if anyone can do it, it's him. If we have any luck at all, we will get him back on track for the clinical trial he was supposed to be in almost six weeks ago. He has to clear the MRI later on this month, but we are staying optimistic that he can get back in. Your continued support and prayers are greatly appreciated.

That's about it for this week, as I have encountered a bit of writer's block. Jen just got home from a zumba class (that's zooooom-ba, you know, like hoooo-mus). She had a blast. She is threatening to drag me there as soon as I am strong enough. Mind you, there were no men in the class tonight. That would make me the only dude there. Hmmmm, a room full of hot, sweaty women. Maybe I'll give it a shot.

Stay cool,

Marc

As you can see from that last post, we all thought he was doing better. In reality, he had a month to live. Looking back, it's hard to believe it would be just a month. He was still animated, engaged, and so willing to try to win his battle. We had no idea how little time we really had left.

Haiku Monday – Day 112

Jul 23, 2012 3:48pm

Not sure why, but I am really tired today. Perhaps a weekend hangover. I am trying to shake off the cobwebs in my head, but I still feel a little foggy. It could be a lot of things adding up. We are all worried about Harryman as he continues to battle but is very weak. I am physically tired from doing things over the weekend, but I am also tired from still having a low white cell count. I tried to help my bone marrow by giving myself a Neupogen injection. Blah. So here I am, stuck in a bit of a Monday rut, physically and emotionally drained. So, instead of my usual writings, I am going to try to lighten things up and do a Monday Haiku. They are brief, they are fun, they are easy to write, and they have seventeen syllables. My lucky number. Perfect. Here goes.

Monday comes too fast
Nobody reads this drivel
Might go back to bed

On the boat with friends
Sunset is magnificent
Puffy Facebook pic

Cancer really sucks
Multiple Myeloma
Bite me, you suckbag

Must stay positive
I am positive this blows
Yup, positively

Trying to lose weight
Cookouts every weekend
It ain't happenin'

Hair is growing back
Some places it never was
I need some clippers

Back is killing me
Shoulder is still not working
I'm Johnny Junko

Still not back to work
Loving the summer work-free
Retirement now?

No way that happens
Jen sick of me in the house
She loves when I golf

Playing golf is fun
Lost ball in the woods again
Hate this stupid game

Jen sleeping soundly
Crinkling wrappers from my snack
Uh-oh, she's awake

She does not like noise
You see, we are just the same
Not helping, still mad

White cells still too low
Thought juicing veggies might help
So far not so much

Hope you are all well
Thanks for all the kind comments
Stay safe this summer

Harryman is weak
Prayers are with him always
My dad, my hero

Marc

CHAPTER 22 – THE DAY THE BANJO WOULDN'T PLAY

Of course my dad opted for the second fiddle drug because he had to. The other option would have been to just die without a fight. So they started him on the new stuff and also started radiation on his brain. He lost his hair again. It was horrifying to see him go through it. He lost more weight. He was feeble and weak, barely able to walk on his own.

He stopped bringing me my morning coffee the way he had done every day for over fifteen years. He didn't have the strength. It was all too telling. I knew how much those morning sessions meant to him. If he couldn't even do that, it wouldn't be long. Instead, I went to see him at the apartment in the barn.

My parents' place used to be an old crappy apartment that was at the back of the barn and was built over the last five or six stalls in the center aisle. It overlooked the track. It had a beautiful view, but it was a mess. In 1995, after I had completed vet school, the three of us (my brother, father, and I) tore down the old apartment and built a nice cozy little place for my mom and dad. Five years working construction during my high school and college years paid off. We did everything ourselves except pour the foundation. It took us a full year to complete, but it came out amazing. They were so happy there.

MAMA PAJAMA AND HARRYMAN IN THEIR APARTMENT.

For seventeen years, they lived a great life there on the farm. Secluded and quiet, with the horses underneath them, it was all they could ask for. All that changed when we both got diagnosed. Our perfect little world was crumbling around us. No amount of money or persistence could help us. We were at the mercy of what the diseases would bring. In late July, my mask finally came off, but Harryman had to be placed in hospice care in Exeter. He was confined to either a wheelchair or a bed. He needed assistance for everything. He couldn't even get up out of his chair on his own. The frustration on his face was hard to watch.

One day, at the hospice facility, Doug brought his guitar and brought Harryman his banjo. Even though he was deteriorating, he could still pluck that thing. They played a few old folk ditties, and it was as if he wasn't sick anymore. He even sang. But during the fourth song, his fingers just stopped working, and the banjo went quiet. He lifted his palms in the air, with the picks still on his right hand, and just shrugged his shoulders and smiled. That was the last time his banjo came alive under his massive hands.

In early August, we brought him home. He wanted to be in his little apartment and spend his days with Mom. We visited him every day and had a hospice nurse come to help as needed. Most of the nurses that came were fantastic and very caring. He wasn't drinking very well, so I placed a catheter in his arm a few times to keep him hydrated. I'm not sure that's legal, but I didn't care, he was my dad.

He rallied some days, even laughing at times, but he was getting worse each day. The cancer had spread to his hip, and they were radiating him to relieve the pain. He made ten trips with my mother to the hospital for palliative therapy. It helped. After his last dose of radiation, he was pretty wiped out and wouldn't drink anything. We didn't know what to do. He had signed a DNR form, which obviously means Do Not Resuscitate, in case he went into arrest.

I placed another catheter in him to keep him hydrated and he perked up. He started to eat. He was talking and being Harryman, just a much weaker, feebler version. On August 10, when a new nurse came to help, I explained that I had placed a catheter in him to rehydrate him a bit. Her response was one that infuriated me. She asked in a very unsympathetic and pissy tone, "Isn't he a DNR?"

Yes, he's a DNR, but that doesn't mean we can't make him feel a little better. Why do you think we have been radiating him for the last two weeks? The callousness of her comment felt unprofessional that I was left speechless and fuming. DNR, Do Not Resuscitate. That doesn't mean "do not treat." I swear I could have popped her one. If there weren't laws against it, I might have. This was my dad. I would put a hundred catheters in him if I had to.

My anger was a mere projection of what I dreaded: that the end was near. I just didn't need a snarky comment from someone who didn't understand what he meant to us. I didn't say anything at all back to her. I thought it best to walk away. I was that close to losing it. She had no idea what kind of rage she almost unleashed. She's lucky Hardwood Bret ever walked this earth. I was definitely the scorpion.

Again, I was that guy. Except this time I was able to hold my tongue like a civilized person. She had probably seen hundreds of people suffering and die from cancer, and just saw me prolonging his agony. I can see how she would be upset with what I had done for the sake of Harryman. I was still in a fairly fragile state of mind but was slowly becoming me again and tempered my anger.

He died on August 13. It was the worst day of my life. It still is. In a matter of three days, he went from a brilliant man to someone unrecognizable as the disease spread quickly to his brain and shut down a mind that had touched so many lives in a positive way.

I think that may have been the hardest part; watching him deteriorate into something that wasn't him anymore. On the morning of August 12, he fed himself pancakes. That evening, he couldn't find his mouth with his fork. Later that night, he couldn't speak. And twenty-four hours later, he was gone. He died at home with the three of us surrounding him. He died surrounded by love. Something he gave unconditionally to us his whole life. The world is now a worse place without him.

Whenever anyone dies, it is difficult not to ask the question of what this life is all about. Hell, I ask myself that question all the time. It just seems harder to answer when someone close to you passes. I guess that is what religion is for, but even the staunchest Christian has his or her faith rattled from time to time. Religion aside, and the idea that heaven awaits aside, the question of what this life is for can be answered in one word. Harryman.

It is how he lived his life that I believe is the reason we are here as human beings. He touched nearly everyone he met in a constructive fashion. He was the George Bailey of today. In the classic Christmas movie *It's a Wonderful Life*, James Stewart plays the character of George Bailey. He gets a rare gift from an angel named Clarence Odbody, AS2 (Angel Second Class), so titled because in over two hundred years, he still hasn't earned his wings. Clarence enables George to see what the world would have been like if he never existed. Our poor protagonist was down on his luck, contemplating suicide, imagining things would have been better if he were never born at all. Instead, he got to see how much of an impact he had made on the world while he was in it. He was shown that he had in fact *had* a wonderful life after all.

It's hard to even begin to fathom what the ripple effect would have been if Harry Mitchell was never here. He taught high school in Arlington, Massachusetts, for over twenty years and impacted so many young lives. Adults today still mention him on Facebook, about how he helped them become who they are. He taught a class called behavioral science, which I had the honor of sitting in on one day. He had an agenda, but it was all in his head. He never brought notes to class, and he never had a plan book. It's funny, his class was a lot like our mornings with coffee. He talked about everything from the psychology of how humans interact to what was going on politically. He helped mold the minds of hundreds of young men and women.

At the end of the movie, George's angel finally earns his wings by helping our main character see the light. At the end, a bell rings, which signifies that the angel got his wings. Harryman may not have helped out any angels, but he gave a whole lot of us here on earth wings to fly. All of my close friends, and our cousins as well, were all touched by him teaching us a way of life. He gave a perspective that few others were able to. The world, or perhaps just our microcosm of it, is a better place because of his existence. I don't need Clarence to show me what it would have been like without him. I wouldn't want to see it. Ironically, I wouldn't have been able to, since I never would have been born. Some people might argue that wouldn't have been such a bad thing, but those are just the guys I played floor hockey against…and maybe the "hat" Nazi…and the maskless dude…crap, maybe the list is longer than I think. Oh well, nobody is perfect.

He was by far the most generous man I ever met. He was loving and tough at the same time. Giving and sensitive. My friend Jay said it best when he wrote to me saying that he gave meaning to the phrase, "he would give you the shirt off his back." He literally would have done it. Although I'm pretty sure that never happened. Probably because he wore a 2XL and the rest of us wouldn't fit into any of his stuff. He always was a hefty fellow. And often times he smelled like a horse, so no one really would have wanted one of his grungy shirts anyway.

His less than snappy attire and Farmer Brown attitude often concealed his gifted mind and sharp sense of humor. There weren't many subjects he couldn't debate you on and either make you feel ignorant or persuade you to think a different way. But he didn't argue in a way to put you down; it was more to inform and direct. His years of teaching made him fun to listen to, even if it was about politics. His somewhat liberal views sparked many a Christmas fireworks show with our more conservative cousins. Clashing political views, mixing with Greek blood and ouzo…not so good. It got ugly sometimes. But his voice never wavered, he never got angry. He just dug in.

He was perhaps the first horse whisperer, before there even was such a term. But he just spoke to them, he didn't bother whispering. He once said that you could learn 80 percent about training a horse in just a few months, but it would take a lifetime to learn the last 20 percent. As a kid, I didn't understand the concept. As an adult and veterinarian…I'm still learning that last 20 percent. How right he was. He was one of the more underrated trainers in New England until Honey's Best came along, and people started to see that he sort of knew what he was doing. As a standardbred driver…well, it's a good thing Doug came along and took over the reins. Let's say he was serviceable in the sulky, and for many years he did our stable proud.

His music with the Tripjacks is still some of my favorite stuff to listen to. His group (along with Len Phillips and Phil Miller) traveled the country back in the sixties as a folk trio and performed at venues all over the map, including the 1964 World's Fair in New York. They were close to making it to the big time, but some little flash-in-the-pan band called the Beatles hit the scene and made folk music all but obsolete. His smooth baritone voice and plucking on the banjo is something we will always cherish.

THE TRIPJACKS PERFORMING AT "KINGSTON DAYS" IN 2011. FROM LEFT TO RIGHT: PHIL MILLER, LEN PHILLIPS, HARRY MITCHELL

He taught so many of us as kids how to be a real person. He did it by example and never with a heavy hand (unless you lied to him). He was tireless in teaching us the right way and how things were supposed to be done. He hated liars and cheats. It was the golden rule around the house. Don't lie. You could have accidentally burned down a church, stolen a car, and spanked a nun along the way, but if you told him the truth, everything would be okay. Lie to him, and, well…we didn't. None of us wanted to disappoint him.

But he did have flaws. He wasn't perfect. He ate too much. He walked into the house with dirty shoes nearly every day, even after being told countless times to take them off. He never closed a single drawer or cabinet after he used them. I'm not sure why our cabinets even had doors. It was crazy. Thank goodness the refrigerator closed on its own. But that was Harryman. With his faults came so many strong attributes that made the little things seem even more insignificant. He was one of a kind and, of that, the very best.

He was a true force of nature without ever being forceful. He was smart and witty without ever being pretentious. He was loving and caring without condition. Simply put, he was a beautiful person. We will miss him always. It really *was* a wonderful life. And sadly, it is now gone.

Hey, Harryman, see you in the winner's circle.

HARRYMAN LOVED FOOD. AND LIFE.

***

Aug 27, 2012 8:15pm

Hello everyone. I took a bit of a hiatus from writing since my dad passed away just to gather my thoughts. It's never easy when you lose someone close to you. We miss him every day, but even though his life has ended, ours must go on. His positive outlook and ability to stay upbeat in tough times was something we all marveled at. We now have to use his strength to help us through it. Even in his final weeks, he would tell us to stay out of the darkness. If one of us would get emotional and start to cry, he would look at us and say, "Don't go there, it's been a great run." True enough, but it's still hard at times. When I find myself slipping into the dark, I hear his words and try to stay strong. There aren't many times I've seen my dad cry, but toward the end, when surrounded by his closest friends and family, he had a momentary break. As he wiped his eyes, he said he was crying not because he was sad, but because "it was so damn good." Even in times of sorrow, he saw the light. He was amazing.

As in many people's lives, music has always been a large part of our family. With my father being in a folk group since the sixties, my brother being a performer today, and my mother being a fairly polished piano player, there was always music in the house. Apparently, the gene pool skipped me and denied me any talent as a musician, but I learned to appreciate music by listening to the three of them. My iPod is filled with a crazy number of songs from all reaches of the musical spectrum (I even have some country songs and hip-hop dabbled in there). I have different playlists for different moods. After Harryman was gone, and I was feeling myself slipping into a place he told me not to go, I could hear his voice telling me to find something to help. I scanned my playlist and found the one labeled "Cool Waves" and hit the shuffle button. The first song that played was Maureen McGovern's version of the "The Morning After." It was chilling how fitting the song was. It was what I needed to hear. The following is an excerpt from the lyrics, which had me crying, not from sadness, but from hope.

There's got to be a morning after
If we can hold on through the night
We have a chance to find the sunshine
Let's keep on looking for the light

There's got to be a morning after
We're moving closer to the shore
I know we'll be there by tomorrow
And we'll escape the darkness
We won't be searching anymore

Today Jen and I went to the farm and sat down at the screen house near the pond with Doug and my mom. It was a place my dad would love to sit and relax on a day just like today. It was perfect. The small fountain in the center of the water was bubbling softly. A large blue heron stalked baby bass on the far shore, and sun turtles swam around near the banks closest to us. He would have loved it. The farm was, and still is, a sanctuary for all of us. It is something that is hard to explain to people how much the land means to the family. It's like our third brother. People have often asked us if we would ever sell the farm. We couldn't even imagine it. Harryman is in every part of the farm. Every fence post. Every tree he planted. Every board he fixed in the barn. Even every trench or mound he made playing with his tractor, instead of leaving the land flat. He was not a perfectionist. He is in everything. Today was a good day. He was with us, and he was smiling.

HARRYMAN AND GOOCH DOWN AT THE SCREENHOUSE
BEFORE ONE OF OUR ANNUAL BONFIRE PARTIES.

Life goes on. I cannot be sure there is anything after this life, but I am certain that I am here right now. There is time for mourning and there is time for sorrow. But it cannot be something that consumes you. If you let it, it will suck you down into the darkness, and it can be hard to find the light to get out. There's got to be a morning after, if we can hold on through the night. Tomorrow will be a good day. Harryman would have made sure of it.

Love,

Marc

CHAPTER 23 – THE BATTLE WITHOUT HIM

And so my battle continued. Without my muse. Without his laugh. Without his support. Without my morning coffee with Harryman. I still had a great team with me, however. Jen, Doug, and my mom were always there. Never wavering. No game is ever won without a team. Our team was still strong, even without our star player. We needed to press on.

My treatment continued on course. We had his memorial service at a local restaurant, and I was far enough removed from my transplant that I could finally go out in public and eat a more unrestricted diet. It was a very nice service, where anyone who wanted to say something about my dad got up and spoke. It was quite moving. Perhaps the most touching scene was when one of the Tripjacks starting singing my father's memorable song "This Little Light of Mine." Slowly everyone in the room joined in for an a capella version of the old folk song. It really was a great moment. The only thing it lacked was Harryman's deep baritone voice. It was hauntingly absent.

I continued taking my drugs. The Acyclovir against shingles, the Gabapentin for the neuropathy, oxycodone for the pain when I needed it (although I wasn't the junkie I was in the hospital), and they started me back on the Revlamid again. Man, do I hate that drug. I take it for twenty-one days (once a day), and then get a seven-day reprieve.

Each month I have to call an eight hundred number and take a survey that makes sure I understand the drug and all of its harmful side effects. It takes about twenty minutes to do, and it's completely automated. One of the stipulations is that you don't share your Revlamid with anyone. Seriously? Like there's anyone out there who wants to take this stuff? I'm sure if people knew I had that drug in the house, they'd be casing my joint to steal it. Who wouldn't want back pain, muscle aches, anemia, and nausea? Oh yeah, it's really a hot black market item. So let me just stop you right there and tell you not to harass me with phone calls asking me to share any with you. They strictly prohibit this.

After taking the automated survey, I then get transferred to a nurse. She then goes over everything all over again. This takes another twenty minutes. I've been on the stuff for two years. You would think I would know what to do at this point. It doesn't matter; they have to ask me the same questions, give me all the side effects that I might get, and make sure that I am taking it properly. And of course make certain I don't share it with anyone. Got it. Don't share it with anyone. Every time the nurse asks me that, I always retort back, "Who the hell would want me to share this with them?" It's good for a laugh on the other end of the phone. Since I get a different nurse every time, the joke never gets old.

Once a month I have to go to my local oncologist and get an intravenous chemo treatment called Zomeda. It's supposed to help me live longer; something like an extra eight months is the average, they tell me. Whoo-hoo, eight months! But I do it anyway. Eight months is eight months, right? *Play till you hear the whistle.* Try googling that drug some time. There are dozens upon dozens of absolute horror stories about what it has done to some people. It can cause some serious side effects with the bones, especially involving the jaw. If you ever read some of those testimonials on the Internet, you would never even consider taking it. But again, I take it anyway. So far I haven't had any real bad effects. Maybe if I had read those reports before I took it, I would have opted not to in the first place. It's scary reading.

One day, when I went back to Dana Farber for my bimonthly checkup and another lovely bone marrow biopsy, I asked Dr. Norton's nurse if I would be on Revlamid indefinitely. I was hoping she would say that I could eventually wean off of it. Maybe she would say yes, I would be on it the rest of my life. It's really vile stuff. Her response was not even close to what I had expected (or I guess wanted) to hear. These were her exact words.

"Oh no, when you get bad, they'll have to do something else, like put you back on Velcade or have another stem cell transplant."

How wonderfully reassuring. Not *if* you get bad one day... *when* you get bad. Isn't that special, and so very sensitive. I wasn't impressed with her answer. As a veterinarian, I took the news in stride. I'm not naïve. I know that this thing is going to get me one day, and reality is reality. But I was expecting a reply more along the lines of "yes, as long as everything goes the way it is right now, you will keep taking it regularly." Now that would have been sugar-coated and easier to swallow. I shrugged it off, but wondered what other patients might think if she said the same thing to them. They might really get depressed. She certainly told it like it was. I give her credit for shooting straight.

As the summer wore on, I was able to play golf again. My strength wasn't there, but at least I was on the course, back in the game. It was a moral victory for sure. And no, they didn't give me relief from the sand traps. I just held my breath and waited for the dust to clear. How much bacteria could be in a sand trap any-way? My shoulder, although still nonfunctional above my head, had no impact on my golf swing. The muscle that I had lost wasn't instrumental in driving the ball, but I couldn't use it to check wind speed, that's for sure. The numbness in my right hand didn't help my grip, but each week it improved a little. By fall, I had complete function back.

Veteran's Day

Nov 12, 2012 9:01pm

I won't lie. Like for everyone, some days are tougher than others. Today was kind of one of those days. I went over to the farm today to help Doug with some fence repair. This is something he and my father would do on a regular basis. It never ends with repairs on the farm. Entropy, it's a bitch. Karma's inbred cousin.

So there we were, putting in posts to replace the old wooden ones that were broken. Doug was in the tractor, and I was holding the posts while he used the bucket to set them in. Driving the tractor was Harryman's job. Man, did he love his tractor. It's not one of your backyard toys, it's a real farm model. Harryman bought it in the mideighties and it still runs great. It must have ten thousand hours on it. It has a fairly large bucket in the front, four-wheel drive, PTO in the back; the whole nine. That thing is a workhorse. If that tractor could talk, the stories it could tell. It made me sad to think he won't ever be in that seat again.

I don't know how Doug and my mother do it every day over there with so many reminders of him constantly hitting them in the face. And I wasn't there every day like the two of them, doing the chores together side by side. Laughing, talking, fighting. In a moment...gone. The finality of death can be overwhelming, and although it is supposed to get easier, so far it hasn't. We are all dealing with it separately, yet together. We all had different relationships with him (Mom, me, and Doug), and his strength was something we fed off of, and he made us stronger. We now have each other. And sometimes it doesn't feel like it's enough. But it has to be; and it will be.

And then there is this thing that I have. This multiple myeloma. I have to stay strong and do everything I can to stick around. I can't bear the thought of either one of them, or Jen, having to say good-bye to me as well. And this too makes me sad. When I'm in a funk, I try to remember how lucky I am to be surrounded by such great people, and it makes me wonder when that day will come that I get too sick to fight anymore. Is it next year? Two years? Ten years? Maybe next month? It can drive you insane if you let it. So I don't. At least not very often.

Last night I went to watch Doug play ice hockey in Exeter on the team that I used to play on. It was fun to watch, and I am eager to play again, but not sure when that realistically can happen. I'm still weak, not to mention out of shape, and the drugs are making it hard for me to exercise due to the fatigue. So I'm sitting there feeling sorry for myself, when this mentally challenged guy sits next to me and I start talking to him. Here's a guy that will never play hockey, nor ever even have the chance to, and there I am sulking. Makes me want to slap myself upside the head. What a cry baby I am.

Seriously, there are people that have it so much worse than what I'm whining about. Sure, I got a bum rap, but when I start thinking about all the diseases out there, accidents that can happen, and all the bad shit that can go down, it makes me...well, pretty damn uneasy that maybe something else is lurking around the corner. But it also makes me thankful for what I have.

So I try not to dwell on it. But sometimes it's hard not to think about. What else have you got in store for me? Talk about tempting the fates. That's not something I say out loud. That was a rhetorical question by the way (in case the fates are listening). I am not literally asking what more is in store, just so we're clear.

How about that election huh? So thankful that crap is over. For all those of you that voted for Obama, please, be gracious. Like I always said when we won a game against a tough opponent...act like you've been there before. Don't run around screaming like a little kid. Show some respect. And for those of you that voted for Romney, please, don't be a sore loser. Shake hands, walk away. You lost. Big deal. We're all in it together despite what you think. And for all of you that didn't vote...WTH?

Let me just say this about the election and all the people who were mailing us stuff and calling the house incessantly, and even those people on Facebook who thought that lobbying on a social network could sway someone's vote. I don't like onions. As a matter of fact, I really hate them. Guess what? I don't eat them. And even when chefs think that the meal would be enhanced if they laced it with onions, I kindly ask them to not put them in my food. Sometimes, however, they try to get me to eat them by conveniently "forgetting" my request. Doesn't matter, I still won't eat them. You would literally have to cram them down my throat. So I don't. And I'm happy.

Here's the thing. I never tell other people not to eat them. Even when they stink up the table and they are offensive to me, I don't interfere. It's their choice.

So...next time there's an election and one of the choices is an onion, scream all you want about how you find them so deliciously appetizing. Good for you. You like them. Eat them. Order them all you want. But please...order them for yourself. I do not like them today. Chances are pretty good I won't like them tomorrow.

Finally, I want to say thanks to all the men and women who have served our great nation to give us our freedoms, including our right to vote and more importantly the freedom to express our feelings about it, without worry or consequences.

Marc

It was a tough winter. Thanksgiving and Christmas without Harryman were hollow. We got together, just the four of us, Doug, Mom, Jen, and me, and had some nice dinners. They were meals that Harryman would have thoroughly enjoyed. He loved food. Not having him there wasn't easy. It's a void that we will never be able to fill. His absence did only one thing positive for me. It gave me a stronger incentive to stick around. Seeing the profound effect of his loss on the family only makes me understand what would happen if I were to expire. I need to fight this thing as long and hard as I possibly can.

All of us find it hard not to cry when we get together for such gatherings. But my father was adamant that we not go into the darkness. He wanted us to move forward and continue living our lives, even if it meant without him. I think it was easier for him to say; since he wouldn't be the one dealing with the loss. Still, I have a feeling he would have dealt with losing one of us better than we were dealing with losing him. As I said, he was wired differently.

Even toward the end when we sat together and one of us would start to weep over him, he would say, "Don't go there, I don't want you to go there." He was right, but grieving is inevitable. It is how it has to be. There is no way you can just shut down your emotions and be a robot. When we grieved, we tried to do it in short segments and not go into a complete cavern of depression for more than a few minutes at a time. After letting out some of the sorrow, his voice would ring in our heads, and we would come back to a more normal state of mind.

I had survived a year with cancer and was slowly starting to work again. No more working six days a week. I was lucky to manage two days a week. The fatigue was remarkable. After working a full day, I found that I would lose nearly the entire next day to sleep. I wasn't the man I used to be. The old workhorse was weak and tired and now needed to be used sparingly to prevent a complete breakdown. I had to be careful with how much energy I expended each day.

CHAPTER 24 – PRESSING ON

My philosophy was simple. No doubleheaders. If I worked one day, I would take the next day off from anything physically straining. This applied to everything. If I went out to dinner one night, I wouldn't play golf or exercise the next day. If I golfed on a Saturday, Sunday would be a down day. It worked out pretty well. It kept my energy up enough so that I could do some of the things that I enjoyed without completely wiping myself out.

Each twenty-one-day cycle of Revlamid was almost seamless. No sooner did I have seven days off and start feeling just a little bit better, I would start right back up again. My white cell counts continued to hover in the 2.5 range (normal is at least 3.8), and my red blood cells were always low. It made for a continued fatigue factor that no amount of mental toughness could shrug off. It was real, and there was no way around it.

Each month I would get the Zomeda infusion. My oncology department right next door decided not to renegotiate with the doctors and let them all go. I had a decision to make. Stick with my primary guy, who was Dr. Hobbs, or stay in Exeter and start with someone new. I asked Dr. Norton at Dana Farber about it, and he said Donny was one of the best multiple myeloma doctors around. Well, that made my decision fairly simple. I followed him up to his Hooksett, New Hampshire, office.

No longer could I travel just ten minutes down the road. I now had to schlep forty minutes up toward Concord. I didn't want to risk anything. So far he had been right on with all the moves, and if not for him, I probably wouldn't be here. I figured it was a small price to pay for the expertise that he carried. Besides, he and Dr. Norton were fairly tight, and that couldn't hurt either. Figures, though; nothing is ever easy.

I slowly eased my way back into work. We had lost quite a bit of revenue with my absence, partly because I worked longer hours than the relief vets, partly because we lost clients, and in part because we had to pay relief vets to cover for me. It was a triple whammy. One of the confounding things that occurred was that several clients asked for their records so they could go to another vet because they couldn't see *me* anymore. What the hell? I'm pretty sure that wherever they're going, they won't see me there either. It was a real head scratcher. If they really liked me that much, it would have been nice if they just kept coming to my hospital and supported me. What was I thinking? That was too logical.

We had closed the practice to new clients as well so as not to overwhelm the staff. Once I started back part time, we opened it back up, and slowly the business started to grow again. At first I wasn't sure the clients recognized me. I was still bald, and my face was grotesquely swollen from the steroids. Yes, and from the weight gain from eating too much. But I'm going to blame most of it on the steroids. I could pull the skin from my cheeks out, like, four inches off of my face. It was ludicrous. I barely recognized *myself* for that matter.

If I worked too much, the neuropathy bothered me quite a bit, although the Gabapentin helped. It didn't look good for my floor hockey comeback when I waddled in at six o'clock from a long day in the clinic. If that's how I felt after just walking, how would I feel after playing a full game? It didn't matter; my training had to start somewhere. The way we left it, so close to a championship, had left a bitter taste in my mouth. Not bitter like the Mepron did, but bad enough. I needed something to look forward to, another goal, other than just surviving the stem cell transplant.

One of the goals was to play golf again. Check. Still sucked at it, but I played, and that's what mattered. I never walked the course, that's for sure, but I never did before all this either. If I wanted a workout walking, I'd just walk, thank you very much. They rent carts for a reason. The pros have caddies that carry their bags around for them so they don't get winded before their next shot. No sir, no walking the course for me. I know, I know, there are plenty of you out there who play golf just because you can get out and stroll around the course and get some exercise. Good for you.

It's hard not to have fun spending four hours out in the sunshine with good friends playing a game you love. We never play for money; we just encourage one another and have a good time. We don't drink on the course either. If we wanted to get drunk, we could go to a bar or stay home, for that matter. When we play, we want to play our best and enjoy the game for what it is. We call ourselves the KGL (Kingston Golf League). It's really just a title. There are no matches, no set schedules, just a group of guys who regularly get together when we can and bang around a silly white ball. It's usually the core of three of us, with any number of fill-ins that are available on any given weekend.

That was all behind me now, with the winter of 2012–13 in full swing. It wasn't a particularly cold winter outside, just in our hearts. We missed him badly. It was our first Thanksgiving, our first Christmas, and our first New Years without him. Things would never be the same. They say that time heals all wounds. I'm not so sure that's true. Some wounds never do. And some just leave an awful scar that reminds us of how bad the wound was. The farm was still alive, though. My brother and mom saw to that.

They continued to board horses there, having as many as fourteen head to take care of. And Doug continued singing and playing his guitar at his gigs, carrying on our father's passion and commitment to music that Harryman did for fifty years with the Tripjacks. It seemed that the group would never sing their songs again, that his banjo was silenced forever.

Phil and Lenny, the surviving duo of the Tripjacks, visited the apartment every now and then and hung out with us for a night. As amazing as it may sound, Doug picked up Harryman's old five string and started playing. As I closed my eyes and listened to the music, it wasn't Doug playing the instrument in my head. I could see my father, almost feel him. It was as if he were actually there. I couldn't help myself from breaking down. When I opened my eyes, full of tears, I wanted it to be him. Instead, it was the hands of my brother that plucked out the old folk song. It was a bitter-sweet moment. His music still lived, even though he wasn't there. It was difficult for my mind to gather it all in. I never closed my eyes again while they played. It was too hard.

Honestly, I don't know how Doug does it. First, he just picked up the banjo and played the thing. He's a guitarist. It's a whole different instrument, all different chords, and a completely different strum and plucking scheme. How the hell could he do it? His ear for music is creepy. I guess it's his idiot savant thing. He can't read music, but if he hears it, he can play it. Second, he was playing the part of Harryman. I can't imagine how emotionally difficult that was the first time he did it. Not only was he playing the songs, he was singing them too. I'm not sure what prompted him to do it. Perhaps it was for the Tripjacks who remained, perhaps for my father, perhaps for himself. Whatever the reason, his music is still with us. Every month or so, Lenny and Phil come up to New Hampshire from Massachusetts and sit down in their regular spots as Doug sits in Harryman's chair, and they bang out the old songs.

CHAPTER 25 – PLAYING THE GAME

Spring finally came after a very dark winter, and it definitely helped the mood of all of us. We had to keep plugging along. I started running on the treadmill when my legs weren't aching or my muscles weren't too tired. I was aiming for the summer floor hockey league in Hampton. It's an outdoor rink with a cement floor. Paul and Doug agreed to play as long as I made it back. They weren't going to play without me. After playing as a line for over twenty years, we had a connection on the floor that was like none other I've had in sports.

Each of us knew where the other one was. Most times we didn't even have to look for each other. We had done it for so long that we functioned as one. Communication was usually silent, made with a head nod or a look, to keep our opponents from knowing what we were planning. We won together and we lost together. I can't remember a single argument between us on the court. If one of us made a mistake, we might point it out, but constructively, never in a negative way or in a shouting match. And we had each other's backs.

There were more than just a few incidents where the gloves were dropped, and we all stood up for each other. Paul was an animal. I usually caused the problem, and he usually ended it. In a game at Hooksett one night, we were playing a team called the Green Hornets. They were notorious for being chippy. In the first ten minutes of the game, eighteen penalties were called. I'm not exaggerating. It was a rough one. At one point, Doug accidentally caught a guy in the head with his stick. The dude freaked out and jumped him. He had pulled his jersey over his head and was swinging at him wildly. Doug was defenseless in that position.

Well, that's all I needed to see. Before I knew it, I was over the boards, making a beeline to his attacker. He was clear on the other side of the rink, so I was in full flight just before I reached him. The guy's head was down, as somehow he was bent over Doug, engaged in battle. In a split second, I decided it best not to put my knee flush into his temple, thinking I might seriously injure him.

Instead, I thrust my knee into his ribcage and separated him from my brother. He collapsed to the ground and was done. That's when it really started. A guy on my blind side sucker-punched me (although I had it coming) and smashed the visor of the helmet into my upper lip, splitting it wide open. I backpedaled fifteen feet before tumbling over in a backward summersault and crashed into the boards. The player who hit me and another guy jumped on top of me and started throwing haymakers. I put the guy who got me first in a headlock and covered up, checking to see if all my teeth were still in, all the while being punched from behind. I was more concerned about my mouth than what the guy was doing to me.

Out of the corner of my eye to my left, I saw Paul. In about ten seconds, he laid three guys out. After dispensing the first two with two swift jabs, a third player came at me from behind the net and was about to pile on. That's when I saw Paul pivot and catch him square in the face. He decleated him, sending him horizontally and flat on his back.

Doug was behind me fending off other would-be attackers, along with the rest of my team, who had all taken on dance partners. There were four or five more of them than us, but when Paul laid out that third dude, things quieted down in a hurry. The two refs who were there did what they could to break it up, but that last punch really did the trick.

When all was said and done, the guy I dropped got carried off by his buddies, and I eventually went to the hospital for countless stitches on the inside of my mouth. My lip had been split all the way up to my nose on the inside, almost completely breaking through the outer skin. Just the tip of my lip had split on the outside. My two front teeth had been loosened badly, and I thought they might be goners, but they held on. I packed myself in ice and went home.

When we got back to the house, I showed Jen what had happened and asked her if she could sew me up, since we had done such things in the past for small cuts. She took one horrified look under my lip, and she just shook her head. I knew it had to be pretty bad if she wouldn't do it. It was a long night in the emergency room. I can still feel the scar with my tongue to this day. Sometimes wounds never heal. Sometimes they leave scars that last forever.

It took only twelve minutes for the fight to break out. But what happened in the minute that followed was all I needed to know about our team. We were tight, and we would always have each other's backs. It wouldn't be the last time it happened, and it's always good for talking about over a few beers when we get together. Someone usually starts with the line, "Remember that bench-clearing brawl up in Hooksett?" Yeah, like we could ever forget it. Good times.

I really missed that. Not the fighting per se (we could have done without that), but the team. How we were as one. And I don't just mean the three of us, although at its core, it was important. I mean the whole team. We were The Rats. We had a way of playing. We had a philosophy. We would play with the same intensity if we were down by five goals or up by five goals. We were full throttle red lined, the entire game. We didn't know a different way. And there was one thing that always stayed true. We never gave up. We played till we heard the whistle. And sometimes, as in Hooksett, we kept going even *after* the whistle was blown.

We called ourselves The Rats because we really wanted a name that was strong yet disliked. No one likes a rat. We didn't want teams to like us. We almost wanted to be hated. It brought out the best in us. And the name defined us. We played like rats. Tough, gritty, clawing, nasty, dirty rats—with a whole lot of finesse. That's what I missed the most: that toughness. You just don't get that being a veterinarian or playing golf. Hockey is a sport that lets that inner rat come out in you. For me, it's liberating. I've been told by opponents I run into from back in the day, "Man, I hated playing against you guys." That's exactly what I'm talking about. We played hard, but we played clean, unless someone wanted to get dirty. Then we got filthy.

I needed that back. Not just to prove to myself that I could do it, but because I loved playing the game so much. It was no longer just about beating cancer and doing it to make a good story where the headlines read, "Poor schmuck gets to play again." I didn't just want to play, I wanted to win. Paul, Doug, and I; we were one big rat. One big scorpion. It was in our nature to play hockey. It was in our nature to win.

One of our old teammates had been asking me for a year for us to join him on his team. He had wanted us to play the summer before, but in my condition, after the stem cell thing, there was no way that could happen. Just walking was a chore. It would have to wait. But a year came and went, and I started training. Some days were harder than others. It was tough to bring myself to do anything physically straining when my muscles ached and the fatigue factor was so high. So on those days, I didn't do a damn thing. I rested. On the days I felt better than awful, I would run or get on the stationary bike, and I started planking.

In May, Jen got out this plank challenge calendar that starts off with a thirty-second plank, where you hold an isometric position on your elbows as if doing a push-up. Slowly they have you work your way up to more time. By the end of the month, I was doing six-minute planks. I was definitely getting stronger. When June came, the street hockey league was starting, and although I wasn't in the shape I wanted to be in, I had lost fifteen pounds and felt I could give it a shot.

Standing there on the right wing, with Paul at center and Doug on the far left wing, was an incredible feeling. I was back. We were back. We all felt it. It had been almost two years, and it felt as if we never stopped playing. When they dropped the puck, I completely lost myself in the game. For forty-five minutes, I didn't have cancer. Never thought about it even once.

That's what street hockey does for me. It completely wipes out any negative thoughts that I might have. During a game, the pain is gone and my head is clear, no matter what else is going on in my life. It's always been that way for me, an incredible escape.

We were rusty, that's for sure. Passes were off. Shots were missed. But it was inspiring to be playing again. I always felt I'd be back again, even though at times it didn't look good. The idea that I could never play again wasn't part of my deepest inner mind-set. In a way, I felt fortunate that it was multiple myeloma and not something else that would truly make that moment impossible. At least with what I had, I could still play the game. Even if I would never be as physically strong as before this evil crawled inside me, I could still play.

We won that first game easily. The league wasn't nearly as tough as the ones we had played in when we were in our prime, even though the guys we were playing against were twenty years younger. Collectively, our front three was 146 years old. But with that age came years of experience together. The teams we were playing didn't have that kind of connection. We were pretty certain that a championship was possible.

The season rolled along, and I could feel my legs getting stronger, my wind was better, and I was gaining speed. Let's just get something straight: I said I was gaining speed, not that I was fast. Never was, never will be. I was back to being the guy who did the dirty work in the corner while Doug and Paul scored the pretty goals. Sure, I lit the lamp my share of the time, even had a few hat tricks, but my job was to be a playmaker and not necessarily a goal scorer. I was the wrecking ball crashing into boards, trying to win the fifty-fifty battles, and coming out with the puck to make a play.

Doug says that sometimes he has to close his eyes when he sees me barreling into a corner. Full throttle; all the time. Paul was the crazed lunatic in the high slot who had to fend off two machetes hacking at him in the middle. Doug was the lone left winger, who dipsy doodled around guys at the blue line, passed off the puck, and then waited for the one-timer to come back to him with his right-handed shot. It had worked for over two decades, and it was still working.

We were the number two seed in the league and had breezed through the quarterfinals and semifinals. The day of reckoning was finally upon us. The chance for redemption. It wasn't a best-of-three scenario like before. It was one game for the championship. It was September, almost exactly two years removed from the last time we were in this spot. But this time we had Paul. He didn't have a parts show to be at, although he was in New York the night before. He had to leave at three in the morning and drive all night to get back in time to play. He said there was no way he was missing it this go around. He better not have; I took the skirt off and everything.

The only thing missing was Harryman. In all the years we played, he rarely missed one of our games. I don't ever remember any other fathers being at those games, but that didn't stop Harryman. He thoroughly enjoyed coming to the games and watching us. He had seen every fight, every goal, every stitch. He even suited up and played net one night when our goalie didn't show up. He was sixty-five years old at the time. We won 10–9. He caught a puck in the neck in an unpadded area that left a bruise the size of a soccer ball. He was a gamer.

He would almost always join us at the rinks, no matter where we went, no matter how late the game. Often he drove us in the old black Chevy Celebrity wagon that faithfully got us to nearly all of our games. We called it the Rat-Mobile. Man, did that thing stink. We left our hockey stuff in there every week, and the perspiration on the jerseys was a feast for bacteria to feed off of, making the inside of the car a rotten fug of old sweat. You could forget about using the air conditioner. That only recirculated the miasma. Some of those summer nights were gag-worthy when you stepped into that thing.

But those days had passed. They were long behind us. Not having him there to see how far I had come was hard to take. The day of the championship was a gorgeous fall day. He would have loved it. Not seeing him on the sidelines just didn't feel right. But he *was* there. He'll always be there.

The opponent we were facing was a pretty strong team of young players. They still weren't the caliber of competition that we used to face in days gone by, but we weren't young men anymore. Our prime had passed us by some fifteen years ago. The teams were evenly matched.

In the first shift, Paul sent me in on the right wing, and I beat the goalie short side with a snap shot, low inside the post. Our bench erupted. I waited two years for that moment. Two years for a second in time. It's crazy what can motivate a person. For me, it was watching that puck hit the back of the net. No drug can give me that feeling. A minute later, Doug scored from the left wing off a tic-tac-toe play from the three of us. From there, it was essentially over.

We won going away, 10–1. Our line scored seven of the goals, and they were seven of the most satisfying goals we've ever potted. The championship was ours. Rats–1, Cancer–0. We shook hands with the other team, and for a brief moment, I wasn't sick. It's a feeling that's hard to describe. After being down as low as I was at one point just a year before to be back holding a championship trophy and knowing that I was instrumental in its winning, was emotional for all of us.

IN THE FRONT ROW FROM LEFT TO RIGHT ARE ME, PAUL, AND DOUG.

On our way back home in the van, we tried to count the number of championships we had won since the early nineties, and we lost track at around ten. They were all special. But this one was perhaps the sweetest. No one on the other team knew that I had cancer, nor did I want any of them to know. Because when I was on the floor, I didn't. The comeback was complete, and even though we were up by nine goals, we were still trying like hell to score another with just ten seconds to play. Never lay down. It's a philosophy that has served me well to get through everything that has happened.

I don't know how much longer I have left here on this earth. None of us do. That's not for me to decide. Remember, there's a malevolent bus roaming around out there, just waiting to pick any one of us off at any moment. When the time comes, and the game is finally over, I know that I will have played as hard and as long as I could. I am a Rat. I am the scorpion. Except that I will not ask for a ride across the river on a turtle…or a frog, for that matter. I will stay right where I am. I will fight until there isn't any fight left. And right now, the game is still on.

I also don't know how many more seasons I'll have the ability to play street hockey, even if I wasn't diagnosed with this dreadful thing. I'm not getting any younger, and it seems the teams we play against are doing just that. As long as I have Doug on the wing and Paul at center, I will continue to play, even if I need a walker. The way I see it, I'm not dying from cancer; I'm living with it. We may be down 6–3 with a minute left, but that's a lifetime in hockey. Never give up. Don't ever give up. There's still time left on the clock, and I'm going to play till I hear the whistle.

Epilogue

It's a bit ironic that I ever wrote a book, let alone a second one. I was never encouraged about my writing in any of my classes in high school. As a matter of fact, they were the worst grades I received in all twelve years of public schooling. I never got a grade higher than 85 in any of the numerous writing classes that I took. Almost every grade was an 80. I'm not sure if it was because they expected more from an honors student, or it was just that my writing wasn't that good. I still don't know.

As a matter of fact, in my last English class as a senior that I took, my journalism teacher used one of my papers to show how *not* to write. Mr. Martin spent the whole lecture critiquing a short piece I called "Student Government: Is it for Real?." It was quite embarrassing. He just kept going on and on about how awful it was, pointing out grammatical errors and fragmented sentences. The whole paper was dotted, dashed and slashed with his red pen. And I just slumped down lower and lower in my chair. It really had an impact on me. It literally took the pen out of my hand. I thought it was fairly well written, and there he was tearing it to shreds. Writing wasn't in my future. He made that clear.

After being ripped by Mr. Martin, I never wanted to write again. He was one of the better teachers at the school and I very much respected his opinion. Maybe he was just trying to get more out of me, but it did just the opposite. Although I took a few writing classes in undergrad in order to fulfill my curricular requirements for vet school, I was disinterested in writing and found myself pathetically revamping old pieces that I had written in high school. Shamefully, I was just plagiarizing myself.

It wasn't until I was forty years old that I found myself in need of telling the story of how one horse in particular changed my life. That was Honey's Best. If not for her, I wouldn't have become a vet and we wouldn't have enjoyed so many great moments at the track as a family. It spawned an idea that other horses also gave me inspiration, and I was motivated to tell their stories as well. The result was my first book, *Hoofprints in the Sand*.

As I reflect back on the good fortune we had, breeding a farm mare to a local stallion, now gives me a chance to pause and think about the incredible luck I have had in my life, even though I often joke that I am the unluckiest human alive. And that's what really is the most unbelievable part in all of this; that I am here at all. Not because I have survived cancer, and that I'm still alive, but that I was even created in the first place.

The genome for our DNA has over 3 billion base pairs. The combinations of two people's genetic coding coming together to be exactly you are boundless. This goes for your parents and grandparents and the hundreds of generations before you. They all had to line up exactly the way they did to become the person you are. The odds that all of those perfect strands of DNA randomly weaved together to produce you is like hitting Powerball a hundred times in a row. And that's just a guess; it's probably a lot higher. It's mind blowing really.

If you're looking for inspiration, just look in the mirror. The astronomical statistical odds of you becoming you are nothing short of a miracle. I consider the fact that I am alive and able to even be here to fight cancer a blessing. If I find myself saddened when I think about losing my dad, or what life would be like if I were gone for the rest of my family, I just think how grateful I am to even be here. Having moments of emotional release is okay, it's part of what makes us human. However, if that sadness lingers and lasts for days, weeks or even longer, then there may be a clinical problem that needs to be addressed.

In my case, I was fortunate enough to get a disease that is at least treatable for a while. Others aren't so fortunate. Some people get cancer that gives them mere months to live. Depression can play a large role in how you spend whatever days you have left, and it can be crippling if you let it. It's not easy to tell someone not to be depressed when they have fallen into that cavern of darkness. It is a symptom of a disease, no less than coughing is a symptom of bronchitis.

You can't tell someone to stop being depressed any more than you can tell someone to stop coughing. It needs to be treated. My message to anyone out there struggling with depression is to get professional help. You are not alone. There are support groups and doctors that specialize in treating depression. I implore you to make the effort to try to enjoy whatever time you have left.

Remember, you are a miracle, and you are worth fighting for. Life is fleeting, for all of us. Every day we have is a gift. I learned it the hard way. I was working too much, and living too little. It almost killed me, but I learned. It's never too late to start living, even when you're dying. The fact remains, no one gets out alive. Some of us just get there sooner. When it is my time and the whistle blows; in my heart, I will know that I have played hard and scored as many goals as possible. I hope you do the same.

Made in the USA
Middletown, DE
14 February 2015